PENGUIN BOOKS

CHURCHILL AND ORWELL

Thomas E. Ricks writes The Long March column for *Task & Purpose* and is also the military history columnist for *The New York Times Book Review*. He is a former adviser on national security at the New America Foundation. He was previously a fellow at the Center for a New American Security and a contributing editor of *Foreign Policy* magazine, for which he wrote the prize-winning blog *The Best Defense*. A member of two Pulitzer Prize–winning teams, he covered U.S. military activities in Somalia, Haiti, Korea, Bosnia, Kosovo, Macedonia, Kuwait, Turkey, Afghanistan, and Iraq. He is the author of several books, including *The Generals*, *The Gamble*, and the number one *New York Times* bestseller *Fiasco*, which was a finalist for the Pulitzer Prize.

Praise for *Churchill and Orwell*

"Both subjects, he tells us in this page turner written with great brio, are 'people we still think about, people who are important not just to understanding their times but also to understanding our own.' . . . What comes across strongly in this highly enjoyable book is the fierce commitment of both Orwell and Churchill to critical thought."
—*The New York Times Book Review*

"An elegantly written celebration of two men who faced an existential crisis to their way of life with moral courage—and demonstrated that an individual can make a difference." —*San Francisco Chronicle*

"Readers of this book will realize, if they needed reminding, that the struggle to preserve and tell the truth is a very long game." —*Los Angeles Times*

"Another one is a book by Thomas Ricks about Winston Churchill and George Orwell. The two never met, but their parallel lives and their views of how society should function, notions of individual freedom, limitations of politics, and so on—extraordinarily harmonious thoughts in different places, really very impressive. I went in assuming [they'd be at odds], but quite the reverse. Really, very interesting." —John Le Carré

CHURCHILL

AND

ORWELL

THE FIGHT FOR FREEDOM

THOMAS E. RICKS

PENGUIN BOOKS

PENGUIN BOOKS
An imprint of Penguin Random House LLC
375 Hudson Street
New York, New York 10014
penguin.com

First published in the United States of America by Penguin Press,
an imprint of Penguin Random House LLC, 2017
Published in Penguin Books 2018

Photograph credits appear on page 340.

ISBN: 9781594206139 (hardcover)
ISBN: 9780143110880 (paperback)
ISBN: 9780698164543 (e-book)

Printed in the United States of America
3 5 7 9 10 8 6 4

DESIGNED BY MEIGHAN CAVANAUGH

Dedicated to all those who seek

to preserve our freedoms

CONTENTS

———————

CHURCHILL

AND

ORWELL

CHAPTER 1

THE TWO WINSTONS

On December 13, 1931, a fifty-seven-year-old English politician, still a member of Parliament but quite unwelcome in his own party's government, stepped out of a taxi on New York's Fifth Avenue. He was in New York to begin a speaking tour in an attempt to recover some of the small fortune he had lost in the stock market crash two years earlier. Being English, and perhaps distracted by his troubles, he looked the wrong way down the avenue, and did not see the automobile that, traveling at about thirty miles per hour, knocked him to the pavement and dragged him for a spell, cracking some ribs and slashing open his scalp. Had he died, he would be remembered today by a few historians specializing in early twentieth-century British history. But he did survive. His name was Winston Churchill.

Almost six years later, on May 20, 1937, another Englishman awoke before dawn and moved out of his uncomfortable quarters in a trench on the front lines of the Spanish Civil War in northeastern Spain, not far south of the Pyrenees Mountains. Though serving as a soldier, he really was a writer, a minor author of mediocre novels that had not been selling well. He considered himself a leftist, but in his latest work, in which he had turned to journalistic sociology, studying the poor of England, he had caused a minor fuss and perhaps lost a few friends by criticizing socialists. Still, in Spain he was serving as a member of the progovernment socialist forces of the Spanish Republic. He was a tall man, and as he moved along the west-facing trenches to check on the members of his squad, his head was silhouetted by the sun to the east, rising behind him. A Nationalist sharpshooter about 175 yards away spied him and fired a copper-plated 7mm bullet. It was a well-aimed shot, sending the bullet through the base of the Englishman's neck, where it just missed a carotid artery. Stunned, he fell to the ground. He knew he had been hit, but in his shock could not tell where. Informed that he had been shot through the neck, he composed himself to die within minutes, because he had never heard of someone surviving such a wound. Had he expired then, he would not be remembered today except perhaps by a few literary specialists in minor mid-twentieth-century English novelists. But he did not die. His name was Eric Blair, but his nom de plume was George Orwell.

On the surface, the two men were quite different. Churchill was more robust in every way; born twenty-eight years before Orwell, he outlived him by fifteen years. But in crucial respects they were kindred spirits. In their key overlapping years in the middle of the century, the two men grappled with the same great questions—Hitler and fascism, Stalin and communism, America and its preemption of Britain. They responded with the same qualities and tools—their intellects, their confidence in their own judgments even when those judgments were rebuked by most of their contemporaries, and their extraordinary skill with words. And both steered by the core principles of liberal democracy: freedom of thought, speech, and association.

Their paths never crossed, but they admired each other from a distance, and when it came time for George Orwell to write *1984,* he named his hero "Winston." Churchill is on record as having enjoyed the novel so much he read it twice.

Despite all their differences, their dominant priority, a commitment to human freedom, gave them common cause. And they were indeed vastly dissimilar men, with very different life trajectories. Churchill's flamboyant extroversion, his skills with speech, and the urgency of a desperate wartime defense led him to a communal triumph that did much to shape our world today. Orwell's increasingly phlegmatic and introverted personality, combined with a fierce idealism and a devotion to accuracy in observation and writing, brought him as a writer to fight to protect a private place in that modern world.

One hazard in taking a dual approach to the two men is that Churchill is such a loud and persistent presence. Look at any key event of the 1940s and he is there, participating in it, or speechifying about it, and then some years later, writing about it. Debating Churchill was like "arguing with a brass band," a member of a British Cabinet once grumbled. The political philosopher Isaiah Berlin observed that Churchill saw life as a pageant, with himself leading the parade. "I must say I like bright colours," Churchill once wrote. "I cannot pretend to feel impartial about the colours. I rejoice with the brilliant ones, and am genuinely sorry for the poor browns."

Together in the mid-twentieth century these two men led the way, politically and intellectually, in responding to the twin totalitarian threats of fascism and communism. On the day that Britain entered World War II, Churchill stated, "It is a war, viewed in its inherent quality, to establish, on impregnable rocks, the rights of the individual, and it is a war to establish and revive the stature of man." Orwell expressed the same thought in his plainer style: "We live in an age in which the autonomous individual is ceasing to exist," he fretted two years later.

Orwell and Churchill recognized that the key question of their century ultimately was not who controlled the means of production, as Marx thought, or how the human psyche functioned, as Freud taught, but rather how to preserve the liberty of the individual during an age when the state was becoming powerfully intrusive into private life. The historian Simon Schama has described them as the architects of their time. They were, Schama said, "the most unlikely of allies." Their shared cause was to prevent the tide of state murder that began rising in the 1920s and 1930s, and crested in the 1940s, from continuing to rise.

One day in the 1950s, one of Churchill's grandsons poked his head into the old man's study. Is it true, the child inquired, that you are the greatest man in the world? Churchill, in typical fashion, responded, "Yes, and now bugger off."

The "Great Man" theory of history is much denigrated today. But sometimes individuals matter greatly. Churchill and Orwell have had lasting impacts on how we live and think today. These two men did not make the prosperous liberal postwar West—with its sustained economic boom and its steady expansion of equal rights to women, blacks, gays, and marginalized minorities—but their efforts helped establish the political, physical, and intellectual conditions that made that world possible.

I had long admired them, separately, but they became one interrelated subject for me when, while taking a break from covering the Iraq War, I studied the Spanish Civil War of 1936–39. Researching Orwell's role, I realized that both he and Churchill had been war correspondents, as I was then. Orwell covered and participated in the Spanish war, and Churchill had played a similar dual role in the Boer War of 1899–1902.

Who were these men, what arguments did they use in preserving a space for the individual in modern life, and how did they come to those views?

This book concentrates on the fulcrum point of their lives, the 1930s and 1940s. The heart of both men's stories is in the same crucial period from the rise of the Nazis until the aftermath of World War II. In this period, when so many of their peers gave up on democracy as a failure, neither man ever lost sight of the value of the individual in the world, and all that that means: the right to dissent from the majority, the right even to be persistently wrong, the right to distrust the power of the majority, and the need to assert that high officials might be in error—most especially when those in power strongly believe they are not. As Orwell once wrote, "If liberty means anything at all, it means the right to tell people what they do not want to hear"—most especially, for him, facts that they did not want to acknowledge. He pursued that very specific right all his life.

Churchill helped give us the liberty we enjoy now. Orwell's writing about liberty affects how we think about it now. Their lives and their works are worth better understanding in that context. In turn, we will better understand the world we live in today, and perhaps be better prepared to deal with it, as they dealt so well with theirs.

Let us now turn to them as young men, setting out on the paths of their lives.

CHAPTER 2

CHURCHILL THE ADVENTURER

On a typically damp December day in the south of England in 1884, Winston Churchill, then a small, ten-year-old redhead new to Miss Thomson's School in Brighton, was entertaining himself in art class by yanking another boy's ear. Finally, the victim counterattacked, stabbing his tormentor, young Winston, in the chest with a penknife.

Churchill was unembarrassed to admit that he was "a troublesome boy." Even so, he omitted this incident from his own autobiographical writings, perhaps because even his own mother blamed him for it. "I have no doubt Winston teased the boy dreadfully—& it ought to be a lesson to him," Jennie Churchill wrote to Winston's father, who was in India. After all, she reasoned, the blade of the knife sank only a quarter of an inch into her son's flesh—deep enough to make the point, but too shallow to cause serious injury. A month later, Lord Randolph Churchill, his dissolute father, receiving the news while in India, responded airily, "I hope there will be no more stabbing."

Parents who treated a boy as Churchill's did might nowadays be accused of criminal abandonment. His father, a rising man in the Conservative Party, appears to have barely spoken to this son of his. Writing decades later, Winston could recall having only "three or four long intimate conversations with him." While at school in Brighton, on the seaside about sixty miles south of London, Churchill was chagrined to read that his father had traveled there to give a speech but had not stopped by to see him. "You never came to see me on Sunday when you were in Brighton," he chastised his father in a letter. Later, when he was at Harrow School, Churchill mounted a campaign to have his father visit him there for a special prize day. "You have never been to see me," he chided. He noted plaintively that his school was just thirty minutes by train from London. "If you take the 11.7 from Baker Street you will get to Harrow at 11.37." He also wrote to his mother, "Do try to get Papa to come. He has never been." Lord Randolph did not go.

Churchill's mother had her own pursuits. Jennie Jerome Churchill, "a beautiful, shallow, diamond-studded panther of a woman," as one Churchill biographer put it, cut a wide swath through late Victorian society, taking perhaps nineteen lovers, by one conservative estimate. Others have estimated that she slept with two hundred men during the course of her life, but careful biographers cast doubt on that as extreme. "The number is suspiciously round," argued one of the best of them, the British politician Roy Jenkins.

At any rate, concludes Con Coughlin, an expert on Churchill's early life, Lady Randolph Churchill enjoyed "an active social life, to put it mildly." At a time when tattoos were largely seen only on the people of the shadier side of the waterfront, she exhibited a serpent inked on her left wrist. After the early death of her first husband—Winston's father—she shocked London society by marrying a dashing young man her son's age. For good measure, after divorcing that man, she took a third husband who also was the same age as Winston. Late in life, she reportedly sorrowed that "I shall never get used to not being the most beautiful woman in the room."

On one Christmas vacation, Churchill's busy parents fobbed him off to his grandmother, the Duchess of Marlborough. Several weeks later, she wrote to them with relief, "Winston is going back to school today. *Entre nous,* I do not feel sorry for he certainly is a handful."

At the first school Churchill attended, flogging was used freely, to the point of causing screaming and bleeding. "How I hated this school," Churchill wrote. Eventually his parents transferred him to that small, enlightened academy in Brighton where Churchill, who may have suffered from some sort of attention deficit disorder, wisely was allowed to pursue only the subjects that interested him, which he recalled as "French, History, lots of Poetry by heart, and above all Riding and Swimming." But even there, though happier, Churchill managed to be ranked last in conduct.

Later in school, his housemaster found that Churchill was notable for "his forgetfulness, carelessness, unpunctuality, and irregularity in every way." Despite these flaws, as a teenager he somehow learned to write. "I got into my bones the essential structure of the ordinary British sentence—which is a noble thing," he wrote. His ability with the English language would become his major asset in both his careers, politics and writing. He would go on to publish some fifteen million words in his lifetime. But his formal education stopped there, and all his life he would have large gaps in his knowledge.

Churchill emerged from school, he recalled, "considerably discouraged." His parents considered him not clever enough to become a lawyer, so he was shunted to the army, a common destination for dull offspring of the British aristocracy. The ground force was easier on the dim-witted than the Royal Navy, which was seen as more important to the defense of the island nation and so was more inclined to a meritocratic approach. But even with that low bar, it took three tries before Churchill was admitted to Sandhurst, the British army's academy for its infantry and cavalry branches. He was accepted into the cavalry, for which competition was easier, as many young men could not afford the expense of keeping a line of horses and servants to tend them. As Churchill put it, "Those who were at the bottom of the list were accordingly offered the easier entry into the cavalry." The choice also appealed to Churchill's fondnesses for comfort and pageantry. Not only could he ride instead of walk, but also, he noted, "the uniforms of the cavalry were far more magnificent than those of the Foot."

His father's letter to him about finally being accepted to Sandhurst, written in August 1893, is worth quoting at length to understand the impossible burden of the disappointed parent that Churchill would carry all his life. It is brutal. Lord Randolph wrote to his son:

> *With all the advantages you had, with all the abilities which you foolishly think yourself to possess & which some of your relations claim for you, with all the efforts that have been made to make your life easy & agreeable & your work neither oppressive nor distasteful, this is the grand result that you come up among the 2nd rate and 3rd rate class who are only good for commissions in a cavalry regiment. . . .*
>
> *I shall not write again on this matter & you need not trouble to write any answer to this part of my letter, because I no longer attach the slightest weight to anything you may say about your own acquirements & exploits. . . .*
>
> *You will become a mere social wastrel, one of the hundreds of the public school failures, and you will degenerate into a shabby unhappy & futile existence. If this is so you will have to bear all the blame for such misfortunes yourself.*

Lord Randolph Churchill was dying at the time, probably of syphilis, which may explain his somewhat crazed tone. "He was in the grip of the progressive mental paralysis from which he was to die," wrote his grandson, Winston's son, Randolph. Still, even while dying he had enough energy to continue to disparage his son, who wrote to his mother plaintively that, in the view of Lord Randolph, "I can never do anything right." The father would die in January 1895, when Winston was twenty years old.

With his father's passing, a fuse seems to have been lit in Winston. A son who could survive such an upbringing would either be thoroughly damaged or, with some luck, enormously self-confident. Churchill was very lucky. The death of his father seems to have liberated him. For the next several years, he would rocket from England to India to the Afghan border, back to England, off to the Sudan, back to India, back to England, and then to South Africa, all in the course of building a brilliant young career.

Late in life, Churchill would claim that "I gained a lot by not overworking my brain when I was young." Typically, he tried to make a plus out of this minus, arguing in 1921 that "it is a mistake to read too many good books when quite young. . . . Young people should be careful in their reading, as old people in eating their food. They should not eat too much. They should chew it well."

He did not attend a university. His true education seems not to have begun until he was almost a grown man, serving as a young cavalry officer in Bangalore, India. There, far from home, in the winter of 1896, "the desire for learning came upon me." Restlessly, he chewed through Aristotle, Plato, Macaulay, Schopenhauer, Malthus, and Darwin.

Most significantly, he consumed Gibbon's *The History of the Decline and Fall of the Roman Empire*. "I was immediately dominated by both the story and the style. All through the long glistening middle hours of the Indian day, from when we quitted stables till the evening shadows proclaimed the hour of Polo, I devoured Gibbon." Gibbon's influence on Churchill's prose style is immediately apparent. This sentence, picked almost at random from the depths of the third volume of Gibbon's history, could easily have been penned by Churchill: "When their long lances were fixed in the rest, the warriors furiously spurred their horses against the foe; and the light cavalry of the Turks and Arabs could seldom stand against the direct and impetuous weight of their charge." Compare that with this passage from Churchill's account of the Battle of Omdurman, outside Khartoum, in 1898: "As the successors of the Saracens descended the long smooth slopes which led to the river and their enemy, they encountered the rifle fire of two and a half divisions of trained infantry, drawn up two deep and in close order and supported by at least 70 guns on the river bank and in the gunboats, all firing with undisturbed efficiency." He set himself to reading twenty-five pages of Gibbon every day, and twice as many of Thomas Macaulay's five-volume *History of England*.

George Orwell once asserted, "Good prose is like a window pane." But if Churchill's prose were a window, it would be the stained glass glowing at the end of a cathedral's transept. His style can be ornate at times, even gaudy, but he knew what he was doing. He was intoxicated by language, reveling in the nuances and sounds of words. "He likes to use four or five words all with the same meaning, as an old man shows you his orchids; not to show them off, but just because he loves them," observed his wartime doctor, Charles Wilson.

Isaiah Berlin observed that "Churchill's language is a medium which he invented because he needed it. It has a bold, ponderous, fairly uniform, easily recognisable rhythm which lends itself to parody (including his own) like all strongly individual styles." Not everyone approved. The novelist Evelyn Waugh, possibly the only person to prefer Churchill's malignant, alcoholic son Randolph Churchill to Churchill himself, would mock Churchill as "a master of sham-Augustan prose."

Like many autodidacts, Churchill would proceed through life intensely confident of what he knew and happily ignorant of what he did not. He knew what he knew, but there were vast amounts of literature he never read, nor seemed to be aware of. He met Henry James at a lunch in 1903, but understandably was less interested in the commentary of the

Master than he was in another American at the table, the beautiful young actress Ethel Barrymore. Twelve years later, he found himself at another meal with James and again ignored him, giving a fellow guest the impression that "he had never heard of Henry James & he could not think why we all listened with such reverent attention & such misplaced patience to this rather long-winded old man. He disregarded him, he contradicted him, he interrupted him, he showed him no consideration whatsoever."

When his friend Violet Asquith, later Violet Bonham Carter, then aged nineteen, at a dinner party quoted to him Keats's "Ode to a Nightingale," he had not heard of it, despite its being one of the hundred or so most famous poems in the English language. He must have taken note of her surprise, because the next time they met, he had memorized the poem—and, for good measure, all six of Keats's odes, which he then proceeded to recite to her, one by one. His doctor once wrote that he appeared not to have read *Hamlet* until he was past the age of eighty, but this remains uncertain, as he had quoted parts of the play to others earlier in his life. At any rate, concluded his wartime advisor Sir Desmond Morton, Churchill's factual knowledge, measured overall, "was astonishingly superficial."

When Churchill was in public, he was rarely quiet—and to Churchill, almost everything was public. The only activity Violet Asquith remembered him practice in silence in his entire life was painting, a hobby he picked up when middle-aged and out of office in a kind of political exile. In conversation, when he exhausted his own thoughts, he would keep himself talking by reciting great chunks of poetry, often by Byron or Pope.

Like many writers, especially those who make their living at it, Churchill developed a workmanlike attitude toward the job. "Writing a book is not unlike building a house," he once commented, with materials to be assembled and placed atop a firm foundation. He meditated on the importance of the solid sentence, and then on the shaping of paragraphs, which "must fit on to one another like the automatic couplings of railway carriages."

Having learned to write, and finishing his task of self-education, Churchill felt himself ready to take on the world. He went looking for wars to write about, with the intention of shedding some glory on himself and using that as a platform to launch himself into politics. For the next several years he would pursue combat frantically. In 1897, when minor fighting broke out on the Afghan-Indian border between the British and local Pashtun tribes, he pushed his way from his post in Bangalore to the action on the northwest fringe of the subcontinent, a journey of some 1,500 miles. When he could not find a military billet in the operation, his mother wrangled a job for him, covering the conflict for the London *Daily Telegraph,* beginning his long relationship with that newspaper. Then, when the inevitable casualties caused a billet to come open, he shifted over to active service. By the middle of the month, he would be assigned to the 31st Punjab Infantry.

In fact, what he witnessed was not a war, but a few weeks of skirmishing. The operation in September 1897 is remembered today only for the fact that Churchill was there and came under fire. "Nothing in life is so exhilarating as to be shot at without result," he memorably noted.

His comrades may have found him overexcited by the experience. Lieutenant Donald McVean, who briefly shared a tent with him during fighting on the Afghan border, wrote in his diary that Churchill's sole fear in combat was that he would be wounded in the mouth.

The fighting with the Afghan tribes was the only war Winston had, so he ran with it. He managed in two months of writing to pump up the few weeks of minor action that he had witnessed into a small book, *The Story of the Malakand Field Force.* Had it been written by anyone else, it likely never would have seen print. But the young man was backed by a formidable force back in London. His mother approached a literary agent and a publisher about turning his dispatches into a book. When it was published a few months later, she promised her son that "I will 'boom' it judiciously," which she did, talking it up to London's book reviewers and newspaper editors.

The Story of the Malakand Field Force is a jejune volume, a bit too pleased with its wit as it relates the events of the brief British offensive. When Christians fight Muslim tribesmen, Churchill remarks with heavy-handed irony, "Luckily the religion of peace is usually the better armed." There is a bit of tough-guy posturing in Churchill's prose: "About half a dozen shots were fired into camp, without other result than to disturb light sleepers." Anyone who has ever been rousted from sleep by having shots fired over them is likely to find this not credible, in part because one does not know how long it will go on or whether it will intensify.

His own confident assessment of the book was that "my style is good—even in parts classic." That overshoots the mark. Still, the glimmerings of the future Churchill are visible in his inaugural effort.

Perhaps most important for Churchill, his book received some complimentary notices. For this young man, after two decades of feeling ignored, neglected, and abused, being applauded was a welcome and unaccustomed pleasure. "Reading the positive press served as a great tonic," states Simon Read in his study of this phase of Churchill's life. "Never before had Churchill been praised in such fashion. He had grown accustomed as a student to hearing his father and teachers voice their disappointment."

CHURCHILL IN AFRICA

And so young Winston Churchill was launched. He took leave from the military, took a ship home to England, and toured London as a freshly published author. He used the book to make new connections with important men, and then used those contacts to get himself included in the

British expedition then forming to fight Islamists in the Sudan. There, just one year after his first taste of combat, he participated in another round of fighting, riding in a cavalry charge outside Khartoum, in a battle in which the British massacred Sudanese tribesmen. He turned this into another book, *The River War*. He then went back to India, participated in a polo tournament, and wound up his affairs in the army.

His eyes were on the prize of a political career. With his newspaper dispatches and two books, he had made enough of a name for himself to be tapped to run for Parliament. In July 1899, at the age of only twenty-five, he stood for election, losing narrowly. It was a respectable enough showing to mark him as a comer.

His martial luck held. Another fight on the periphery of the empire was brewing. Less than four months after the election, he was off to South Africa to cover what would soon become the Boer War. He did not mean to suffer. He brought with him two cases of wine, eighteen bottles of whisky, and six each of port, brandy, and vermouth. He arrived in South Africa at the end of October 1899. When he returned to England less than a year later, he was famous.

His adventure started on November 15, 1899. He had been in South Africa barely two weeks when he was aboard a British military armored train being sent to the front as part of a reconnaissance operation. "Eager for trouble," as he recalled, he found a place aboard it. No sooner had the train begun chugging into Boer-held territory than it was taken under fire by enemy light guns. The engineer accelerated, and part of the train derailed, likely encouraged by Boer undermining of the rails.

Churchill leaped into action. For more than an hour, while under fire, he helped the British commander organize the men, clear the track of the overturned cars, and then recouple the engine. Finally, the engine began to retreat at a walking pace. It was laden with the wounded, with others on foot sheltered on the far side of the engine. Then, contrary to a hastily devised plan, the engine began to speed up, leaving behind the infantry.

Churchill told the engine driver to stop on the far side of a bridge over the Blue Krantz River, so he could walk back along the track to rally the infantry. As he approached, he saw men, but they were not British. A man on horseback with a rifle approached. Churchill reached for his pistol and found his holster empty—he had taken it out to ease his work restarting the train. He surrendered and became a prisoner of the Boers.

For this young dervish of a man, becoming a POW was close to torture. He was held, along with other British officers, in a school building in Pretoria, the Boer capital. "Hours crawl like paralytic centipedes. Nothing amuses you. Reading is difficult, writing, impossible. . . . I certainly hated every minute of my captivity more than I ever hated any other period of my life," he remembered. He protested that he was a war correspondent; the Boers responded that he had been armed and was seen helping the British military in the fighting.

One night in mid-December 1899, after being held less than one month, he climbed a wall, evaded a sentry—some bribery may perhaps have been involved there—and then followed the stars to a railroad he knew was about half a mile away. He crouched near a train as it began to puff out of a station. "Then I hurled myself on the trucks [cars], clutched at something, missed, clutched again, missed again, grasped some sort of hand-hold, was swung off my feet—my toes bumping on the line." He climbed inside a pile of empty coal sacks and fell asleep. There was, he thought, no lullaby more pleasing "than the clatter of the train that carried an escaping prisoner at twenty miles an hour away from the enemy's capital."

It was a perfect adventure for a young imperialist of promise. Heading for the border of Portuguese East Africa, about 275 miles away, he slept in the countryside by day and jumped trains by night. Running low on food and energy, he made his way to the house of a Scottish mine manager, sympathetic to the British cause. Churchill portrays this as a lucky accident, but one must wonder whether he had been told to seek out this man, who stashed him two hundred feet below ground at the bottom of a disused mineshaft. There Churchill was provided with candles, whisky, cigars, and chicken, as well as a copy of Robert Louis Stevenson's thriller *Kidnapped*. Meantime, arrangements were made to hide the young fugitive inside a hole made in a cargo of wool bales on another freight train heading to the Portuguese colony. Arriving at Lourenço Marques, the capital of Portuguese East Africa, he reported to the British consul. For fear of Churchill's being retaken by Boers in the town, the diplomat that night put him aboard a steamer back to South Africa. There Churchill gave a speech and then rejoined the British forces in his dual role of officer and correspondent, which then was considered quite acceptable.

In the months afterward, he reveled in the articles arriving from the British newspapers about his adventures. "The papers had . . . been filled with extravagant praise of my behavior," both in the incident of the train and then in his escape, he noted. "I became for the time quite famous." His thoughts were really no longer on the war, which was breaking down into small guerrilla actions.

After some more desultory reporting, he headed home to use his growing fame to relaunch his political career. When he got home in the summer of 1900, his mother was not there to greet him—she was preoccupied with marrying her second husband, Captain George Cornwallis-West, a handsome man twenty years younger than her and just sixteen days older than Winston. Years later, Churchill would devote an entire chapter of his memoir to the incident of "The Armoured Train." Rightly so, because this incident was the springboard for his jump from minor celebrity to major figure in British public life.

From the start, Churchill was regarded by many of his peers as not quite correct in his breeding, character, and temperament. "In Tory and social circles he . . . was an outsider, a pusher, thruster, and self-advertiser," noted Violet Asquith. Indeed, by October, just twelve months after being a prisoner and then a fugitive, he was elected a member of Parliament.

THE ADVENTURER BECOMES A POLITICIAN AND HUSBAND

The rocket ride was just beginning. Just four years after entering the House of Commons, Churchill abandoned the Conservative Party and became a Liberal, one reason that Conservatives would long tend to distrust him. In April 1908, aged just thirty-three, he was invited by H. H. Asquith, the newly chosen prime minister (and father of Violet), to become a member of the Cabinet. Unimpressed, King Edward VII told his son that Churchill "is almost more of a cad in office than he was in opposition."

In the same year, Churchill wooed and married the woman who would be his closest confidante for more than half a century. For years, he had pursued one woman, then another, with indifferent results. He grew extremely close to Violet Asquith. Yet he seemed to find romance awkward. She apparently expected him to propose. He did not. Rather, in the spring of 1908, he became interested in another, far less prominent woman, Clementine Hozier, offspring of a minor branch of impoverished Scots aristocracy who had at one point taught French to supplement her income.

In August 1908, Violet learned that Churchill had proposed to Clementine. "Whether he will ultimately mind her being as stupid as an owl I don't know," she wrote to her own best friend, Venetia Stanley. "He did not wish for—though he needs it badly—a critical, reformatory wife who would stop up the lacunas in his taste etc. and hold him back from blunders." In one of those odd complications of British aristocratic life, Violet's father would a few years later fall in love with Violet's friend Venetia. During Cabinet meetings about the Great War, he distracted himself by writing love letters to her.

It is unlikely that Violet would have been tolerant of Churchill's lack of romantic imagination in any case. A few years later, he was standing alongside her—she remained a close friend—at the stern rail of a yacht cruising the Adriatic. "How perfect!" she sighed.

"Yes," Churchill responded. "Range perfect—visibility perfect." He proceeded to tell her how the coastline towns could be bombarded.

Clementine Hozier herself came from a tangled background. Some biographers believe that her natural father was Bertram Mitford, the grandfather of the six Mitford sisters, who would cut a wide swath across the Britain of the 1930s and 1940s. "Clementine was not entirely sure as to the identity of her father," notes the writer and politician Boris Johnson.

For Churchill, Clementine's personality would prove far more significant than her parentage. Marrying Clementine was perhaps the wisest choice Churchill made in his life. Reserved, quietly observant about the world, she was not him, and absolutely unlike his mother: she had known the fear of lacking money, and the life of the anonymous citizen. Nor was she a potential politician herself, as Violet was. Rather than outshine or rival him, she would anchor him when he was manically high and buoy him when he was miserably down. As she asserted to him years later, "Just becos' I am ordinary & love you I know what is right for you & good for you in the end." Winston and Clementine were wed in September 1908, just weeks after the engagement was announced. Perhaps significantly, at the ceremony, "Bertie" Mitford sat next to Clementine's mother.

In 1911, Churchill achieved the high post of first lord of the admiralty, overseeing the Royal Navy. He held that post into World War I. In 1915, he was seen as one of the major architects of the British landings at Gallipoli, in Turkey. The operation was a disaster. After nine months of fighting, the Allies withdrew from the peninsula, having suffered more than fifty thousand dead, and with little to show for those losses.

Churchill, taking much of the blame for the failed Turkish campaign, suddenly found himself out of a job. He was stunned. "Like a sea-beast fished up from the depths, or a diver too suddenly hoisted, my veins threatened to burst from the pressure," he recalled. Mulling the events of the war, he added, "I had great anxiety and no means of relieving it." Looking for a way to occupy and calm himself, he took up painting. It would serve him well as a distraction for many decades.

But withdrawing from public life and contemplating the English countryside proved insufficient to ease his misery—or to offer him a path back to prominence. He did not feel he was to blame for Gallipoli, but still saw the need to do penance for it, so he volunteered for service in the war in France. He arrived at the front in November 1915 and wound up commanding a front-line battalion for several months. "It is a wild scene," he wrote to Clementine. "Filth & rubbish everywhere, graves built into the defences & scattered muck on all sides; & about this scene in the dazzling moonlight troops of enormous rats creep & glide, to the unceasing accompaniment of rifle & machine guns & the venomous whining & whirring of the bullets which pass overhead." For all that, he was surprised at how much better he felt in France than he had in England. "I have found happiness & content such as I have not known for many months."

After a lifetime of champagne and rich food, living shoulder to shoulder with others in the mud was as close as he ever would come to experiencing the life of the common man. Even so, he took steps to ease his situation. He asked his wife to ship to him "large slabs of corned beef; stilton cheeses; cream; hams; sardines—dried fruits; you might almost try a big beef steak pie: but not tinned grouse or fancy tinned things. The simpler the better: & substantial too; for our ration meat is tough & tasteless."

Clementine, sensitive to his mood swings, also sought to steady him when his spirits plummeted at the front. "Darling," she wrote in February 1916, "one of the letters I received yesterday was written in a somber mood. Do not I pray of you let this mood deepen & permanently tinge your heart & mind."

When he came home on leave, she felt he paid too much attention to politics and too little to her needs. She gently chided him. "My Darling these grave public anxieties are very wearing—When next I see you I hope there will be a little time for us both alone." She did not quite state that she needed more sexual intimacy, but came close: "We are still young, but Time flies stealing love away & leaving only friendship which is very peaceful but not stimulating or warming." Pamela Digby, who would marry Randolph Churchill during World War II, and who had intimate conversations with Clementine about her problems with him, recalled decades later that she came away with the impression that Churchill men had small carnal appetites. Her sex life with Randolph left much to be desired, Pamela told her biographer. "When it came to sex, Randolph, like some other Churchill men, did not seem all that interested. It did not help that he drank too much to perform well or often." Arguing against this report is the fact that Winston and Clementine had children born to them in 1909, 1911, 1914, 1918, and 1922.

Churchill's section of the front was relatively quiet, because at that point in the war, most of the action was around Verdun, farther to the south. Even so, his battalion suffered casualties. In May 1917, it was sufficiently depleted that it was withdrawn, to be consolidated with other units. Churchill took that as an opportunity to head home and return to politics. By July of that year, he was back in the Cabinet as the minister of munitions.

He was defeated for reelection in 1922 and lost another vote in 1923. In April 1924, he wrote to his wife, who was vacationing in France, that he and the children were enjoying themselves in the countryside. "I drink champagne at all meals & buckets of claret & soda in between, & the cuisine tho' simple is excellent. In the evenings we play the gramophone & . . . Mah Jongg." The same year, he was returned to Parliament, just as a Labour government took office for the first time. But with his Liberal Party in turmoil, he then left the Liberals to rejoin the Conservatives. After that act, he reportedly crowed, "Anyone can rat, but it takes a certain amount of ingenuity to re-rat." He was not entirely welcomed back by his old Conservative comrades. Among Tories, wrote his friend and political ally Lord Beaverbrook, "he was hated, he was mistrusted, and he was feared."

Even so, at the end of 1924, when the infant Labour government fell and the Conservatives took power again, he was rewarded with the important post of chancellor of the exchequer, the equivalent of a finance minister or secretary of the treasury in other countries. This was psychologically significant for him because being named to that position had been the pinnacle of his father's meteoric career. Lord Randolph had held it for just five months in 1886.

But by the end of the 1920s, he was following his father in another way, squabbling with his party's leaders and expecting his will to be obeyed. Instead, after 1929, when the Conservatives were replaced by a second Labour government, he found himself out of power. His finances were in tatters as a result of his stock market speculations. As he tried to recover, he occupied himself with writing and with lecturing—which is how he found himself on Fifth Avenue in December 1931, distractedly looking the wrong way as an American automobile sped toward him.

CHAPTER 3

ORWELL THE POLICEMAN

I f Churchill spent his early years in the pursuit of power and prominence, Orwell spent his own in pursuit of a core theme. Ultimately,
he would find it: the abuse of power. It is the thread that runs
through all his writings, from his early works to the very end.

———— ◆ ————

The writer we know today as "George Orwell" was born as Eric Blair in
June 1903 in Bengal, India, where his father, the son of an officer in the
Anglo-Indian army, was a low-ranking bureaucrat in the Indian Civil
Service's department responsible for overseeing the growing and process-
ing of opium. Most of the drug grown and processed was exported to
China, which helped to balance large British imports of Chinese tea, por-
celain, and silk. Indeed, in the mid-nineteenth century, the opium trade
accounted for 15 percent of India's revenue. His mother was from a
French family, the Limouzins, who grew tea in Burma.

But he was not to stay long in Burma as a child. When he was less than a year old, his mother packed up him and his older sister and took them to England, where they lived in Henley-on-Thames, west of London. For a few years, the toddler would live not far away from Winston Churchill, who was serving there with a squadron of the Oxfordshire Hussars. In his first winter, at the age of seven months, he suffered a bout of bronchitis.

The first word spoken by young Eric Blair may have been, at the age of about eighteen months, "beastly." Like Churchill, Orwell was an unhappy young man. His brother-in-law Humphrey Dakin, who had known and sincerely disliked Orwell since he was a child, described him as "a little fat boy . . . always whining. And sneaking, telling tales and so on." He eventually had two sisters, one younger, one older. Despite later coining the famous phrase "Big Brother," he had no brothers, older or younger.

Like Churchill, Orwell saw little of his father, who traveled from Burma to visit his family in 1907, and then moved in with them when he retired in 1912. "I barely saw my father before I was eight," Orwell noted. By that time, the boy had been shipped off to boarding school. The distant figure of Orwell's father "appeared to me simply as a gruff-voiced elderly man forever saying 'Don't.'" So began Orwell's lifelong skepticism of authority.

Young Eric hated his first boarding school, St. Cyprian's, in East Sussex. He described it later so vehemently in an essay, "Such, Such Were the Joys," that the article was not published during his lifetime for fear of libel suits. "At eight years old you were suddenly taken out of this warm nest and flung into a world of force and fraud and secrecy, like a gold-fish into a tank full of pike," Orwell remembered.

At school, alone and afraid, Orwell became a bed wetter. This led to a beating by the headmaster, who chanted "you dir-ty lit-tle boy" in time with the swinging of the bone-handled riding crop. After his first beating, Orwell reported to his fellows that it had not hurt. This proud remark was overheard by someone in authority, so the boy was recalled for a second thrashing so severe that the riding crop broke. This led Orwell to the calculation that he lived in a world where it was impossible to be good—he had not wanted to wet the bed, he had tried to stop it, but it still happened. He called this grim realization "the great, abiding lesson of my boyhood."

He also came to realize that he was attending school at a reduced rate—that is, as a scholarship student. This was not an act of charity on the part of the school. Rather, his job was to succeed academically and get into a top-level school, Eton or Harrow, and so burnish the lower school's reputation. One can see the beginning of the adult socialist in the boy's realization that the richer students were never beaten, no matter how they behaved. "It was the poor but 'clever' boys who suffered. Our brains were a gold-mine in which he [the headmaster] had sunk money, and the dividends must be squeezed out of us." He emerged from the school persuaded of two ugly rules of life: that the strong would always beat the weak, and that any project he attempted would fail.

Yet he did as he was bid and won that prized scholarship to Eton. Oddly, upon graduating from there at age nineteen, rather than try to enroll in a university, he joined the Indian Imperial Police, which sent him to Burma. Even now, it is hard to fathom what he was thinking in doing so. One of the lessons he had learned at school, he wrote, was "break the rules, or perish." There was nothing about him that recommended him as an enforcer of any sort of law, let alone one built to enforce colonial repression. Yet for the next four years of his life that was his job. Perhaps he wanted to see for once what it was like to be on the side of the strong, to himself be one of the authorities.

So, like Churchill, Orwell came of age in a remote part of the British Empire. In his case, it was in Upper Burma, about 1,600 miles southeast of the Afghan borderlands where Churchill had ridden twenty-five years earlier, and which he chronicled in *Malakand Field Force*. Orwell lived in

Burma from the end of 1922 to the middle of 1927, working as an officer of the Imperial Police. He could go there because the British had annexed the uncolonized central and northern sections of Burma in 1886, in an action supervised by Winston's father, Lord Randolph Churchill, then serving briefly as the British secretary of state for India.

Making a poor early impression on his superiors in the police, Orwell was shipped off to the town of Katha, at the northern end of the Burmese rail line, and just eighty miles from the Chinese border. It was there, at that remote town on the Irrawaddy River, that he matured, developing the perspective that would shape his writing throughout his career. Consider this closely observed moment, from his early essay "A Hanging," of his helping escort a condemned Hindu man forty yards to the gallows:

> Once, in spite of the men who gripped him by each shoulder, he stepped slightly aside to avoid a puddle on the path. It is curious, but till that moment I had never realised what it means to destroy a healthy, conscious man. When I saw the prisoner step aside to avoid the puddle, I saw the mystery, the unspeakable wrongness, of cutting a life short when it is in full tide. This man was not dying, he was alive just as we were alive.

From his years there, Orwell produced his first novel, *Burmese Days*, really more a memoir than a work of pure imagination. As he put it in a letter years later, "Much of it is simply reporting what I have seen."

The book is best read as a study of the abuse of power in its various forms. He wrote in "Shooting an Elephant," one of his finest essays, that he was seeing there every day

> the dirty work of Empire at close quarters. The wretched prisoners huddling in the stinking cages of the lock-ups, the grey cowed faces of the long-term convicts, the scarred buttocks of the men who had been flogged with bamboos . . .

He quit his police post when he was still a young man, just twenty-four years old. He went back home and began knocking around London and Paris. He actually would finish *Burmese Days* several years later, and it would be published after the second book he wrote, *Down and Out in Paris and London*. But in Orwell's own life, Burma came before Paris and London.

His account of his time in Burma is straightforward. The antihero of *Burmese Days* is Flory, a bored, disaffected, vaguely liberal colonial lumber merchant living in a small colonial outpost in far northern Burma along the Irrawaddy River. He resembles what Orwell might have become had he stayed another ten years—an unhappy man of "about thirty-five," with black, stiff hair, a cropped black moustache, and sallow skin. "His face was very haggard . . . with lank cheeks, and a sunken withered look around his eyes." The major difference between Orwell and Flory is the character's most noticeable physical feature—a port-wine birthmark staining his left cheek, an attribute that makes him acutely self-conscious.

Flory meets Elizabeth Lackersteen, a young British woman who had been sent to Burma to find a husband. She does not really like him, and in fact is disdainful of his interest in art and literature and increasingly wary of his sympathy for Burmese life and culture. She only really warms to him when he conforms to the imperial manner, as when he shoots a pigeon. Yet that imperialist part is the facet of himself that he despises and wishes he had the courage to rise above. Even so, Elizabeth is somewhat desperate, suffering nightly gropes by an uncle with whom she is staying. Given her difficult circumstances, she appears willing to settle for Flory, until a scheming Burmese minor official, a corrupt subdivisional magistrate, maneuvers to embarrass Flory by having him publicly denounced by the Burmese mistress Flory has thrown out. This provokes Elizabeth to sever ties with Flory. Miserable over the embarrassment and the abandonment, facing deep emotional isolation, Flory shoots himself. After he dies, the "hideous" birthmark fades away.

All this is served up in a stew of social and political machinations by the British and Burmese over small issues of prestige and face, such as which Burmese will be invited to join the town's European Club, which has been told by higher British authorities to liberalize its racist admission policies. With its observations of endless, tiny, cruel exertions of social power, the novel feels sometimes as if it were a combination of Jane Austen and E. M. Forster, whose *Passage to India* appeared four years before Orwell began drafting his own novel of the waning empire.

Setting his scene, Orwell writes early in the novel, "In any town in India the European Club is the spiritual citadel, the real seat of British power, the Nirvana for which native officials and millionaires pine in vain." This particular club, small and isolated, had lagged behind others and had never invited in a "native" member. When required to do so, three of the club's members vigorously object. "Little pot-bellied niggers breathing garlic in your face over the bridge-table," sneers one, in an intentionally ugly sentence. But of the two other members, Flory likes the idea, while the de facto chief of the British community, the paternalistic Mr. Macgregor, is resigned to carry out his instructions.

The twists in the plot almost always carry a larger point, given the fairly clumsy ideological framework Orwell uses. For example, a British woman sighing about the "laziness" of her servants remarks, "In some ways they are getting almost as bad as the lower classes at home." When a visiting British officer kicks the club butler, he is upbraided by a member who says, "It's our job to kick the servants, not yours." Flory tells an Indian doctor, his sole true friend, that he was ashamed to be living "the lie that we're here to uplift our poor black brothers instead of to rob them." The empire, he asserts, rests on erecting banks and prisons and calling that progress. In sum, Flory says, "The British Empire is simply a device for giving trade monopolies to the English—or rather to gangs of Jews and Scotchmen." There is no hint that Orwell was being ironic in that double ethnic swipe, especially given his close identification with Flory. Historically, it is accurate that the export of opium from India to

Burma was dominated by two companies, the Scottish firm of Jardine Matheson and an Iraqi Jewish family, the Sassoons, who became British. (Siegfried Sassoon, the memoirist and poet of World War I, was part of that family.)

It is a minor novel, but not a bad one. It is better than Churchill's early work (and especially Churchill's rightly forgotten sole work of fiction, *Savrola*), but that is in part because Orwell at this point in his career was a more seasoned writer.

If Orwell had not gone on to write other far more powerful works, today *Burmese Days* probably would be remembered as an obscure but occasionally interesting literary study of empire. As a young man, he recalled many years later,

> I wanted to write enormous naturalistic novels with unhappy endings, full of detailed descriptions and arresting similes, and also full of purple passages in which words were used partly for the sake of their sound. And in fact my first completed novel, *Burmese Days,* which I wrote when I was thirty but projected much earlier, is rather that kind of book.

Yet it remains a readable story, most notable nowadays for its insights into the nature of the empire and of imperialism generally. "No European cares anything about proofs," asserts U Po Kyin, the Machiavellian Burmese official, in the novel's first scene. "When a man has a black face, suspicion is proof"—an observation he cleverly uses to his advantage. The narrator later reminds the reader that Flory "had forgotten that most people can be at ease in a foreign country only when they are disparaging the inhabitants"—not a universal truth, but certainly accurate in describing the sad little British community of *Burmese Days.*

At the end, Flory is miserable, self-loathing, and in despair. His last words are a lie. "Master wouldn't hurt you," he reassures his terrified dog. He then shoots the pet and himself.

Orwell initially had Flory write his own epitaph, but excised it from the final version of the book: "Learn from me how not to live." At the novel's end, Flory is just one more victim of the empire. One of the points of the novel is that the English people, as well as the Burmese, are crippled by the imperial system.

This is perhaps the most important consequence of Orwell's time in Burma: If at school he learned to be skeptical of authority, in Asia he learned how the exercise of power can corrupt a person. He hated what he saw it do to himself and feared what would have happened to him had he remained in the role of enforcer of colonial law. As he put it in "Shooting an Elephant," "When the white man turns tyrant it is his own freedom that he destroys. He becomes a sort of hollow, posing dummy, the conventionalized figure of a sahib." This conclusion amounted to a wholesale rejection of his own background in the bureaucracy of the British colonies.

It is difficult now to invoke how this novel of the British in Burma must have felt like a slap in the face to those middle-class Englishmen who ran the everyday affairs of the British Empire. Even into the 1930s, it was common in English culture to portray the empire as a force for good, transmitting education, trade, and the rule of law into the far reaches of Asia and Africa. It was unusual for a British writer to portray it instead as a force of evil, driven by the basest of motives. "I thought it was a bit wet at the time if you follow me," recalled Orwell's brother-in-law Humphrey Dakin, himself a civil servant. "He was looking for dirt and squalor and that sort of thing and he found it." For fear of libel suits from people who recognized themselves in the story, the book was published first in the United States. Others contemplated more direct responses, with his old police trainer supposedly vowing that if he ever again encountered Orwell, he would horsewhip him.

The key conclusion that Orwell took away from his time in Burma was that "the oppressed are always right and the oppressors are always wrong." Orwell went on to write that it was "a mistaken theory, but the natural result of being one of the oppressors yourself."

To do penance for his time as an oppressor, Orwell would dive into a lengthy process of self-abnegation upon returning to Europe. He spent some time living as a tramp in England. Then, in the spring of 1928, he hurled himself into the underworld of Paris. He lived and worked in filthy conditions. He suffered his first round of pneumonia, the beginning of a series of lung ailments that would pain him for the remaining two decades of his life. He went hungry. This was mainly of his own volition—he had an aunt in Paris, Nellie Limouzin, who would look out for him if he asked. But that was not what he was looking for. He later told a friend that he lost his savings when they were stolen by a girl named Suzanne, "a little trollop" he had picked up in a café. "She was beautiful, and had a figure like a boy, an Eton crop, and was in every way desirable." And he began to write for publication, placing his first essays in French and English newspapers late in 1928. He still was writing under his own name, Eric Blair.

He returned from France to England at the end of 1929. He moved in with his parents, who had relocated to the southeast coastal town of Southwold, which was favored by retired Indian civil service officials. He made a little money tutoring, and then got a job teaching in a minor secondary school. He also wooed Brenda Salkeld, a well-read gym teacher. He proposed repeatedly to her, and ultimately accepted her refusals. He went on to have a short romance with another woman.

He then set out to experience the British underlife. He picked hops with tramps in fields. He slept on the pavement in Trafalgar Square. He tried to get arrested. He moved from shelter to shelter, where the men were fed swill and treated like dogs.

He then combined his experiences in England and France into a kind of fictionalized memoir that was published in 1933 as *Down and Out in*

Paris and London. It would be the first time he published under the name "George Orwell," combining a very English first name with that of an estuarial stream south of Southwold, the River Orwell.

Orwell was writing at a time when it was considered legitimate for the wealthy not only to ignore but indeed to disdain the way most of the people around them lived and worked. The British novelist Vita Sackville-West and her husband, the talented mediocrity Harold Nicolson, are good examples. They considered themselves the crown of creation—good, decent, tolerant, cultivated people, the best sort of people produced by the best part of the best nation on Earth. "I am a happy, honest, loving man," Nicolson once confided to his diary. Among those with whom he shared his love was Guy Burgess, who would be revealed in the 1950s to be part of an aristocratic ring of Soviet spies recruited around H.A.R. "Kim" Philby at Cambridge in the 1930s.

Nicolson was a snob to the bone. He once wrote to his wife, "We are humane, charitable, just and not vulgar. By God, we are not vulgar!" He was pleased to agree with the supercilious comment by another of his lovers, the literary critic Raymond Mortimer, that "the masses do not care for truth in the way that we care for it."

"I hate democracy," Sackville-West once confided to Nicolson. "I wish *la populace* had never been encouraged to emerge from its rightful place. I should like to see them as well fed and well housed as T. T. cows, but not more articulate than that." ("T. T. cows" were those that had been tested for tuberculosis, which was still a threat in the England of the mid-twentieth century, as George Orwell would learn.) In another letter a week later, she added how relieved she was not to be a common drudge. "Wouldn't it be awful if one were a person who just existed, getting through one day after the other, all filled up with idiotic little preoccupations that had not importance at all? I mean washing up and cleaning the front doorstep and gossiping about one's neighbours?"

So it was with some justification that Orwell could pose the question in *Down and Out,* "What do the majority of educated people know about poverty?" It was exactly the "vulgar" world of working and surviving, the existence of the vast majority of humankind, in which he sought to immerse himself and then describe to the world. At times he rubs the reader's nose in it, as when early in the book he neutrally describes "Charlie," a young French ne'er-do-well who is a regular at the neighborhood bar, relating how he paid to rape a twenty-year-old woman being held captive. "I pulled her off the bed and threw her on to the floor. And then I fell upon her like a tiger! . . . More and more savage, I renewed the attack. Again and again the girl tried to escape; she cried out for mercy anew, but I laughed at her." It probably was a mistake for Orwell to devote six pages of his short book (it is 213 pages long) to this Poe-like horror story. It is a distraction from his real theme, which is to depict the issues that preoccupied the poor of Paris and London in the 1930s: getting enough to eat, staying warm, sleeping just enough to rise and go back to work, and getting drunk on cheap wine on Saturday night.

It was a book he had to write for himself as much as for the reader, an essential step on his journey through life and into literature. By immersing himself in the filth, fatigue, and hunger of the poor worker, Orwell was atoning for his previous colonial life. In Burma he had voluntarily joined the European oppressors. Now as penance he would voluntarily live among the oppressed of Europe. "I came to understand that it was . . . an act of expiation for having served the cause of British colonialism by spending five years in Burma as an officer of the Imperial Police," observed the philosopher A. J. Ayer, who was working for British intelligence when he met Orwell in Paris at the end of World War II.

Down and Out, which was published in January 1933, is most important as a transitional work for Orwell, part of his search for himself as a writer and observer. It is a little uncertain, shaky in tone, especially in its opening third. Like many young writers, he was susceptible to the lure of the easy shock, as with the rape scene. Another passage early in the book suggests that he is a poverty tourist, not locked into that world. It comes as he is hungry and sees an insect fall into his glass of milk. His immediate conclusion is, "There is nothing for it but to throw the milk away and go foodless." Someone genuinely suffering prolonged hunger, rather than making an excursion into it, likely would pluck out the bug and drink up. The poor are accustomed to the company of insects.

Down and Out sometimes reads like a lurid guidebook to the exotic world of the urban poor. In several places in the book, Orwell limns the status structure within a segment of proletarian society—a concern that seems quite British in an unconscious way on his part. In the restaurant where he works, the top of the pyramid is occupied by the hotel manager, then the maître d', and then, in descending order, the headwaiter, the head cook, the personnel chief, the other cooks, the other waiters, the apprentice waiters, the dishwashers, and the chambermaids. Near the book's end, the narrator returns to England to live on the streets of London, where he discerns a clear caste structure among its beggars. "There is a sharp social line between those who merely cadge and those who attempt to give some value for money." The most prosperous are street performers, such as organ-grinders, acrobats, and sidewalk artists. Below them are those who affect to sell matches, bootlaces, or lavender, to sing hymns—the pretense being necessary, he explains, because actually asking for money for nothing is a criminal offense. Like a proper travel writer, Orwell even provides a glossary of street life, defining slang words such as "gagger," "moocher," and "clodhopper," the last being a street dancer.

Orwell was just twenty-five years old when he went to Paris, and the book's flaws are those of a young writer still learning his craft. Orwell had an overworked sense of smell, so at times *Down and Out* seems more about the stench of the downtrodden than about their sufferings or modes of survival. On his morning commute on the Paris Metro, he "stood jammed in the swaying mass of passengers, nose to nose with some hideous French face, breathing sour wine and garlic." Unlike in *Burmese Days*, we are not told if the garlic breathers are pot-bellied. He was especially sensitive to that pungent plant, finding during a spell farming one winter in Morocco in 1939 that his milk became undrinkable after his small farm's cow ate wild garlic. But he did manage to cook with it. Later in the book, he is repulsed by "sheets [that] stank so horribly of sweat that I could not bear them near my nose." There are eight other instances in the book of Orwell noting the scents of his environment, most of them repugnant.

There are two points to be made here. First, sensitivity to odor is a tic of much of his writing. Second, and more unsettling, it is the smell of humanity that repels him. When he notes the smells of nature, even of the barnyard, it is almost always with approval. In contrast, he is always ready to be horrified by mankind.

Another more repellent thread runs through the book—a kind of quick and casual prejudice against the Jews he encounters. In a coffee shop he sees, "In a corner by himself a Jew, muzzle down in the plate, . . . guiltily eating bacon." The animallike "muzzle" in that sentence is particularly disturbing. At another point he recounts a tale told by his friend Boris, a former Russian soldier, of being offered the sexual services of a Jewish girl for fifty francs by her father—"A horrible old Jew, with a red beard like Judas Iscariot." Orwell's playing with this offhand sort of anti-Semitism appears in some of his other work. It is little consolation that he is an equal opportunity bigot, as when in *Down and Out* he approvingly quotes the proverb "Trust a snake before a Jew and a Jew before a Greek, but don't trust an Armenian."

The fact of the matter is that Orwell was always tin eared about Jews. During World War II, Orwell would write extensively against anti-Semitism, but in the course of doing so he failed to reexamine his own writings of the previous decade. After the war, he had surprisingly little to say about the Holocaust, one of the major events of his time. He remained strongly anti-Zionist throughout his life, but that probably should be seen more in the context of his enduring distaste for nationalism rather than the anti-Semitism of some of his early writings. Even so, his friend the journalist Malcolm Muggeridge would conclude that "he was at heart strongly anti-Semitic."

At its best, *Down and Out* depicts how the struggle to get by grinds down people every day. That basic fact of working life is most vividly shown in the middle of the book, about his time washing dishes for that hotel restaurant. It begins with a descent into the underworld with many of the characteristics of the Inferno, such as the lower circle to which the narrator is relegated:

> He led me down a winding staircase into a narrow passage, deep underground, and so low that I had to stoop in place. It was stiflingly hot and very dark, with only dim, yellow bulbs several yards apart. There seemed to be miles of dark labyrinthine passages—actually, I suppose, a few hundred yards in all. . . .
>
> One of the passages branched off into a laundry, where an old, skull-faced woman gave me a blue apron and a pile of dishcloths. Then the *chef du personnel* took me to a tiny underground den—a cellar below a cellar, as it were—where there were a sink and some gas ovens. It was too low for me to stand quite upright, and the temperature was perhaps 110 degrees Fahrenheit.

Here he arrives at one of the book's most memorable passages, in which he juxtaposes the steamy squalor of the kitchen with the pristine splendor of the adjacent dining room of the hotel, which we are told is one of the most expensive in Paris. The patrons eat among mirrors, flowers, snowy tablecloths, and gilt cornices. But lurking just behind the kitchen door, steps away,

> was disgusting filth. There was no time to sweep the floor till evening, and we slithered about in a compound of soapy water, lettuce-leaves,

torn paper and trampled food. A dozen waiters with their coats off, showing their sweaty armpits, sat at the table mixing salads and sticking their thumbs into the cream pots. . . . There were only two sinks, and no washing basin, and it was nothing unusual for a waiter to wash his face in the water in which clean crockery was rinsing. But the customers saw nothing of this.

His confident conclusion, after mixing with the rich at Eton and then with the poor in the subbasement of a Paris hotel and on the streets of London, was that "the average millionaire is only the average dishwasher dressed in a new suit." As for those who worried about the mob looting in the streets, he responded that "the mob is in fact loose now—and in the shape of rich men." In other words, in Orwell's view, the wealthy were waging class warfare, looting from the poor, but they just were not admitting it.

Orwell now thought himself a writer. He spent the mid-1930s in the bohemian north London neighborhood of Hampstead. He lived above Booklovers' Corner, a secondhand bookstore, writing bad novels in the mornings and evenings and working in the store in the afternoons. He described it as tomblike: a "small dark room, smelling of dust and decayed paper . . . filled to the brim with books mostly aged and unsaleable."

At this point in his life he was hardly on a promising course. "He was not a natural novelist," the writer Mary McCarthy once wrote of Orwell, in a gentle understatement. His limitations as a writer of conventional fiction are immediately evident to anyone browsing those novels of the mid-1930s—*A Clergyman's Daughter* (1935), *Keep the Aspidistra Flying* (1936), *Coming Up for Air* (1939). All of them are close to unreadable. Here is the clumsy opening of *Clergyman's Daughter:*

As the alarm clock on the chest of drawers exploded like a horrid little bomb of bell metal, Dorothy, wrenched from the depths of some complex, troubling dream, awoke with a start and lay on her back looking into the darkness of extreme exhaustion.

In addition to his published fiction, Orwell also wrote two early novels that he threw away. No trace has been found of them. Orwell's friend Jack Common, another socialist novelist, said Orwell wrote his '30s novels as fast as he could, making just enough to live off the proceeds.

These novels were summarized in a devastating aside by the novelist Anthony Powell, who was actually a friend of his: "Apart from projections of himself, the characters of his novels do not live as persons, though they are sometimes effective puppets in expressing his thesis of the moment."

Orwell himself later wrote to a friend who had asked for a copy of *Keep the Aspidistra Flying:*

There are two or three books which I am ashamed of and have not allowed to be reprinted or translated, and that is one of them. There is an even worse one called *A Clergyman's Daughter.* This was written simply as an exercise and I oughtn't to have published it, but I was desperate for money, ditto when I wrote *Keep the A.* At that time I simply hadn't a book in me, but I was half starved and had to turn out something to bring in £100 or so.

Orwell's talent lay elsewhere, still undiscovered by himself. His two great novels, coming near the end of his life, *Animal Farm* and *1984,* would not be naturalistic fiction typical of the twentieth century, but rather variants of genres generally held to be lesser—the fairy tale and the horror story. But reflecting reality more directly than conventional novels often do, both *Animal Farm* and *1984* were built on foundations of politics in its most basic sense of how we organize the public world, and how individuals relate to that organization.

More productively, Orwell in the spring of 1935 met his future wife. Eileen O'Shaughnessy was an attractive, bright young woman who had studied English literature at Oxford, graduating in 1927. At the time of their meeting, she was pursuing a master's degree in psychology at University College London, focusing on the measurement of intelligence and imagination in children.

A few months later, the British edition of *Burmese Days* was published. Orwell now had two books under his belt. He had come to suspect that in his book on Paris and London, he had been looking at the wrong groups of people. "Unfortunately you do not solve the class problem by making friends with tramps," he had realized. "Tramps, beggars, criminals and social outcasts generally are very exceptional beings and no more typical of the working class as a whole than, say, the literary intelligentsia are typical of the bourgeoisie." Now he wanted to plunge into the heart of the British economy, the coal mines of northern England, and to live among the people who toiled in them.

He left his bookstore life in Hampstead in January 1936 and set out to study the working class. On his first night, he stayed in Coventry. "Smell as in common lodging houses," he wrote in his diary. "Half-witted servant girl with huge body, tiny head and rolls of fat at back of neck curiously recalling ham fat."

He traveled north by train and then spent two months moving around the coal mining country near Liverpool. Much of the time he walked miles from town to town, in the rain and snow. On February 12, 1936, he strode through Wigan, a coal and canal town midway between Manchester and Liverpool, dotted with slag heaps and mud puddles. "Bitter wind. They had to send a steamer to break the ice in front of the coal barges on the canal. . . . A few rats running slowly through the snow, very tame, presumably weak with hunger."

The resulting book, *The Road to Wigan Pier*, is the most straightforward of Orwell's nonfiction works. It is not really a narrative. Rather, it follows a brilliant but simple plan, to try to portray factually the lives of the Depression-era working classes in the coal country. This is not to say that it was easy to research or write—to invoke one of Orwell's most famous comments, "To see what is in front of one's nose needs a constant struggle."

Returning south from Wigan, Orwell became a shopkeeper, renting a small two-story cottage in the village of Wallington in Hertfordshire, halfway from London to Cambridge. It was a hamlet of thirty-four houses, two pubs, and a church. The cottage lacked electricity, hot water, or indoor plumbing, but had a front room that had been used as a store. The front door was about four feet high, which must have been difficult for the lanky Orwell to negotiate. In between spells of writing, he sold bacon, sugar, and candy, as well as his own eggs and vegetables. "They had a proper bacon slicer," recalled Fred Bates, a local farm worker. "Beautiful bacon they used to have." The profits from his sales covered the rent of less than two pounds a month.

The book he wrote in that cottage is a mixed bag. The first half of *Wigan Pier* is a collection of closely observed reports on the living conditions of England's poor—where they live, what they eat, how they try to keep warm, how they work, or, increasingly, as the Depression took hold, how they are affected by unemployment. In this half, the writer George Orwell whom we know today emerges for the first time. Some of that was hinted at in *Down and Out*, but here Orwell has matured. This work revels not in repugnant sensationalism, as in the earlier book, but rather on a foundation of small, hard facts. The diet of the workers, he writes, is "white bread and margarine, corned beef, sugared tea and potatoes." Probably because of lack of calcium, he writes, most lose their teeth by the age of thirty. In Lancashire he watches women in the slag heaps outside a mine, "kneeling in the cindery mud and the bitter wind," gathering bits of coal. "They are glad enough to do it. In winter they are desperate for fuel; it is more important almost than food. Meanwhile all around, as far as the eye can see, are the slag-heaps and hoisting gear of the collieries, and [because of the Depression] not one of those collieries can sell all the coal it is capable of producing."

Part of the book amounts to Orwell's *Notes from Underground*—literally. Just as in his Paris and London book he descended into the underworld of the hotel scullery, here he goes down into a coal mine and finds it fits his mental picture of the Inferno. "Most of the things one imagines in hell are there—heat, noise, confusion, darkness, foul air, and, above all, unbearably cramped space." Once at the bottom of the shaft, he must walk stooped for a mile to the coal face through a tunnel about four feet in height. The journey takes Orwell nearly an hour, and leaves him in agony. And, he notes, that is just the miners' commute before they begin work. It is followed by a day of labor, "blackened to the eyes, with their throats full of coal dust." This is Orwell at the heart of the matter.

But Orwell was not yet fully developed as a writer. The second half of the book is an odd, atypically wordy essay in which Orwell dissects English socialism in an attempt to understand why it had failed to seize the imagination of the English middle class, or even gain the emotional loyalty of working-class socialists. This section is as notable for its failures as for its successes, making *Wigan Pier* "a curiously uneven achievement," in the words of Peter Stansky and William Abrahams in their biography of Orwell.

Unusually for Orwell, this second half is poorly observed and, in places, poorly written. It also is occasionally mean-spirited, as when he mocks the middle-class eccentrics associated with English socialism. "One gets the impression that the mere words 'Socialism' and 'Communism' draw towards them with magnetic force every fruit-juice drinker, nudist, sandal-wearer, sex-maniac, Quaker, 'Nature Cure' quack, pacifist and feminist in England." Just eight pages later, he repetitively denounces "all that dreary tribe of high-minded women and sandal-wearers and bearded fruit-juice drinkers who come flocking towards the smell of 'progress' like blue-bottles to a dead cat."

More strikingly, this part of the book also displays one of Orwell's oddest ventures, his attempt to build a political theory upon his hyper-sensitive sense of smell. "The real secret of class distinctions in the West . . . is summed up in four frightful words . . . *The lower classes smell.*" Almost any other fault can be overcome, he asserts. "You can have an affection for a murderer or sodomite, but you cannot have an affection for a man whose breath stinks—habitually stinks, I mean. . . . You will hate him." He goes on about this for several pages in prose probably best understood by those tormented by overdeveloped olfactory receptors, an affliction known as hyperosmia.

It was little wonder that *Wigan Pier* irked many of his friends and fellow socialists. "I thought it was really a terrible book," said Kay Ekevall, one of Orwell's leftist friends at the time. "I thought it denigrated all socialists; it put the working class in a terribly sordid light." She especially disliked how he portrayed coal miners. "The miners were very political in those days; they were more or less the vanguard of the trade union movement. And he seems to have ignored anything that was happening on the positive side of politics and just concentrated on all the sordid aspects." There is an echo here of some of the criticism he received from old imperialists for *Burmese Days.*

Even the man who published the book held his nose in doing so. Victor Gollancz's foreword amounts to an extended apology for producing it under the mantle of his "Left Book Club." He is shocked by Orwell's portrayal of socialists as faddish cranks. He tries to spin the odor theory of class distinction by treating it as the thoughtful confession of a repentant middle-class snob. He simply denounces Orwell's "curious indiscretion of referring to Russian commissars as 'half-gramophones, half-gangsters.'" He also offers up some of the ideological tap dancing that Orwell would mock throughout his later career: "The Left Book Club has 'no policy' . . . it would not even be true to say that the People's Front is the 'policy' of the Left Book Club. . . . In other words, the People's Front is not the 'policy' of the Left Book Club, but the very existence of the Left Book Club tends towards a People's Front." It is not clear what that means, if anything.

Ultimately, what *Wigan Pier* offers, in its confusion and contradictions, is a writer moving forward but still slightly off stride. The best thing about it is that in it, Orwell completed his education and found his true skills and his real subject. His literary method was to discover the facts and lay them out. His perspective was that the powerful would almost always try to obscure the truth.

He could not know it, but at this point in the late 1930s he stood on the cusp of greatness. He had become especially attuned to the gaps between theory and reality, between what people claim to be and what they really are. He was happy, even eager, to grapple with uncomfortable and unpopular truths. It was a frame of mind that prepared him well to write about the deadly collision of ideology and reality, first locally in the Spanish Civil War and then globally in World War II.

Orwell and Eileen O'Shaughnessy married in June 1936, as he was turning the diaries of his northern trip into a book. They walked together from their cottage to the village church in Wallington, which had a population of about two hundred. After the ceremony, the wedding party lunched at the pub.

Eileen as a wife would show a streak of feistiness. When he airily pronounced one morning over breakfast with some houseguests that "bacon manufacturers" had arranged government regulations to make it impossible for villagers to cure their own bacon, Eileen challenged his "sweeping statement." Orwell persisted in blaming sanitary rules, despite his entire lack of evidence. Eileen responded, "That's the kind of statement an irresponsible journalist would make." She also pitched into village life. Learning that a local ten-year-old boy there was illiterate, she taught him to read well enough that he was able to go to school.

The month after their wedding, war began in Spain between the leftist government and rebels—much of the Spanish army and navy, backed by fascists, ultranationalists, and some Catholic organizations. The war immediately captured the attention of the newlyweds. In December, as soon as the manuscript of *Wigan Pier* was finished, Orwell gave it to his publisher. He then pawned some family silver to raise travel funds and set out for Barcelona. Eileen would follow two months later.

He went to Spain to fight fascism, but instead wound up being hunted by communists. This is the central fact of his experience of the Spanish Civil War, and indeed it is the key fact of his entire life. But had a sniper's bullet plunged into his neck just a little differently in May 1937, he would never have written his first great book, *Homage to Catalonia*. And the world never would have met the great writer who holds our attention even now.

CHAPTER 4

CHURCHILL: DOWN AND OUT IN THE 1930S

We now see both men about to enter the periods in their lives that made them people we still think about, people who are important not just to understanding their times but also to understanding our own.

The 1930s were horrible in many ways. There was a growing sense among many people that a new Dark Age was at hand. These fears began with the great economic and social dislocation of the global Great Depression. The long and vicious war that would kill tens of millions in the 1940s began in Asia and was brewing in the West. As the poet Stephen Spender put it, there was a general feeling emerging that his generation might well see "the end of Western civilization."

Many people, especially the young and engaged, thought that liberal capitalist democracy was tired and failing. They saw only two choices available for the way forward, fascism or communism, the dynamic new ideologies beckoning from Berlin, Rome, and Moscow. The end of the Western way of life, and especially the death of liberal democracy, was a common theme in cultural life, discussed daily in newspapers and in private diaries. The historian Arnold Toynbee began the 1930s with the ob-servation that it was becoming common to think that "the Western system of society might break down and cease to work." He closed the decade out in 1939 with a lecture at the London School of Economics on "The Downfall of Civilizations." In 1935, the Shakespearean scholar A. L. Rowse wrote in his diary that it was "too late to save any liberalism, perhaps too late to save socialism." (Two decades later, Rowse would pub-lish an admiring history of the Churchill family.) Louis Fischer, a jour-nalist then sympathetic to Stalinism, wrote to Beatrice Webb in 1936 that "the whole system is bankrupt." In 1937, Harold Lasswell, a leading American political scientist, published an essay predicting the rise of "the garrison state," in which "the specialist on violence is at the helm, and organized economic and social life is systematically subordinated to the fighting forces." After the Munich Agreement between British prime minister Neville Chamberlain and Adolf Hitler in September 1938, Vir-ginia Woolf wrote to her sister Vanessa Bell lamenting "the inevitable end of civilization." Three years later, she would kill herself.

Amid these signs of looming disaster, Winston Churchill was rele-gated to the sidelines. For most of the 1930s, he was isolated from the majority of his own party, and many thought his political career finished. Harold Nicolson saw Churchill and found him "very changed from when I had last seen him. A great round white face like a blister. Incredibly aged. . . . His spirits also have declined and he sighs that he has lost his old fighting power." At about the same time, George Bernard Shaw and Nancy Astor, both political foes of Churchill, traveled together to the Soviet Union and visited Stalin at the Kremlin. When Churchill came up in a discussion of Britain's anti-Soviet policy, Lady Astor dismissed him, assuring Stalin that Churchill was "finished." Shaw seconded the notion, saying that Churchill would never become prime minister. Stalin de-murred, wondering aloud if the English people might turn to Churchill in a crisis.

Churchill ranted so much about India policy (he was against independence) and Germany (he thought the threat was underestimated) that he wore out his welcome with his own party, whose leaders grew determined to keep him out of the Cabinet. Just as Burma had pushed Orwell leftward and away from gainful employment, so India would propel Churchill rightward and away from power, causing him in 1931 to break with Conservative Party leader Stanley Baldwin and resign from the party's business committee. From that point he sharpened his rhetoric, once in the House of Commons likening former Labour prime minister Ramsay MacDonald to a circus freak, calling him "the boneless wonder sitting on the Treasury bench." One reason his foreboding speeches on Germany later in the decade would be greeted with skepticism was that he had been equally intense about the dangers of Indian independence.

He spent much of his time writing books and newspaper pieces. Once when he dropped by the *Evening Standard* to deliver an article, Malcolm Muggeridge, then a young reporter there, saw him and wondered what had happened to him. "There's a guy who's not well, or down on his luck, or dead broke," thought Muggeridge, who sat in the newsroom next to Randolph Churchill, Winston's dissolute son.

As Muggeridge suspected, Churchill faced serious financial problems. They would continue throughout the decade, eventually forcing him to consider selling his cherished country house, Chartwell, which had become his refuge from the world.

In his wartime memoirs, Churchill would refer to the 1930s as his time "in the political wilderness." Some modern academics have disputed the extent of his political exile, but the facts, and contemporary observations, are on Churchill's side.

Churchill's road back to power was long and hard. He remained a wanderer for much of the decade, out of step with his times, which were epitomized by the resolution of the Oxford Union, a university debating society, in February 1933 that it would "in no circumstances fight for its

King and Country." The nation's leaders, often in sympathy with the tone of the Oxford discussion, embarked upon a policy of appeasing Germany, making concessions from a position of weakness.

———————

The nature of appeasement—what it was, how to implement it, when to stop it—became the key issue of British politics for most of the 1930s.

It is important here to remember that a narrow but strong strain of sympathy for fascism, and even for Hitler, ran through part of the English aristocracy. Most prominent of those seen as friendly to Germany was Lord Londonderry, a relative of Churchill's who served in the Cabinet in the early 1930s and then briefly was leader of the House of Lords. Orwell once commented that "whether the British ruling class are wicked or merely stupid is one of the most difficult questions of our time, and at certain moments a very important question." It is possible that he had Lord Londonderry in mind when he wrote this.

While doltish and gullible, Londonderry was also a man accustomed to deference because of his wealth and standing, about which he was quite sensitive. The king called him "Charley" at a time when such familiarity conferred great status. He was a major figure in London society. "The Ribbentrops are intimate with the Londonderrys," Sir Henry "Chips" Cannon, a London socialite and Tory politician, noted in his diary in 1936, referring to the German ambassador to England, soon to become Hitler's foreign minister. After meeting Hitler the same year, Londonderry pronounced the German leader "very agreeable" and called on the British government to find "common ground" with the Germans in fighting communism. He even applauded the German takeover of Austria in March 1938 as perhaps drastic but necessary to avoid bloodshed. A second cousin to Churchill, Londonderry remained cordial with him until a bitter conversation over dinner at the Grillions dining club in October 1938 during which Churchill mocked his politics.

Londonderry was an extreme case, but hardly alone—either in embracing some features of fascism or indeed in doing so while being distantly related to Churchill. Even closer, in several ways, was the relationship between the Churchills and the Mitford family. Churchill's wife, Clementine, was a cousin of the father of the Mitford sisters, and, as noted previously, may even have had closer blood ties, depending on who her natural father really was.

Clementine and Winston's son, Randolph Churchill, at one point was "very much in love" with one of those sisters, Diana Mitford. An artist who had painted Diana's portrait told Nancy Mitford he had heard that Diana had an affair with Randolph, Nancy reported in a letter to Diana. In her next paragraph she mentioned a lunchtime conversation with Fred Astaire's sister, Adele, who had pronounced that "I don't mind people going off & fucking but I do object to all this free love."

In another tangle of aristocratic ardor, a nephew of Clementine's, Esmond Romilly, who had fought in Spain in 1936 for the Republicans, eloped a year later with his second cousin Jessica Mitford. There long were rumors that Esmond was actually Winston Churchill's natural son. Esmond may have helped that gossip along by performing for friends what Jessica Mitford called his "awfully good" imitation of Churchill. At any rate, Esmond, having moved to Canada, volunteered for the air force and would be killed in combat while flying a bomber in 1941.

As for Diana Mitford, she wisely moved on from Randolph Churchill and chose instead to marry an heir to the Guinness brewing fortune. Her next liaison was less well chosen: A few years later, she dumped the Guinness and became involved with Oswald Mosley, leader of the British Union of Fascists. Their wedding in 1936 was held at the house of the Nazi propaganda chief Joseph Goebbels, with Hitler in attendance. A third Mitford sister, Unity, grew friendly with Hitler in the mid-1930s. "I think Hitler must be very fond of her, he never took his eyes off her," observed yet another Mitford sister, Deborah. At a lunch in December 1935, Unity reported to Diana, "He talked a lot about Jews, which was lovely."

Dallying with fascists was not simply a pursuit of the young and the foolish. Neville Chamberlain's sister-in-law, living in Rome, assured Mussolini that the British government would come around to cordial relations with Italy, despite his military adventurism in Africa. To be fair, Churchill in the 1920s had expressed some admiration for the Italian leader. Arnold Toynbee, now nearly forgotten but at the time one of the most prominent of British historians, met with Hitler in 1936 and reported to the British Foreign Office that the German leader genuinely desired peace. "He is convinced of [Hitler's] sincerity in desiring peace in Europe and close friendship with England," recorded Thomas "T. J." Jones, a Conservative Party political operative, after a walk in the countryside with the historian. Waldorf Astor, an American-born peer, explained to Jones that Americans' distaste for the Nazis "is largely due to the intensive and widespread anti-German propaganda being conducted by Jews and Communists. Newspapers are influenced by those firms which advertise so largely in the press and are frequently under Jewish control." Harold Nicolson, dining one evening in May 1938 at one of the more aristocratic London clubs, Pratt's, was taken aback to hear three young lords agree that "they would prefer to see Hitler in London than a Socialist administration." Four days later, Nicolson was visited by Charles Lindbergh, the world's most famous pilot, and a prominent isolationist in America. "He says that we cannot possibly fight since we should certainly be beaten," Nicolson recorded. "He thinks we should just give way and then make an alliance with Germany."

In May 1939, Archibald Ramsay, a Conservative Scottish MP, formed a pro-German, anti-Semitic group called the "Right Club." Its badge featured an eagle killing a snake and the initials "PJ," for "Perish Judah."

The *Times* of London, then co-owned by another member of the Astor clan, John J. Astor, was at the time the daily journal of the British establishment. As Lord Halifax, Chamberlain's foreign minister, put it, in prewar Britain, "Special weight was held to attach to opinions expressed in its leading articles [that is, editorials], on the assumption that these carried some quality of government stamp, if not approbation." The newspaper fervently supported appeasement throughout the 1930s, to the point that it was willing to tolerate and even embrace Hitlerian tactics. Following the "Night of the Long Knives," a series of shocking political murders carried out on Hitler's orders in mid-1934, the newspaper soothed, "Herr Hitler, whatever one may think of his methods, is genuinely trying to transform revolutionary fervour into moderate and constructive effort and to impose a high standard of public service on National-Socialist officials."

In 1937, Geoffrey Dawson, editor of the *Times,* confided to his Geneva correspondent, "I do my utmost, night after night, to keep out of the paper anything that might hurt their susceptibilities." According to the *Times*'s own official history of itself, published in 1952, those who opposed appeasement were all too often "intellectuals, utopians, sentimentalists and pacifists satisfied with a programme of resistance without the means of resistance." The *Times*'s history, with extraordinary nerve, blames those hotheads for making the disastrous policy of appeasement necessary, arguing that the newspaper, "like the Government, was helpless in the face of an apparently isolationist Commonwealth and a pacifist Britain." What this explanation fails to note is that the role of a leading newspaper is not just to follow opinion but to try to shape it, especially when a major government policy rests on faulty assumptions. And it certainly is not the role of a newspaper editor to suppress news on the grounds that it might bother people or force government officials to reconsider their policies.

King Edward VIII himself, during his eleven-month reign in 1936, supported appeasement. According to one account, when Hitler sent troops into the Rhineland in March 1936, breaking the terms of the Versailles Treaty, the king called the German ambassador in London to tell him that he had given Prime Minister Baldwin "a piece of my mind." To wit, "I told the old-so-and-so that I would abdicate if he made war. There was a frightful scene. But you needn't worry. There won't be war."

The king actually would abdicate for other reasons later that same year. During the war, his rightist views and contacts would become a persistent worry for Churchill and British intelligence.

Many of the advocates of appeasement saw themselves as practical thinkers. In their view, they were faced with the fact that a rising Germany could be countered only by a strong European coalition willing to take military action. But, they noted, no such alliance was going to come together. So in their minds, given that lack of an alliance and in view of the slow pace of British rearmament, appeasement was the shrewd move, the favored course of heads much cooler than Winston Churchill's. In a letter in January 1938, Neville Chamberlain stated that "as a realist, I must do what I can to make this country safe."

Despite the arguments made by the *Times* and the prime ministers it vigorously supported—first Stanley Baldwin and then Chamberlain—it is clear now that appeasement rested more on self-delusion than on rational calculation, because it necessarily required faith in Hitler's sanity and trustworthiness. Chamberlain himself told his sister privately that Hitler was "a man who could be relied on when he had given his word." Former prime minister David Lloyd George, after his own meeting with Hitler, pronounced the German leader "a remarkable man" whose head "has not been turned by adulation."

Churchill's response to the arguments of the appeasers was that the Nazi hold on power in Berlin meant that a policy of appeasement eventually would lead to war. "The rise of Germany to anything like military equality with France, Poland or the small States, means a renewal of a general European war," he argued in the House of Commons in April 1933, about three months after Hitler became chancellor and was taking steps to make Germany a one-party state. In another Commons speech near the end of that year, he asserted that "the great dominant fact is that Germany is re-arming, has already begun to re-arm."

A year later, he asked, "What is the great new fact which has broken in upon us during the last 18 months?" His answer: "Germany is rearming.

That is the great new fact which rivets the attention of every country in Europe, indeed in the world, and which throws almost all other issues into the background." He was especially worried by the growing strength of German airpower. "Germany has already a powerful well-equipped army, with an excellent artillery, and an immense reserve of armed trained men. The German munition factories are working practically under war conditions, and war materiel is flowing out from them, and has been for the last 12 months certainly, in an ever broadening flow. Much of this is undoubtedly in violation of the treaties which were signed. Germany is rearming on land; she is rearming also to some extent at sea; but what concerns us most of all is the rearmament of Germany in the air."

The view of the British government remained quite the opposite: The path to peace, many of its leaders believed, was to refrain from an arms race, and even to disarm. Hitler in the late 1930s believed that Britain was too weak to fight, and many British leaders privately agreed with him. When Germany did begin to increase its military might, the official British reaction was to pressure the French government to make concessions that would placate the Germans. Clement Attlee, at the time a leading figure in the Labour Party, spoke for mainstream opinion when he said in 1935 that, in pursuing peace, "we do not think you can do it by national defence. We think you can only do it by moving forward to a new world—a world of law, the abolition of national armaments with a world force and a world economic system." However, by the late 1930s, Attlee would move to support Churchill's view and become a strong opponent of Chamberlain's policy of appeasing Hitler.

Others persisted in the course of appeasement. After becoming prime minister in May 1937, Chamberlain sought to reconcile with Germany by offering it colonial territories to administer. In November 1937, Chamberlain's foreign minister, Lord Halifax, met with Hitler. He came away reassured, telling the Cabinet that the Germans "had no policy of immediate adventure." In March 1938, Attlee would charge that Chamberlain was "proceeding on a policy of negotiation with persons who have shown their belief in force and who exercise force even while he is negotiating with them."

The leaders of the Tory Party felt that as part of keeping Hitler mollified, Churchill must be excluded from a position of leadership. Thomas Jones, who served as consigliere to Prime Minister Baldwin, spent years ensuring that Churchill remained sidelined. In 1934, Jones confided to a friend that "rightly or wrongly, all sorts of people who have met Hitler are convinced that he is a factor for peace." Jones was himself one of these, writing two years later, "We have abundant evidence of the desire of all sorts of Germans to be on friendly terms with us." After himself making the pilgrimage to meet the German leader, Jones reported back to Baldwin, "Hitler believes in you, and believes that only you in this country can bring about the reorientation of England, France and Germany which he desires." Jones went on to make "strongly the case for alliance with Germany," a step that shocked even some political allies.

The result of this policy split was that until the last year of the 1930s, Churchill would be regarded, as the historian Tony Judt summed it up, as an "overtalented outsider: too good to be ignored but too unconventional and 'unreliable' to be appointed to the very highest office." He was derided by other politicians as flighty, with more energy than judgment, immovable in his views but loose in his party loyalties. "We all know that in our politics there is nothing so completely obsolete as the Winston Churchill of ten years before," sneered Liberal Party luminary Herbert Samuel in a parliamentary debate in March 1930. A few years later, Samuel would compare Churchill on defense policy to "a Malay running amok." When Churchill spoke at Oxford University in 1934 about his concern for the safety of England, he was greeted with what Martin Gilbert, his official biographer, called "derisive laughter." In February 1935, Sir Samuel Hoare, a prominent Tory, confided to the editor of the *Manchester Guardian* that "there is scarcely a single Tory who would be willing to accept Churchill as the leader of the party or Prime Minister."

Perhaps most painful of all may have been the cut inflicted by a Conservative MP in May 1935. "Although one hates to criticise anyone in the evening of his days, nothing can excuse the right honorable Member for Epping [Churchill] for having permeated his entire speech with the atmosphere that Germany is arming for war," said Thomas Moore. Another Conservative wrote in his diary after dining with Churchill that he thought him "very unbalanced." Given this torrent of denunciation, it is not surprising that by the end of 1936, Churchill thought for at least a moment that his political career was "finished." Churchill does not say in his own memoirs if he believed this, but he does note that "it was almost the universal view that my political life was at last ended."

The unlikeliness of Churchill ever rising to the premiership became a punch line for his opponents. "Whatever dangers there may be before us in this country, the prospect of a Government formed by Mr. Winston Churchill . . . and others, is not one of the dangers to which we have to look forward," said Baron Ponsonby of Shulbrede with a chuckle in the House of Lords. Ponsonby, whose father had been private secretary to Queen Victoria and whose grandfather had fought at Waterloo, later expanded on that danger, telling the House of Lords that it might be necessary to imprison Churchill at some point: "I have got the greatest possible admiration for Mr. Churchill's Parliamentary powers, his literary powers, and his artistic powers, but I have always felt that in a crisis he is one of the first people who ought to be interned." At about the same time, Lord Maugham suggested that Churchill would best be "shot or hanged."

Churchill's isolation grew even deeper in December 1936, when he sided with King Edward VIII during the crisis over whether the king should step down over his desire to marry an American divorcée, Wallis Simpson. In supporting the king, he was seen as taking a stance against the aristocracy, which was trying to rein in the king, who enjoyed broad popular support. Churchill, by siding with Edward, also was defying his own Conservative Party and its leader, Prime Minister Baldwin. Churchill's advocacy of the king has puzzled historians, especially in light of what later emerged about Edward's fascist sympathies. The best guess is that Churchill's traditionalism, his love of "king and country," muddled his judgment of the man.

When Churchill spoke against his party in the House of Commons, he was booed heavily. Red-faced with anger, he shouted at Baldwin, "You won't be satisfied until you've broken him, will you?" He told a friend later that day that he thought his political career was over.

The king was indeed forced out. At Christmas pageants that month, English schoolchildren shocked their parents and teachers by singing,

> *Hark the herald angels sing*
> *Mrs. Simpson's pinched our king.*

"The upper classes mind her being an American more than they mind her being divorced," observed the dependably snobbish Harold Nicolson.

The Germans remained unsure that Churchill was finished, and continued to study him. One day in 1937, Churchill went to the German embassy to lunch with Joachim von Ribbentrop, then still the German ambassador in London. The Nazis by this point knew well that Churchill was a leading voice in Britain against them. Ribbentrop began by telling Churchill that Germany sought the friendship of England, that it did not seek the dismantling of the British Empire, and that all it wanted was a free hand on the eastern side of Europe, in order to acquire the *Lebensraum,* or "living space," it needed. To achieve that goal, he said, pointing to a map on the wall of the embassy, Germany would have to absorb Poland, Ukraine, and White Russia. All that Germany asked was that Britain not interfere.

Standing before the map, Churchill responded that Britain would not go along with such a plan. Ribbentrop turned away "abruptly" from the map and said, "In that case, war is inevitable. There is no way out. The Fuehrer is resolved. Nothing will stop him and nothing will stop us."

The two sat again. Churchill warned Ribbentrop not to underestimate Britain. "If you plunge us all into another Great War, she will bring the whole world against you like last time."

At this, the German stood. That was not his assessment, he declared with some "heat": "England may be very clever, but this time she will not bring the world against Germany."

Churchill continued to crusade against appeasement. In April 1937, he warned the House of Commons, "We seem to be moving, drifting, steadily against our will, against the will of every race and every people and every class, towards some hideous catastrophe. Everybody wishes to stop it, but they do not know how."

His apprehension grew throughout 1938, when Chamberlain's appeasement policy was at its height, both in practice and popularity.

Churchill's personal low point came on the night of February 20, 1938, when he lay in his bed, sleepless until dawn. He was mulling the fact that Anthony Eden, the foreign secretary, had just resigned over Chamberlain's determination to keep pursuing appeasement. "I watched the daylight slowly creep in through the windows," he wrote, "and saw before me in mental gaze the vision of Death." A month later, he sounded elegiac, telling the House of Commons, "For five years I have talked to the House on these matters, not with very great success. I have watched this famous island descending incontinently, fecklessly, the stairway which leads to a dark gulf."

On May 14, 1938, when the British soccer team played Germany before a crowd of a hundred thousand at the Olympic Stadium in Berlin, its players gave the Nazi salute during the playing of the German national anthem. It did so at the specific request of the British Foreign Office, now led by Lord Halifax. Also that spring, Halifax told the Cabinet that, in the interests of peace, it might be necessary for Britain to pressure

Czechoslovakia to make large concessions to Hitler. "It was a disagreeable business," he conceded, "which had to be done as pleasantly as possible." That uneasy sentence may have been the essence of the appeasement policy—and its epitaph.

At the end of September of that year, Prime Minister Chamberlain, after three short trips to Germany that month, arrived at the Munich Agreement with Hitler. Churchill's political comeback would begin with that pact.

Of course, it did not look like that at first. Chamberlain rode high in the fall of 1938. Pleased with his diplomatic skills, he reported after the first talk, "I had established a certain confidence, which was my aim, and on my side, in spite of the hardness and ruthlessness I thought I saw in his face, I got the impression that here was a man who could be relied upon when he had given his word." At the second of his meetings with Hitler that month, Chamberlain gave in to all of Hitler's demands. The governments of France and Britain instructed the Czechs to give up the heavily Germanic western fringe of their country called the Sudetenland. In doing so, Chamberlain gave Germany a free hand to begin taking apart Czechoslovakia, beginning with one third of its population and its system of frontier defenses. Churchill responded: "The belief that security can be obtained by throwing a small State to the wolves is a fatal delusion." Chamberlain told the Cabinet that he believed Hitler trusted him.

On September 29, Chamberlain flew to Germany for his third meeting that month with Hitler. Returning to London, he proclaimed that he had secured "peace for our time." He was greeted by cheering crowds in the streets.

When the House of Commons met the following week, Chamberlain began by happily telling it, "A cloud of anxiety has been lifted from our hearts." He had, he said, "laid the foundations of peace." He reassured the House that he had no regrets. When the handful of opponents shouted "shame," he responded, "I have nothing to be ashamed of. Let those who have, hang their heads."

Most members of the House supported Chamberlain. George Lansbury, an aging Labour Party official, backed up the Conservative PM by telling the House, "I hear all this denunciation of Herr Hitler and Signor Mussolini. I have met both of them, and can only say that they are very much like any other politician or diplomat one meets." Cyril Culverwell, a Conservative, saluted Chamberlain's "courage, sincerity and skilful leadership." At any rate, he added, "There are only two alternatives, war or appeasement." The sentiment of the majority was with the latter.

Henry Raikes, another Conservative, thought Chamberlain had secured a noble place in history, saying, "We on this side of the House have a right to feel proud that we have been led as we have been led by the Prime Minister. We have a right to believe that instead of there being jeers at his statement that peace has come for our time there should be full appreciation of the fact that our leader will go down to history as the greatest European statesman of this or any other time."

Churchill waited all through that first day of Munich debate, and indeed through the second. On its third and final day, just past five o'clock on the afternoon of Wednesday, October 5, he finally rose to speak. "I will begin by saying what everybody would like to ignore or forget but which must nevertheless be stated, namely, that we have sustained a total and unmitigated defeat."

Lady Astor, his longtime political nemesis, vehemently pro-appeasement, interrupted him, shouting, "Nonsense."

Churchill responded, "The utmost my right honorable Friend the Prime Minister has been able to secure by all his immense exertions, by all the great efforts and mobilisation which took place in this country, and by all the anguish and strain through which we have passed in this country, the utmost he has been able to gain—"

Here he was interrupted again by members shouting, "Is peace!"

Churchill pressed on. "The utmost he has been able to gain for Czechoslovakia . . . has been that the German dictator, instead of snatching his victuals from the table, has been content to have them served to him course by course."

He continued, "We are in the presence of a disaster of the first magnitude." After another brief interruption from Astor, again swatted away, he concluded with an almost Biblical warning: "This is only the beginning of the reckoning. This is only the first sip, the first foretaste of a bitter cup which will be proffered to us year by year unless by a supreme recovery of moral health and martial vigour, we arise again and take our stand for freedom as in the olden time."

But Churchill spoke for history that day, not for other members of the House of Commons. Their view was better captured by Thomas Magnay, a Liberal member of Parliament representing Gateshead, near Tyne, who rhetorically asked, with clear indifference as to the answer, "What is Czechoslovakia?"

Prime Minister Chamberlain ended the three days of debate by emphasizing the personal nature of his commitment:

Anybody who had been through what I had to go through day after day, face to face with the thought that in the last resort it would have been I, and I alone, who would have to say that yes or no which would decide the fate of millions of my countrymen, of their wives, of their families—a man who had been through that could not readily forget.

And so, he said, he would be guided not by parliamentary criticism, but by his own conscience. "When a man gets to my age and fills my position, I think he tends to feel that criticism, even abuse, matters little to him if his conscience approves of his actions." The House of Commons endorsed his policy by a vote of 366 to 144.

In the wake of the debate over the Munich Agreement, Churchill faced a challenge from his own constituency. "The hard fact," writes Roy Jenkins, "is that for six weeks or so in the autumn of 1938, and then on a diminuendo basis for another four months, there was doubt if he would be able to continue to sit as a Conservative MP." On November 4, 1938, the Conservatives of Epping met to consider whether to continue to back him as their representative in Parliament. He won the group's vote by 100 to 44. Jenkins notes that a switch of a mere thirty votes might have changed history, had it forced Churchill to step down and then run in a special election for his seat, probably against a Chamberlainite Conservative.

Chamberlain, meanwhile, enjoyed a burst of popularity. The mayor of Cardiff, Wales, ordered the swastika flag flown in celebration. Peregrine Cust, the 6th Baron Brownlow, who had been the Personal Lord-in-Waiting to King Edward VIII, gave Chamberlain a cigarette case engraved with the map of Europe and a sapphire to mark the location in Germany of each of the three talks between Chamberlain and Hitler— Berchtesgaden, Godesburg, and Munich. Chamberlain reasserted to his Cabinet with confidence at the end of October, "Our foreign policy is one of appeasement." Charles Lindbergh arrived in London and told his hosts that he believed that in the event of war, "the democracies would be crushed absolutely and finally."

But Hitler evidently understood the consequences of Chamberlain's position better than British leaders did. In his words and actions, he began to demonstrate what Munich really meant. In two speeches in early November, he attacked Churchill by name, calling him "mad" and a force for war. Just after those speeches, Nazi thugs carried out a nation-wide assault on German and Austrian Jews, burning hundreds of synagogues and smashing seven thousand businesses owned by Jews. The attacks of November 9 and 10, 1938, now remembered as *Kristallnacht,* for all the shattered shopwindow glass they produced, are seen today by some historians as the beginning of the Holocaust, because they marked the first instance of state-organized mass violence against Jews in Germany and Austria.

Chamberlain reacted to *Kristallnacht* wearily, telling his sister that he was "horrified" yet complaining, "I suppose I shall have to say something on the subject." But he had very little to say about it directly, or even indirectly, when later that month the House of Commons discussed the issue of Jewish refugees. His silence was noticed. Neville Laski, president of the Board of Deputies of British Jews, observed to the editor of the *Manchester Guardian* that Chamberlain had never "expressed a word of sympathy for the Jews in Germany." The prime minister had been similarly reticent in a private meeting with prominent British Jews, he added. Chamberlain was still basking in the afterglow of Munich. His Christmas card that year would proudly feature a photograph of his aircraft, a twin-engine, twin-tailed Lockheed Electra monoplane, when it was flying to Germany.

Churchill was appalled. He privately threatened that "at the next general election I shall speak on every Socialist platform in the country against the government." (Inexplicably, he made no mention of *Kristallnacht* in his multivolume World War II memoirs, even when minutely recounting the steps that led to war, such as devoting several pages to analyzing the implications of the replacement, several months later, of Maxim Litvinov by V. M. Molotov as Soviet foreign minister. It is one of the odder omissions in the memoirs.)

There was money available to bolster British defenses, but Chamberlain warned against doing so. Despite the British government running a surplus of 20 million pounds, he maintained that such a move was unwise. As a former chancellor of the exchequer, he told his Cabinet, the financial position looked "extremely dangerous."

All in all, Chamberlain was pleased with his achievements. He wrote to his sister, "Now it will take some time before the atmosphere is right but things are moving in the direction I want." When the German government asked the British ambassador in Berlin about what to make of Churchill's speeches, the ambassador said not to worry.

In mid-March 1939, Hitler ordered the German army into the rest of

Czechoslovakia, which six months earlier Chamberlain had publicly characterized as "a far away country" that was engaged in "a quarrel . . . between people of whom we know nothing."

The jig was up. With the invasion of truncated Czechoslovakia, it was clear that appeasement had failed, and Chamberlain with it. There has grown up in recent decades a revisionist view that Chamberlain had bought time for Britain to build, but that ignores two key factors. One is that Hitler gained enormously at the same time, for example, taking Austria's gold and Czechoslovakia's arms industry, and also gaining access to more manpower to use in factories and in his army. The other factor is that Chamberlain gave no indication that buying time was his aim, and it is likely that he or one of his political allies, such as Lord Halifax, if in power would have sued for peace in 1940. Some revisionists contend that the delay was intended to give the Royal Air Force (RAF) time to build up, but that argument neglects the fact that Chamberlain funded fighter aircraft only because it was less expensive than building bombers.

We now know that on May 23, 1939, Hitler brought his top military officials to his study in his Chancellery to unfold his plans for war, which, he said, he deemed unavoidable. First, he intended "to attack Poland at the first suitable opportunity." Eventually, there would be a "life and death struggle" with England. He laid out the conditions needed for a German victory there. "If Holland and Belgium are successfully occupied and held, and if France is also defeated, the fundamental conditions for a successful war against England will have been secured. England can then be blocked from Western France at close quarters by the Air Force, while the Navy with its submarines can extend the range of our blockade." He did not mention the United States in this document, according to the translation used in the postwar Nuremberg trials. There is evidence that at this point he envisioned fighting the United States, but only after subduing Europe and the Soviet Union.

As the British watched Hitler expand beyond the borders of Germany, the tone of political banter about Churchill began to change. "The right honorable Gentleman keeps on coming to this House and issuing warnings to the Government," Reginald Fletcher said in a debate in June 1939. "The Government invariably reject his warnings, but over and over again we find them having to adopt his proposals at a far higher price than they need have paid had they heeded him in the first instance." Even then, Chamberlain stoutly resisted bringing Churchill into a position of leadership. The prime minister informed his political ally Geoffrey Dawson, the editor of the *Times*, that he "had no intention of being bounced into taking back Winston."

Pressure in favor of Churchill grew. In August 1939, on the eve of war in Europe, Eleanor Rathbone, an Independent and women's rights activist representing English universities other than Oxford, Cambridge, and London (which then were privileged to each have their own representatives), told the Commons that Churchill "all along has prophesied that these things would happen, but his advice was neglected."

CHAPTER 5

ORWELL BECOMES "ORWELL"

SPAIN 1937

Orwell shipped the manuscript of *Wigan Pier* to his publisher on December 15, 1936, and a week later left for Spain. He stopped in Paris to talk to Henry Miller, a writer he admired. Miller gave him a corduroy jacket to wear to Spain. Orwell arrived in Barcelona around Christmas Day.

So began the most significant seven months of Orwell's political life. What he saw in the Spanish Civil War in 1937 would inform all his subsequent work. There is a direct line from the streets of Barcelona in 1937 to the torture chambers of *1984*.

It was not yet so when he arrived there at the end of 1936. Barcelona, the capital of Catalonia, in northeastern Spain, was a major center of resistance to the rightist war against the Spanish Republic. Orwell went there ostensibly to write about that civil war, but almost immediately joined the antirightist forces. He was almost giddy with delight at finding a genuinely revolutionary atmosphere in Barcelona, where everyone treated everyone else as a comrade. He felt that for the first time in his life he was seeing the working class in command. "Above all, there was a belief in the revolution and the future, a feeling of having suddenly emerged into an era of equality and freedom," he wrote.

Other visitors were similarly intoxicated. Kitty Bowler, a young American antifascist, wrote to her mother, "A new world is in the making here." Lois Orr, another American, liked that the anarchists had adopted Popeye the Sailor Man as their mascot, selling pins and scarves depicting the cartoon mariner waving the red and black flag of their party. But, she noted, Mickey Mouse was deemed to be nonpartisan. (In an essay about Dickens written a few years later, Orwell would observe in an aside that both Popeye and Mickey are "variants of Jack the Giant-Killer.") Arriving in Barcelona, the Austrian Marxist Franz Borkenau felt "as if we had been landed on a continent different from anything I had seen before." Workers were in charge, police were almost invisible, and everyone seemed to be a comrade. Borkenau could not know that the following year he would be tortured by communist Spanish police for his lack of faith in communism. Likewise, Lois Orr would wind up, briefly, in a communist-run jail.

Feeling his way around the city, Orwell asked an Englishwoman how he could get to the front. Suspicious, she asked for his credentials. "He won me over by pointing to the boots over his shoulder," she recalled. It was a persuasive move because it showed that he knew what he was getting into, and perhaps had some military background. In his enlisted papers, he recorded his occupation as "grocer," which was true enough, given his recent foray into village shopkeeping.

He headed out to the front, about seventy-five miles west of Barcelona. He was met there by Bob Edwards, coordinator of British volunteers in the area. Edwards remembered the arrival: "He came striding towards me—all 6 foot 3 of him—dressed in a grotesque mixture of clothing— corduroy riding breeches, khaki puttees and huge boots caked with mud, a yellow pigskin jerkin, a chocolate-coloured balaclava helmet with a knitted khaki scarf of immeasurable length wrapped round and round his neck and face up to his ears, an old-fashioned German rifle over his shoulder and two hand-grenades hanging from his belt."

Orwell being Orwell, the first thing that hit him when he arrived in the combat zone was the pervasive stench: "We were near the front line now, near enough to smell the characteristic smell of war—in my experience a smell of excrement and decaying food." That may be the quintessential Orwell sentence: He offers a straightforward, grim observation, and manages to use the word "smell" three times.

He saw nothing romantic about this front. It was sad, tiring, and at times macabre:

> We had just dumped our kits and were crawling out of the dug-out when there was another bang and one of the children of our company rushed back from the parapet with his face pouring blood. He had fired his rifle and had somehow managed to blow out the bolt; his scalp was torn to ribbons by the splinters of the burst cartridge-case. It was our first casualty, and, characteristically, self-inflicted.

Almost by accident, as he describes it, Orwell had joined a unit raised by the POUM, which stood for *Partido Obrero de Unificación Marxista*— that is, the Workers' Party of Unified Marxism. It was a far-left splinter group, opposed to Franco's fascists, of course, but politically most distinctive for its anti-Stalinist stance. It was vaguely Trotskyite at a time when Trotsky represented a grave danger to the Soviet worldview by providing a focal point for non-Stalinist socialists. This made it anathema to the Soviet-controlled Communist Party in Spain. The POUM newspaper had been the sole one in Catalonia to criticize the show trials that began in Moscow in the summer of 1936, when Stalin finished off most of his old Bolshevik comrades.

Joining POUM was dangerous for Orwell, much more than he perceived at the time, but it also would prove a perfect perch from which to gain perspective on the great ideological crisis of his age. Orwell could not have known that the NKVD, the Russian spy agency deeply involved in Spain at the time, already had cast its cold eye on POUM. Aleksandr Orlov, the head of Soviet intelligence in Spain, had assured his superiors three months earlier that, if and when necessary, "the Trotskyist organization POUM can be easily liquidated." When the crackdown on POUM came in the spring of 1937, Orwell and his fellows would become marked men.

Arriving at the front's trenches, he noted that he was trailed by a dog with the letters POUM painted or branded on its side. It is possible that seeing this politicized animal planted a seed for the book he would write seven years later about Stalinist pigs. Indeed, in those later years, he owned a black poodle he named Marx—though whether for Groucho or Karl remains unclear.

Settling in at the front, he complained, as soldiers always do, that "nothing happened, nothing ever happened." His unit had standing orders to report the ringing of church bells, because the Nationalist troops celebrated Catholic Mass before going out on their major attacks. If they ever actually served as a warning, it goes unreported.

As a soldier, "he was very practical," recalled another British volunteer, Stafford Cottman. Given his paramilitary experience in Burma, Orwell was made squad leader almost immediately, overseeing twelve men. He emphasized keeping rifles cleaned and oiled. He also ventured into the no-man's-land between the opposing trench lines to collect potatoes. The one time he broke discipline was the night he shot a rat, exciting his comrades into thinking they were under attack. Edwards, leading the British fighters in the area, said Orwell had a particular phobia about the rodents that gnawed on their boots at night. Edwards recalled the incident with some irritation: "Everything was quiet, and all of a sudden there was a terrific explosion. It was Orwell. He's shot a rat in his dugout. And the noise vibrated all over the front. And the fascists thought this was the attack, you see. Shells came over, bombing planes came at us. They blew up our canteen and blew up our buses and everything. It was a very costly shot at a rat, that was."

But most of the time, the section of the front where Orwell was posted was quiet, even stagnant, so much so that he mulled heading south to the Madrid area to join the International Brigade. Edwards warned against it, telling him that the political commissar of that brigade was executing members who displayed "Trotskyite tendencies."

In February 1937, Orwell's wife, Eileen, arrived in Barcelona, where she went to work for a splinter group of the British Labour Party, the ILP. She found a room in the Hotel Continental, on the Ramblas, the main street of the city. The hotel was just steps away from the offices of the POUM. In mid-March, she came out to the front to visit him. She reported in a letter to Orwell's literary agent, "I was allowed to stay in the front line dug-outs all day. The fascists threw in a small bombardment and quite a lot of machine-gun fire." To her mother, she omitted any mention of gunfire, stating only, "I thoroughly enjoyed being at the front."

While on sentry duty, Orwell passed the time in part by fantasizing about getting leave and going on a seaside vacation with Eileen. "Then what a rest we will have," he wrote to her in a letter. He also dared to hope that they might "go fishing too"—one of his favorite pursuits. In late April, after 115 days of front-line service, Orwell was indeed given leave to go to Barcelona. Among other things, he wanted a thorough delousing and a warm bath.

But he would not find the beach vacation he had dreamed about. Instead, he came upon a changed city in which "the revolutionary atmosphere had vanished." He also was surprised to find that while he had been poorly supplied at the front, Republican officers were striding about the city well uniformed, with sidearms strapped on. "We, at the front, could not get pistols for love or money," he noted. An official propaganda campaign against the non–Communist Party militias was under way. The Russians supplying the Republican forces had decided that the anti-

Stalinist left was a more immediate threat than the Francoists, leading the NKVD to start its campaign against POUM. This included constructing a secret crematorium near Barcelona to dispose of the bodies of those it killed. A sense of looming danger hung over the city.

The storm broke on May 3, about two weeks after Orwell arrived in Barcelona from the front. He was in the lobby of the Hotel Continental when a friend said to him, "There's been some kind of trouble at the Telephone Exchange, I hear." This was an attempt by the police to regain control over the telephone exchange building, which was occupied by anarchists. The exchange building was diagonally opposite the Hotel Colón, where Churchill had stayed while vacationing in December 1935 and found the food excellent. Officials of the local branch of the Spanish Communist Party also enjoyed the hotel. After the civil war began, they had occupied it and made it the party's regional headquarters.

A few hours later, Orwell was on the Ramblas when shooting began. An American he knew from the front pulled on his arm and said that POUM men were gathering at the Hotel Falcon, at the far end of the Ramblas. There he found POUM officials distributing rifles and cartridge boxes. He spent the night in a cabaret held by the POUM, cutting down the stage's curtain for use as a blanket.

In the morning, barricades were in the streets, made of uprooted cobblestones and the gravel underneath them. Behind one, a fire had been built and men were frying eggs over it. In the Plaza de Cataluña, Orwell reported, "In a window near the last O but one in the huge 'Hotel Colon' that sprawled across its [the hotel's] face they [the Communists] had a machine gun that could sweep the square with deadly effect."

His experience of the street fighting that May is the heart of the book, leading him to meditate on the politics of his time. To his shock, he found his POUM comrades denounced as "Trotskyists, Fascists, traitors, murderers, cowards, spies and so forth." POUM members were particularly vulnerable because their faction was small and poorly armed and they had not expected to have to go underground, and so had not prepared for it.

He was posted as a sentry atop the Poliorama, a theater on the Ramblas that was topped by twin domes that provided commanding views up and down the street. It was located across the street from the Hotel Continental, where he had been staying with Eileen. The rooftop provided a good field of fire from which to protect the POUM's executive offices, just down the road.

While he was there on the roof of the Poliorama, one of his old colleagues from the secondhand bookstore in Hampstead, Jon Kimche, appeared. "Most of the fighting was going on a mile or two away," Kimche remembered. Orwell told him how poorly the POUM militia was trained and equipped. Bored, Orwell read several Penguin paperback books he had bought a few days earlier.

On the afternoon of May 7, some six thousand additional government troops arrived, and the fighting ended. Again, Orwell was impressed by how well these rear-area units were equipped, compared with his frontline unit. To his disgust, the government blamed all the fighting on POUM, because it was the weakest of the leftist factions.

Watching all this, Orwell arrived at some conclusions that clashed with leftist conventions of the era. At a time when leftist solidarity was considered mandatory, the right thing to do, Orwell began to harbor suspicions. Observing the fighting in Barcelona between different antifascist factions, he noted, "You had all the while a hateful feeling that someone hitherto your friend might be denouncing you to the secret police."

In effect, the events in Barcelona forced him to examine the left as he once earlier had scrutinized imperialism and capitalism. He concluded, "The Communist Party, with Soviet Russia, had thrown its weight against the revolution." It was determined to systematically wipe out the anticommunist parts of the left—first POUM, then the anarchists, and then socialists.

But to say this in public was a form of modern heresy. Orwell realized, with shock, that the left-wing newspapers did not report the situation accurately, and did not want to. Rather, they willingly accepted lies. "One of the dreariest effects of this war has been to teach me that the Left-wing press is every bit as spurious and dishonest as that of the Right," he wrote. This set him on his life's work, to push continually to establish the facts, no matter how difficult or unpopular that might be.

On May 10, 1937, he left Barcelona to return to the front, where the POUM was still deployed, despite being suppressed back in Barcelona by the government whose territory it was defending. On May 11, the POUM was denounced in the *Daily Worker* as "Franco's Fifth Column." Posters appeared on Barcelona walls with the headline TEAR THE MASK, showing a face marked POUM, and a fascist face underneath it. It was classic "big lie" propaganda.

The POUM soldiers at the front there had not been told that they were being denounced in Barcelona, and the newspapers from the city remained quiet about the purge.

Orwell expected to remain at the front until late summer. But around dawn on May 20, he was moving through the trenches, checking on the sentries, when he was hit. He knew it was a dangerous time because his trench, facing west, had the rising sun behind it, which silhouetted his tall frame for enemy snipers. Of being shot, he would write, "Roughly speaking it was the sensation of being at the centre of an explosion. There seemed to be a loud bang and a blinding flash of light all round me, and I felt a tremendous shock—no pain, only a violent shock, such as you get from an electric terminal; with it a sense of utter weakness, a feeling of being stricken and shriveled up to nothing. The sand-bags in front of me receded into immense distance." The bullet's impact knocked him to the ground. "All of this happened in a space of time much less than a second. . . . I had a numb, dazed feeling, a consciousness of being very badly hurt, but no pain in the ordinary sense."

The American sentry with whom he had been speaking started toward him. "Gosh! Are you hit?" The American, named Harry Milton, recalled, "I thought he wouldn't make it. He had bitten down hard on his lip, and

I thought there must be a lot of damage. But he was breathing, and his eyes were moving."

Orwell provides one of the best accounts ever written of what it is like to be badly wounded by a bullet and expecting to die soon. He knew he had been shot, but could not tell where. When informed that it was a neck shot, "I took it for granted that I was done for. I had never heard of a man or animal getting a bullet through the middle of the neck and surviving it." Blood dribbled from a corner of his mouth. He assumed that a carotid artery had been severed, which would mean that he had only a few minutes to live. "My first thought, conventionally enough, was for my wife. My second was a violent resentment at having to leave this world which, when all is said and done, suits me so well."

But the minutes passed and he did not die. He could not know that, with enormous luck, the bullet had shot through the tiny space of about one centimeter between the carotid artery and his larynx, with the impact bruising his vocal cords. A bit to the left or right, or more tumble in the high-velocity bullet, and he likely would have died that day. Because the shot hit him at an angle, the bullet passed out the back of his neck without severing his spine, even though it apparently grazed a nerve, causing the temporary paralysis of one arm.

He was carried on a stretcher about a mile to a field hospital, where he was given a shot of morphine, and then was taken to a larger military hospital in the nearby village of Sietamo, just east of the provincial capital of Huesca. His old comrades dropped by, expressed pleasure that he was alive, and then relieved him of his watch, pistol, flashlight, and knife, knowing that all those likely would be stolen from him in the hospital, and that the gear was needed at the front. For weeks, his voice was a croak that sounded like the grinding brakes of an old Model T, and could not be heard from more than two yards away, reported his battalion commander, Georges Kopp.

But his troubles were just beginning. After recuperating, he was discharged from the Spanish army as an invalid. On June 15, Andreu Nin, the head of the POUM, had been arrested and then disappeared, likely killed by the NKVD. The party was outlawed on June 16.

Orwell returned to Barcelona on June 20 to find the Soviet crackdown on the POUM in full swing. In a scene out of an early Hitchcock film, upon arriving in Barcelona he went that evening to meet his wife, Eileen, at the Hotel Continental. She saw him across the hotel lobby, smiled casually, and then hissed in his ear, "*Get out!* . . . Get out of here *at once*." He began to leave. A friend ran into him on the long set of stairs winding from the lobby down several flights to the front door on the Ramblas and repeated the admonition, telling Orwell to move along quickly before the hotel staff alerted the police. Then came a third warning, from a sympathetic hotel employee: "The POUM's been suppressed. They've seized all the buildings. Practically everyone's in prison. And they say they're shooting people already." Orwell quickly came to realize that "the 'Stalinists' were in the saddle, and therefore it was a matter of course that every 'Trotskyist' was in danger."

Orwell became a fugitive. That night he slept in the ruins of a church. He would continue to wander the streets for a few days until he and his wife could get their papers in order to leave the country. When he encountered old comrades walking by, each would ignore the other, "as though we had been total strangers. That was dreadful." There is an early whiff of *1984* in his resentment of how the police state could intrude on such friendships.

Six secret policemen came in the middle of the night to search his wife's hotel room for incriminating documents. They were thorough, emptying drawers and suitcases, probing under the bath and radiator, holding garments up to the light. But the one thing they did not do was look in the bed, because his wife had remained in it. Orwell would describe the scene with affection. "One must remember that the police were almost entirely under Communist control, and these men probably were Communist Party members themselves. But they were also Spaniards, and to turn a woman out of bed was a little too much for them. This part of the job was silently dropped." This was fortunate, because the Orwells' passports were hidden in the bed with her.

Ernest Hemingway, also in Spain at the time, provides an illuminating contrast to Orwell. He was as politically naive as Orwell was observant, in part because his macho posing got in the way of seeing accurately. In *For Whom the Bell Tolls,* his novel of the Spanish Civil War, the hero thinks to himself, in what is supposed to be a hardened, wise way, "He had learned . . . if a thing was right fundamentally the lying was not supposed to matter. There was a lot of lying though. He did not care for the lying at first. He hated it. Then later he had come to like it. It was part of being an insider."

In the same chapter, "Karkov," a Russian journalist, presented by Hemingway as extremely intelligent, summarizes the POUM. It was "never serious," Karkov informs the hero. "It was a heresy of crackpots and wild men and it was really just infantilism. There were some honest misguided people. There was one fairly good brain and there was a little fascist money. Not much. The poor P. O. U. M. They were very silly people. . . . Poor P. O. U. M. They never did kill anybody. Not at the front nor anywhere else. A few in Barcelona, yes." Hemingway also provides the Russian with an alibi for the execution of Nin, the POUM leader: "We had him but he escaped from our hands." Eight years later, Orwell's friend Malcolm Muggeridge would encounter Hemingway in postliberation Paris and come away unimpressed: "boozy, preoccupied with the image rather than the reality."

When the Orwells fled the country on June 23, they considered themselves lucky to get out alive, because many of their friends did not. Orwell did not know it, but a few weeks later, on July 13, an indictment was handed up in Barcelona that charged him and his wife with spying and treason. It began, "Their correspondence reveals they are confirmed Trotskyites." It added that Orwell "took part in the events of May"— the street fighting in Barcelona.

Once at home, he sat down to write *Homage to Catalonia,* his first great book. Like the best war memoirs, it rigorously resists overdramatization. The book is true to the fact that all wars are essentially the same in consisting of long stretches of stupefying boredom mixed with moments of fear and shock. Cold and hunger were greater enemies than the fascists in distant trenches, out of range of the Republic's rifles.

The book begins as a very good tale of going to war, and then, two thirds of the way through, when Orwell runs into the Stalinist crackdown on other leftists in Barcelona, turns into a noirish political thriller. In that narrative, Orwell hammers home two points. The first is that Soviet-dominated communism should not be trusted by other leftists. The second is that the left can be every bit as accepting of lies as the right.

Orwell knew that neither of these themes would win him friends on the British left. By splitting with the conventional, pro-Stalinist left, Orwell made a move that paralleled Churchill's earlier distancing of himself from the profascist elements of the British aristocracy. Orwell knew that many of his British socialist friends believed that lying was not only permissible but mandatory if it helped the Soviet cause.

The book ends beautifully, and unexpectedly, with Orwell's appreciation of the Edenic landscape of southern England as he arrives home— and then with a warning to the inhabitants of that green and pleasant land:

It was still the England I had known in my childhood: the railway-cuttings smothered in wild flowers, the deep meadows where the great shining horses browse and meditate, the slow-moving streams bordered by willows, the green bosoms of the elms, the larkspurs in the cottage gardens; and then the huge peaceful wilderness of outer London, the barges on the miry river, the familiar streets, the posters telling of cricket matches and Royal weddings, the men in bowler hats, the pigeons in Trafalgar Square, the red buses, the blue policemen— all sleeping the deep, deep sleep of England, from which I sometimes fear that we shall never wake till we are jerked out of it by the roar of bombs.

This is a wonderful sentence, worth reading aloud. It is closely observed, it is infused with his love of England, and it is, most of all, eerily prophetic. It was written in mid-1937, at a time when British leaders were seeking peace through appeasement, and much of the population voiced support for pacifism. Orwell was on a very different course. As he put it in a book review that was published in February 1938, "If someone drops a bomb on your mother, go and drop two bombs on his mother."

Orwell, arriving home, had become the writer we know today from *Animal Farm* and *1984*. Burma had made him an anti-imperialist, but it was his time in Spain that developed his political vision and with it the determination to criticize right and left with equal vigor. Before Spain, he had been a fairly conventional leftist, arguing that fascism and capitalism were essentially the same. Until this point, Orwell still clung to some of the views of the 1930s left.

He would leave Spain resolved to oppose the abuse of power at both ends of the political spectrum. After Spain, observed the literary critic Hugh Kenner, he would be "a leftist at odds with the official left." "It is unfortunate that so few people in England have yet caught up with the fact that Communism is now a counter-revolutionary force," Orwell wrote in September 1937.

After Spain, wounded in body and spirit, he followed a far more independent course. "The Spanish war and other events in 1937 turned the scale and thereafter I knew where I stood," he explained in "Why I

Write," a marvelous essay produced between finishing *Animal Farm* and starting *1984*. "Every line of serious work that I have written since 1936 has been written, directly or indirectly, against totalitarianism and for democratic Socialism, as I understand it." He was careful to distinguish socialism from communism, which he lumped with fascism as essentially undemocratic. By the end of his life, he would believe that "a communist and a fascist are somewhat nearer to one another than either is to a democrat."

From Spain on, his mission was to write the facts as he saw them, no matter where that took him, and to be skeptical of everything he read, especially when it came from or comforted those wielding power. This became his faith. "In Spain, for the first time, I saw newspaper reports which did not bear any relation to the facts," he wrote a few years later. He continued:

> I saw great battles reported where there had been no fighting, and complete silence where hundreds of men had been killed. I saw troops who had fought bravely denounced as cowards and traitors, and others who had never seen a shot fired hailed as the heroes of imaginary victories; and I saw newspapers in London retailing those lies and eager intellectuals building superstructures over events that had never happened. I saw, in fact, history being written not in terms of what happened but of what ought to have happened according to various "party lines."

Back at his village cottage, Orwell wrote and gardened, but did not reopen the shop. The vicar of the church, likely suspicious of the politics of this couple just returned from Spain, dropped by for a chat. The churchman "doesn't approve at all of our having been on the Government side" in Spain, Orwell wrote to one of his war comrades. "Of course we had to own up that it was true about the burning of churches [by

Republican forces], but he cheered up a lot on hearing they were only Roman Catholic churches."

In March 1938, six weeks before *Homage to Catalonia* was published, Orwell's lungs began to bleed. He was briefly hospitalized. In April, the book was released. In September, he and Eileen left to winter in Morocco to nurse his respiratory system, a trip made possible only because an anonymous benefactor sent him three hundred pounds.

Today *Homage to Catalonia* reads like a five-alarm warning about the future, a vision of the nightmarish collision of fascism with communism, with neither side brooking any other choice. In his introduction to the first American edition of the book, issued in 1952, the literary critic Lionel Trilling called it "one of the most important documents of our time." In 1999, the conservative American magazine *National Review* named it the third most important nonfiction book of the century. Coming in first was Churchill's memoirs of the Second World War; in second place, between Churchill and Orwell, was, appropriately enough, Alexander Solzhenitsyn's *Gulag Archipelago*. Orwell was the only writer to have two entries in the top ten; his *Collected Essays* ranked fifth.

But the reception in 1938 was far chillier. Coming on the heels of *The Road to Wigan Pier*, the new book confirmed that he was a renegade in English literary circles. Orwell's regular outlets, both for his books and his journalism, were not interested in publishing his views on Spain. Victor Gollancz had under protest published *The Road to Wigan Pier* a year earlier, but a direct attack on Stalinism was just too much for him. To be fair, Gollancz had a sense of the market. In April 1938, when the book was published by another house, it was reviewed warmly but did not sell well, and fewer than 1,500 copies were purchased during Orwell's lifetime. The physical book itself became a victim of the bombs Orwell had foreseen in its final paragraph: In 1941, the printing plates for the original edition were destroyed in a German bombing raid on Plymouth, England.

Homage to Catalonia is a wonderful book, certainly among Orwell's best. Even so, perhaps inevitably, an unresolved moral question hangs over it. In it he concludes that despite all he saw happen in Barcelona—friends disappeared, probably shot by a secret police regime backed by the Soviets—he still thinks it would be better if the communist-backed Republicans defeated the fascists. The communists might be the enemies of the noncommunist left, but even so, he asserts, "Whatever faults the post-war government might have, Franco's regime would certainly be worse."

Orwell hinted at this contradiction. Even as he urged the defeat of Franco, he acknowledged that the generalissimo was more than anything else "an anachronism," a feudalist representing the interests of the military, the rich, and the Church. Orwell said as much in a chapter of the book that was included in the first edition but has since been dropped from most editions: "Franco was not strictly comparable with Hitler or Mussolini." Also, his anecdote of the chivalrous secret policemen who would not discomfit his wife also hints that he understood that Spain, for all its problems, was not Germany or the Soviet Union. There certainly was large-scale brutal repression in post–civil war Spain, with tens of thousands of antifascists executed and thousands more held in concentration camps. One has only to visit Franco's chilling tomb, in the Valle de los Caidos, a stadium-sized cavern built in part by the labor of leftist political prisoners, to intuit the brutal atmosphere of Spain in the 1940s. It is a cathedral of death.

Also, once in power, Franco proved to have no answer at all. He had no program. He was unadaptive, backward looking. After his death in 1975, the transition to a democracy got under way relatively expeditiously. In the national elections of 1982, the center-left Socialist Workers' Party, which had been banned from 1939 to 1977, prevailed and went on to govern for fourteen years. It is impossible to know whether a victory of the Soviet-backed government would have been better for Spain, but with the benefit of hindsight, it's certainly an open question.

In the end, however, such counterfactualism is unproductive. One could as easily conclude that had the Republicans won, they would have been ousted by the Nazis early in World War II. A German occupation of Spain, or just of its major Mediterranean and Atlantic ports, would have made Allied operations far more difficult in 1943 and 1944.

Churchill's position on Spain at first was that he would prefer that neither side win, but that if victory had to occur, then he would prefer that Franco emerge triumphant. But as Hitler began to show his strength, especially with the takeover of Austria in March 1938, his position shifted. It was not in Britain's interests for fascism and its allies to dominate Europe. So Churchill stated in December 1938, "It would seem today that the British Empire would run far less risk from the victory of the Spanish government than from that of General Franco."

Orwell's political education was not quite finished. The final step would come when Hitler's Germany signed a nonaggression pact with Stalin's Russia on August 23, 1939. With that agreement, the totalitarian right made peace with the totalitarian left. This had the effect on Orwell that the Munich Agreement had on Churchill eleven months earlier, confirming his fears and making him all the more determined to follow the dissident political course he was on, in defiance of his mainstream leftist comrades. "The night before the Russo-German pact was announced I dreamed that the war had started," Orwell wrote. "I came downstairs to find the newspaper announcing Ribbentrop's flight to Moscow. So war was coming, and the Government, even the Chamberlain Government, was assured of my loyalty."

The agreement between Nazi Germany and the Soviet Union brought an extraordinary moment for the left in the West. For years, the final defense of Western supporters of the Soviets had been that, for all of Stalin's excesses, communism was the only ideology strong enough to stand up to fascism. But now the two totalitarian stances were supporting each other, even if only at arm's length.

For Orwell, this was a final moment of clarity. From this point on, his target was the abuse of power in all its forms, but especially by the totalitarian state, whether left or right. His subtheme would be the hypocrisy of some in the left in believing that it was not only permissible but mandatory to suppress the facts if doing so helped the Soviet cause. Many had turned a blind eye to a series of catastrophes, from the Ukrainian famine to the Moscow show trials, and now, to the Nazi-Soviet pact. He would not.

As war loomed near the end of the decade, Orwell's greatness, however evident today to readers of *Homage to Catalonia,* was not at all widely recognized by his contemporaries. He was seen as a minor and somewhat cranky writer. Orwell's reputation looms so large today that few people grasp that he was for most of his life a relatively obscure figure. Writers such as H. G. Wells and Aldous Huxley, now receding into the past, were far more prominent then. Orwell is never mentioned in memoirs and diaries of notables of his time, figures such as Anthony Eden, Hugh Dalton, Lord Halifax, Clement Attlee, Henry Channon, Oliver Harvey, or Sir Alexander Cadogan. The best-known diarist of the era was Harold Nicolson, who mentions Orwell nowhere in his five hundred pages, even though they had a minor connection in that one of Nicolson's lovers, the literary critic and editor Raymond Mortimer, once scrapped with Orwell over the politics of the Spanish Civil War.

Cultural histories of the 1930s written shortly after the decade do not mention him. He is nowhere to be found in *The Long Week-End: A Social History of Great Britain, 1918–1939,* by the poet Robert Graves and the historian Alan Hodge, published in 1940. Even Malcolm Muggeridge, a sympathetic mind, did not see fit to mention Orwell in his own study

The Thirties, written at the end of that decade. Only in retrospect is it clear that between 1936 and 1939, Orwell became the "Orwell" we know today.

Orwell spent the summer of 1939 mainly at his cottage in Hertfordshire, watching over his garden and ducks and chickens, and taking notes on the news as Europe slid toward war. He once advised a friend that it was unwise to name one's chickens "because then you can't eat them." On August 24, he planted seventy-five leeks and noticed that the larkspurs were "coming out" in "five different colours." The same day, he noted in his diary that his wife had been to the War Office, where she was working in "the Censorship Department," and came away with the "impression that war is almost certain." On August 30, he reported that a friend told him that "a few weeks back W. Churchill expressed very pessimistic views to him." The next day, he observed, "Blackberries are ripening. . . . Finches beginning to flock." On September 1, he drily recorded, "Invasion of Poland began this morning. Warsaw bombed. General mobilisation proclaimed in England, ditto in France plus martial law."

CHAPTER 6

CHURCHILL BECOMES "CHURCHILL"

SPRING 1940

Churchill spent much of August 1939 on vacation in France, painting landscapes and mulling the looming war. He was full of ominous premonitions. "This is the last picture we shall paint in peace for a very long time," he commented to a fellow artist. Back in England near the end of the month, he gazed out of an automobile window at a peaceful countryside view of growing corn and slowly said, "Before the harvest is gathered, we shall be at war."

On the morning of Friday, September 1, 1939, before all the wheat was ripe, the German army invaded Poland.

Two days later, at nine o'clock on the bright, clear Sunday morning of September 3, the British government delivered a final message to Berlin: Unless Germany reversed its invasion of Poland, Britain and France would be compelled to declare war. At eleven, that ultimatum expired. Fifteen minutes later, Prime Minister Chamberlain spoke over the BBC, declaring that a state of war existed between Britain and Germany. As he finished, air-raid sirens began to wail.

Chamberlain was publicly distraught. "This is a sad day for all of us, and to none is it sadder than to me," he said. "Everything that I have worked for, everything that I have hoped for, everything that I have believed in during my public life, has crashed into ruins." His words were entirely accurate, but probably not appropriate. The issue at hand was far bigger than the personal feelings or political future of Neville Chamberlain. The fate of Europe and perhaps of the world was at stake.

Churchill understood this. Waiting to speak that day in the House of Commons, he later recalled, "I felt a serenity of mind and was conscious of a kind of uplifted detachment from human and personal affairs." When he stood to talk, he tried to convey that sense to the House.

Churchill struck a surer, clearer note than the prime minister. "This is not a question of fighting for Danzig or fighting for Poland. We are fighting to save the whole world from the pestilence of Nazi tyranny and in defence of all that is most sacred to man. This is no war for domination or imperial aggrandisement or material gain; no war to shut any country out of its sunlight and means of progress. It is a war, viewed in its inherent quality, to establish, on impregnable rocks, the rights of the individual, and it is a war to establish and revive the stature of man."

George Orwell may not have believed those words coming from Churchill, but he certainly agreed with the principles stated in them, especially the last sentence about the rights and place of the individual. Years later, he would write, "Intellectual liberty . . . without a doubt has been one of the distinguishing marks of western civilisation." He also commented that "if this war is about anything at all, it is a war in favour of freedom of thought."

Six days after Churchill's speech, Orwell wrote to the British government asking to be given a role in the war effort. This was to prove to be a long, frustrating struggle for him.

People react to war in different ways. One response is to be overwhelmed by events and stunned into inaction or social withdrawal. No one could accuse either Churchill or Orwell of this. Both men were energized, leaping into the fray intellectually.

By the close of that Sunday, September 3, 1939, Churchill was back in government as a member of the Cabinet. He was made first lord of the admiralty, the British equivalent of secretary of the navy and the post he had held at the outset of World War I. It had taken another major war to force the Conservatives to open the door to him. (Meanwhile, in Munich on that same Sunday, Unity Mitford walked into a park and shot herself in the head. The bullet lodged in her brain, causing much damage, but she did not die until nine years later.)

On September 11, Churchill received an extraordinary message from the American president. "I shall at all times welcome it, if you will keep me in touch personally with anything you want me to know about," Franklin Roosevelt wrote. Churchill responded with alacrity. FDR's message of September 11 was the first of about 800 he would send to Churchill during the war. Churchill would respond with even more, a total of 950.

It was unusual, even highly irregular, for an American president, ostensibly neutral and at peace, to be communicating directly with a British Cabinet member involved in a war. The reason likely was that neither Roosevelt nor Churchill trusted Joseph P. Kennedy, then the American ambassador in London, and, of course, the father of the future president John F. Kennedy. Harold Ickes, a key aide to Roosevelt, wrote in his diary, "The President thinks that Joe Kennedy, if he were in power, would give us a Fascist form of government." At one point Kennedy told Roosevelt that he believed that events would make it necessary for the United States to implement, "possibly under other names, the basic features of the Fascist state: to fight totalitarianism, we would have to adopt totalitarian methods." FDR muttered to another associate around the time of the Munich Agreement that he considered Kennedy "disloyal to his country."

And indeed, earlier on that same day, Kennedy had sent to Roosevelt and to Cordell Hull, the secretary of state, a "Triple Priority" message recommending that the United States enter into peace negotiations with Hitler. That may well have been what pushed FDR to contact Churchill. Roosevelt already had tried to reach out to the British government, writing to Prime Minister Chamberlain in January 1938. He had been rebuffed. At the Foreign Office, Anthony Eden fretted then that "we have snubbed President too much." In his World War II memoirs, Churchill would express "amazement" that Chamberlain had given Roosevelt a cold shoulder: "The lack of all sense of proportion, and even of self-preservation, which this episode reveals in an upright, competent, well-meaning man, charged with the destinies of our country and all who depended upon it, is appalling. One cannot today even reconstruct the state of mind which would render such gestures possible."

On the sparkling late summer day of Sunday, September 17, Churchill inspected part of the British fleet in Scotland's saltwater Loch Ewe, including the antisubmarine nets at the loch's mouth, and then began the drive across the highlands to the train station in Inverness. It was a warm, dry day, so he interrupted his journey by picnicking by a hill stream. As he was sitting in that idyllic spot, some grim memories of World War I crept over him, chilling him despite the abundant sunshine. "Somehow the light faded out of the landscape" as he considered his situation, and the globe's: "Poland in its agony; France but a pale reflection of her former warlike ardour; the Russian Colossus no longer an ally, not even neutral, possibly to become a foe. Italy no friend. Japan no ally. Would America ever come in again? The British Empire remained intact and gloriously united, but ill-prepared, unready. We still had command of the sea. We were woefully outmatched in numbers in this new mortal weapon of the air." In that moment of reflection he girded himself for war.

Two weeks later, Churchill delivered his first major speech since returning to the Cabinet, and then gave a successful national radio broadcast. For the following six years, he would stop only when forced by pneumonia to take bed rest. He was such a busybody in the first days of the war that, in mid-September, after he wrote a memorandum critiquing the state of the Royal Air Force, Chamberlain decided to have a "very frank talk" with him, instructing Churchill to restrain himself. Undeterred, Churchill sent thirteen analytical letters to Chamberlain by mid-October. "Winston's ceaseless industry is impressive," the prime minister's aide John Colville, still a skeptic of Churchill, wrote in his diary a few months later. Churchill's habit of scrutinizing documents and questioning details sent a needed jolt of energy into the vast military bureaucracy below him. His fierce determination gave Colville the sense that if England fell, Churchill would go underground and carry on the fight as a partisan leader.

People noticed how much Churchill was rejuvenated by the war. Malcolm MacDonald, the son of the former prime minister and himself a minor political figure, was struck that Churchill "has not appeared so fit for twenty years." This was despite his continuing large daily intake of alcohol. Harold Nicolson recalls a friend coming away from lunch with Churchill "rather shocked by . . . the immense amount of port and brandy he consumed." On a typical day, according to his aide Sir Ian Jacob, Churchill drank champagne and brandy with lunch, then, after his afternoon nap, had two or three glasses of whisky and soda, then champagne and brandy with dinner, followed by more whisky and soda. Jacob noted that he also sometimes accompanied his breakfast with white wine.

The war did not go well under Chamberlain in the fall of 1939 and winter and early spring of 1940. By May, it was clear that he would have to give up the premiership. Many expected the foreign secretary, Lord Halifax, to step up. Halifax, who had been one of the architects of appeasement, was the preferred candidate of both the Conservative Party and of King George VI. Had Halifax been willing to take the prime ministership instead of Churchill, he very likely would have entered into peace talks with the Germans.

But Halifax was worried. He sat in the House of Lords, and that made it difficult to lead the Commons, he observed. His hesitation left only Churchill.

MAY 10, 1940

On the morning of May 10, having been informed that the Germans had begun invading Holland and Belgium, and knowing he likely would take office later that day, Churchill breakfasted on fried eggs and bacon, and then enjoyed a cigar. It was a hearty meal for an aging man on shaky ground. He was sixty-five years old, at a time of life when many people then retired. Instead, after decades of striving, he was on the verge of achieving his lifelong ambition to be the prime minister of Great Britain.

It would be an extraordinary day. His first meeting was at six o'clock that morning, with the ministers of war and air. At seven, there was another meeting, of the Military Co-ordination Committee. The full War Cabinet met at eight at the prime minster's residence, reviewing the forlorn state of affairs—Germany was bombing Belgium and northern France, German paratroopers were landing in Belgium, British fighter squadrons were being moved to France. The HMS *Kelly* had been torpedoed off Belgium.

Given all this, Prime Minister Chamberlain's first thought was that he should remain in office until the crisis passed. A message arrived later that morning at Churchill's office: "Mr. Chamberlain was inclined to feel that the great battle which had broken upon us made it necessary for him to remain at his post." No, came the response from Churchill's allies: The crisis made it all the more urgent that Chamberlain give way to a new national government.

Churchill then received officials of the Dutch government. "Haggard and worn, with horror in their eyes, they had just flown over from Amsterdam."

There was a second War Cabinet meeting at 11:30 A.M., to review more news of German bombings and paratroops. Then the Military Co-ordination Committee met again at one in the afternoon. Churchill lunched with Lord Beaverbrook, the newspaper baron and his sometime political ally.

The War Cabinet met again at 4:30 P.M. News arrived that German firebombs were being dropped in Kent, in southeast England. The Germans had taken the Rotterdam airport. Six British fighters had been sent to intercept the German paratroop planes over Holland; only one returned. A War Office message arrived reporting that German tanks and infantry had entered Belgium. Chamberlain then finally came to the point: He had decided to resign.

Chamberlain went to see King George VI. The king suggested that Halifax succeed Chamberlain. "I thought H was the obvious man," he wrote in his diary. But when Chamberlain said that Halifax was not the right fit at the moment, "I asked Chamberlain his advice, & he told me Winston was the man to send for."

The king summoned Churchill, and the formalities of asking Churchill to form a government were observed. Outside Buckingham Palace, Churchill turned to his bodyguard, who congratulated him. Churchill teared up and replied, "I hope that it is not too late. I am very much afraid that it is. We can only do our best."

Churchill returned to his office at the Admiralty to form a government. He wrote to Chamberlain asking for his continued counsel and service. He asked Halifax to remain as foreign minister. He asked the leader of the Labour Party, Clement Attlee, to come see him that evening, and when he did, invited him to join the government and to submit the names of other Labour members who might join the Cabinet.

The Labour men actually were more at ease with him than were the Conservatives. John Colville wrote in his diary that day that Churchill was damned four times over, as "the greatest adventurer of modern political history . . . a half-breed American whose main support was that of inefficient but talkative people of a similar type." He viewed Churchill's ascension, he added, a bit unnecessarily, with "total horror."

Neither Churchill's memoirs nor Martin Gilbert's exhaustive biography mentions it, but Churchill had one other meeting on May 10. He dined that night with a senior intelligence officer, William Stephenson, whom he was sending to America. He gave Stephenson three goals for his mission: Get military aid for Britain, counter enemy intelligence in the Western Hemisphere, and "eventually to bring the United States into the war." It may have been the most significant order Churchill issued in the entire war, and it came just a few hours after he had become prime minister.

Churchill went to bed at 3:00 A.M., "conscious of a profound sense of relief. At last I had the authority to give directions over the whole scene." For the first time in his life, he lay his head on the pillow as prime minister. "Ten years in the political wilderness" had ended, he later wrote.

But for how long? There was a good chance he would be an interim leader, and indeed there were people betting that that was the likely outcome.

His own party did not rally to him even after he took office. Regarding the new prime minister, J.C.C. Davidson reported to his political ally, the former prime minister Stanley Baldwin, "The Tories don't trust Winston." This was no idle observation, given that Davidson was a former chairman of the Conservative Party. He hoped that Churchill would be a short-timer, predicting that "after the first clash of war is over it may well be that a sounder Government may emerge." Peter Eckersley, a Tory MP, predicted that "Winston won't last five months."

Churchill sometimes got in a few digs of his own: Later that year, when a factory owned by former prime minister Baldwin was bombed by the Germans, Churchill tartly remarked, "Very ungrateful of them."

On May 13, 1940, when he entered the House of Commons for the first time as prime minister, he received less applause than did Chamberlain, the outgoing premier. "In the early weeks it was from the Labour benches that I was mainly greeted," he would recall. Moved by some of the welcoming speeches, Churchill mopped his moistening eyes.

At 2:54 that afternoon, he rose to speak. He introduced his War Cabinet—the five most powerful members of the new government—and then struck a trumpetlike note: "I have nothing to offer but blood, toil, tears and sweat," which echoed the lines in Byron's poem "The Age of Bronze" that reproached British land barons for living on the "Blood, sweat, and tear-wrung Millions."

He went on to deliver a powerful speech, all the more vigorous for its simplicity:

> You ask, what is our policy? I will say: It is to wage war, by sea, land and air, with all our might and with all the strength that God can give us; to wage war against a monstrous tyranny never surpassed in the dark, lamentable catalogue of human crime. That is our policy.
>
> You ask, what is our aim? I can answer in one word: It is victory, victory at all costs, victory in spite of all terror, victory, however long and hard the road may be; for without victory, there is no survival.
>
> Let that be realised; no survival for the British Empire, no survival for all that the British Empire has stood for, no survival for the urge and impulse of the ages, that mankind will move forward towards its goal.

This is rhetoric on par with Orwell's best essays—although, of course, preserving the British Empire was hardly a goal of Orwell's. Speaking not just to the House but to the British nation and the world, Churchill was laying down a new, harder line. He had not become prime minister as a man of peace, and would not be one. His was a policy of war in pursuit of victory. There would be no more talk of finding a compromise with Germany, perhaps of giving up colonies as part of a settlement.

Orwell, surprisingly for a leftist, was encouraged by Churchill's rise to power. "For the first time in decades we have a government with imagination," he wrote.

Churchill was not just rallying the nation. He also needed to stabilize his own position. It was not clear to many other political leaders that he was the man for the long haul, and might rather be only a caretaker during a moment of crisis.

From mid-May to mid-June 1940, there was no certainty in Churchill's position. The question of dealing with the Americans—and getting them involved in the war—continued to preoccupy him. On the morning of May 18, as he began his ninth day as prime minister, he told his son, Randolph, while shaving that he expected not only that Britain would survive the war but that it would win. "I mean we can beat them," he explained.

Randolph, surprised, replied, "I'm all for it, but I don't see how you can do it."

Churchill dried his face, then turned to look at his son, and said, with urgent vehemence, "I shall drag the United States in." He made a similar point when he told Royal Navy leaders, "The first thing is to get the US into the war. We can settle how to fight it afterwards."

Ambassador Kennedy continued to underestimate Churchill. He saw German victory on the horizon. "The situation is terrible," he wrote to his wife on May 20, 1940. "I think the jig is up. . . . The English will fight to the end but I just don't think they can stand up to the bombing indefinitely." In early June, Kennedy wrote to his son Joe Jr. that "I can see nothing but slaughter ahead." To be fair, the American ambassador in Paris, William Bullitt, took a similar stance, advising FDR in May 1940 to consider the possibility that the British would form a fascist government that would seek an armistice with Germany. "That would mean that the British navy would be against us," he warned.

Churchill understood that 1940 would be hard. The question really was whether he and Britain had more staying power than those two

American ambassadors believed. In mid-May, walking across from Downing Street to the Admiralty building, he was cheered by a crowd. "As soon as we were inside the building, he dissolved into tears," wrote his military assistant, General Hastings "Pug" Ismay. Churchill explained his emotion to Ismay: "Poor people, they trust me and I can give them nothing but disaster for quite a long time."

DUNKIRK

Just how much disaster, even Churchill could not know. The key point in his first weeks in office was the British retreat to the coastal French town of Dunkirk, just west of the Belgian border, in late May 1940. Several hundred thousand British and Allied troops were encircled by the Germans. Had the Germans attacked aggressively, they would have captured a quarter of a million men, stripping Britain of its army. This would have put enormous pressure on Britain to enter into peace talks, something that could have forced Churchill to step down.

But the Germans did not thrust into the beach areas. Instead, a crushing force of nine Panzer divisions stopped just short of Dunkirk. A British general was puzzled, writing in his diary, "The German mobile columns have definitely been halted for some reason or other."

Some junior officers on the other side also were surprised. "We could not understand why we let so many get away," recalled Hans von Luck, commander of a Panzer reconnaissance company at the time.

And so the British were able to begin their evacuation from the beaches. Even today, there are some unresolved questions about why Dunkirk went so well for the British. One group of historians argues that Hitler, still hoping for a peace settlement with the British, stopped his tanks in order, as military historian Stephen Bungay put it, to "avoid inflicting a humiliating defeat on the British" that would make them less willing to negotiate. The historical record is mixed, but one quite persuasive piece of evidence is that Hitler's order stopping his ground forces was sent unencrypted, making it possible for the British to hear and understand it immediately as a kind of peace offering. Later in the war, Hitler took to complaining that he had been too nice to the British. For example, Walter Warlimont, a general in the German military headquarters, reported that Hitler stated, "Churchill was quite unable to appreciate the sporting spirit of which I have given proof by refraining from creating an irreparable breach between the British and ourselves. We did, however, refrain from annihilating them at Dunkirk." Indeed, after the war, German commanders being debriefed confirmed that they had been ordered to stop about eight miles outside Dunkirk. "My tanks were kept halted there for three days," said Field Marshal Gerd von Rundstedt. "If I had had my way the English would not have got off so lightly. But my hands were tied by direct orders from Hitler himself." When one of Rundstedt's subordinate generals told Hitler in a small meeting that he did not understand why such an order was issued, Hitler replied that "his aim was to make peace with Britain on a basis that she would regard as compatible with her honour to accept."

However, some serious historians believe it possible that all this talk of stopping in hopes of peace was a cover story concocted to explain away Hitler's bungled decision. For example, Ian Kershaw, the author of a two-volume biography of Hitler, concludes that Hitler's claim that he had purposely let the British escape was "no more than a face-saving rationalization," while Gerhard Weinberg in his massive history of the war dismisses it flatly as "a fabrication."

A third possibility, supported by Alistair Horne, a leading military historian, is that Hitler aimed to reserve the delivery of the coup de grâce at Dunkirk for the Luftwaffe, the most politically loyal of his armed forces. He cites the German Panzer commander Heinz Guderian, who wrote that one of the orders telling him to halt stated, "Dunkirk is to be left to the Luftwaffe."

Whatever the tactical situation at Dunkirk, the result was that most of the British troops made it home, albeit without most of their weapons, artillery pieces, and vehicles. About three hundred thousand men were brought out—two thirds British, the remainder French. One who did not make it was Orwell's wife's brother, a major in the Medical Corps, who was hit in the chest by shrapnel and died in Belgium hours before he was to be evacuated. The loss plunged Eileen into a deep depression for about eighteen months, recalled one of her friends. "Her hair was unbrushed, her face and body thin. Reality was so awful for her that she withdrew." Yet as Michael Shelden, one of Orwell's biographers, notes, her pain was not reflected in Orwell's letters or diaries, let alone his journalism and literary criticisms. "He did not talk about such things to other people," Shelden states. Rather, he told people that work had worn her down and that she needed "a good rest."

The important point often neglected in discussions of the Dunkirk evacuation is that Hitler's hopes for a peace settlement with the British were not unfounded. We know now that even as the Dunkirk operation was under way, the British government was mulling whether to seek peace terms. On May 27, 1940, as ragged British troops were disembarking from ships and boats all along the southeastern coast of England, the five members of the War Cabinet of Churchill's new government debated the wisdom of entering into peace negotiations. Churchill was vehemently against any such move, arguing, "Even if we were beaten [later], we should be no worse off than we should be if we were now to abandon the struggle."

Halifax, who favored some sort of peace talks, wrote in his diary that night, "I thought Winston talked the most frightful rot." Halifax's view was that England's negotiating position was stronger while France was still in the war—as it would be for another two weeks—and while English aircraft factories had not yet been bombed. He also felt that the goal of Britain should not be to try to fight and defeat Germany, but rather to hold on to as much of British independence as possible in some kind of peaceful coexistence. It was an astonishing argument to make, given that the prime lesson of the Chamberlain government was that it was folly to negotiate with Hitler from a position of weakness.

Even so, Churchill needed to thread a narrow course here. Two British politicians who have written about Churchill make different but complementary observations about his situation at this decisive point. The politician and writer Boris Johnson, who in mid-2016 became the British foreign secretary, notes that Churchill was "fighting for his political life and credibility, and if he gave in to Halifax he was finished." Equally true is Roy Jenkins's point that Churchill needed to overcome the Halifax position without doing so in such a way that led Halifax and Chamberlain to resign from the Cabinet. Churchill at this point did not command enough loyalty in the Conservative Party to survive such a departure. If they left, "his government would be untenable," observes Jenkins, himself a Labour member of Parliament for decades and several times a senior Cabinet official in the 1960s and 1970s.

Halifax grumbled to Sir Alexander Cadogan, also at the War Cabinet meeting on May 27, that he felt that he could no longer work with Churchill. Churchill, perhaps sensing that a breach was looming, invited Halifax for a quiet walk in the garden. There he spoke in terms of "apologies and affection," Halifax told his diary.

The buttering up concluded, Churchill the following day showed his teeth. In another Cabinet meeting he stated flatly that there would be no surrender, and that as long as he was in office, he would not parley with the Nazis. "If this long island story of ours is to end at last," he vowed, "let it end only when each one of us lies choking in his own blood on the ground." At about the same time, he wrote in a note to a subordinate, "England will never quit the war whatever happens till Hitler is beat or we cease to be a State." It was an admirably strong, succinct statement, especially coming from a man who had been in office fewer than three weeks. Until that point, writes John Charmley in his detailed biography of Churchill, there was "a good deal of support for the idea of at least opening talks to find out what Hitler's peace terms might be." After this point, there was no question that Britain would fight. Simon Schama, perhaps a bit ardently, describes Churchill's defeat of the Halifax position as "the first great battle of the Second World War." Yet it is hard to fault Schama's enthusiasm. Churchill's swaying of his War Cabinet that day may have been the single most important moment in World War II.

The Germans, not privy to these internal debates of the British government, would continue to hope for months that what they called "Churchill and his gang" would be ousted, clearing the way for some sort of peace agreement. What's more, their intelligence sources misinformed them that British political trends continued to favor that outcome. Joseph Goebbels, the chief Nazi propagandist, told his staff in June, "A compromise government will be formed. We are very close to the end of the war." The Swedish ambassador to London told his government the same month that it looked as if there would be peace talks, and that "Halifax may succeed Churchill." For another month, Hitler would continue to mull the possibility of Churchill being replaced by some combination of Halifax, former prime minister David Lloyd George, and Chamberlain.

CHURCHILL'S GREAT RHETORICAL CAMPAIGN OF 1940

On June 4, 1940, as the evacuation from Dunkirk proceeded, Churchill knew as he went before the House of Commons that he would be presenting to it the details of one of the worst days in British history. The British Isles stood the closest they had come to being conquered in four hundred years.

He spoke artfully, managing at once to depict the German eviction of a British army as a humiliating rout and to frame it as a wondrous event. "When a week ago to-day I asked the House to fix this afternoon as the occasion for a statement, I feared it would be my hard lot to announce the greatest military disaster in our long history," he began. He had feared then, he told the House, that perhaps only twenty thousand or thirty thousand British soldiers would be brought home, which would mean that several hundred thousand would be killed or taken prisoner. Rather, he said, "A miracle of deliverance, achieved by valour, by perseverance, by perfect discipline, by faultless service, by resource, by skill, by unconquerable fidelity, is manifest to us all."

He was an unlikely figure as a war leader. He stood perhaps five foot seven and had a round head perched atop a pear-shaped body. Yet it was around this time that he became the rallying point for the English people.

This is Churchill at his best—and his most manipulative. "We must be very careful not to assign to this deliverance the attributes of a victory. Wars are not won by evacuations. But there was a victory inside this deliverance, which should be noted. It was gained by the Air Force."

About thirty minutes into his speech, Churchill ended powerfully, with an operatic presentation of the future:

> We shall fight in France, we shall fight on the seas and oceans, we shall fight with growing confidence and growing strength in the air, we shall defend our island, whatever the cost may be.
>
> We shall fight on the beaches, we shall fight on the landing grounds, we shall fight in the fields and in the streets, we shall fight in the hills; we shall never surrender, and even if, which I do not for a moment believe, this island or a large part of it were subjugated and starving, then our Empire beyond the seas, armed and guarded by the British Fleet, would carry on the struggle, until, in God's good time, the new world, with all its power and might, steps forth to the rescue and the liberation of the old.

On the face of it, this was an odd way to steady a frightened public. As Stephen Bungay has observed, the phrases about the locations of fighting followed the likely pattern of a tenacious combat retreat, withdrawing from the coast and airstrips to the cities and fields, and then up into the remoter hills. He also ventured into the previously unspeakable prospects of a German victory and of British starvation. He was talking about the unthinkable, and he was doing it on the national stage.

Yet this grim talk did not dismay the British people. Instead, it braced them. Harold Nicolson, an admirer of Churchill's and a veteran of Parliament, wrote to his wife, "This afternoon Winston made the finest speech I have ever heard. The House was deeply moved."

In wartime, people will believe the worst if they are not told the truth, or something close to it, perhaps mixed with a vision of the way forward. Having been given that, they were somewhat reassured. Joan Seaman, a civilian in London, recalled, "I remember being very frightened indeed when France collapsed because I thought it was going to be us next. Really frightened. Until I heard the speech that Churchill made on the radio about fighting on the beaches. I suddenly wasn't frightened anymore. It was quite amazing."

During that summer of 1940, Churchill's voice became "our hope," recalled C. P. Snow, the physicist and novelist. He continued: "It was the voice of will and strength incarnate. It was saying what we wanted to hear said ('we shall never surrender') and what we tried to believe, sometimes against the protests of realism and common sense, would come true."

Compare the strength of Churchill's words of June 4 with those issued about the same time by a lesser man, Duff Cooper, then serving as Churchill's minister of information. "It will be necessary to withdraw our army from the positions they now occupy, but it will not be a defeated army," Cooper said, managing to be both trite and misleading. "It will be an army whose courage is still high and whose confidence is still unshaken, and every officer and man burning with desire to meet the enemy in combat. . . . As the danger increases so does our courage to meet it." There is nothing inspiring in those words. If anything, there is, underneath the clichés of men who cannot wait to get back into the fight, an air of quiet panic. When a politician offers nothing but empty and deceptive rhetoric, he is implicitly conceding something very close to defeat.

In fact, there actually was good reason to panic. The British army was in a frightful state in the months after Dunkirk. "Britain was not just expelled from Europe, it was partly disarmed," concluded military historian Cathal Nolan. Left behind in the sand dunes of the Belgian coast were 700 British tanks, 880 heavy artillery pieces, 11,000 machine guns, and some 64,000 vehicles, now all the property of the Wehrmacht. The numbers of what the British army had on hand once it was back home that summer are stunning even today. British ground forces on English soil possessed only 200 first-rate tanks, about as many as are in one modern U.S. Army armored division. One lesser division, the 1st London, fielded only 23 artillery pieces and entirely lacked armored cars and machine guns. Anthony Eden, then overseeing the army as the secretary of state for war, confided to a journalist that for a brief period, England was capable of sending into combat only one trained and equipped brigade—that is, just a few thousand men. Yet there were enough weapons around that sixteen times that June, civilians were shot by British militiamen at anti-invasion roadblocks.

As Britain braced for invasion, Major William Watson of the Durham Light Infantry reported that some of his men were still in the uniforms they had been wearing when they escaped from Dunkirk. Another soldier, Douglas Goddard, was sent on patrol on the southeastern coast with some of his riflemen carrying only five bullets each. The Royal Air Force also had lost 250 modern fighter planes in just ten days in May 1940, and entered June with a total of about 500 remaining.

THE FRENCH COLLAPSE

Churchill was everywhere at this time. He went to France repeatedly to try to buck up French leaders, stunned into political disarray by the swift

German advance into their country. He met with some at the French Foreign Ministry while smoke drifted into the room from outside, where workers were pushing wheelbarrows of archived documents to toss onto bonfires in the courtyard behind the ministry building. Smoke from his cigar wreathed his head, leaving him, mused the French secretary of war, "crowned like a volcano." The French officials told him that their military plans had not provided a strategic reserve of soldiers to throw into the fight. Stunned, he asked if he understood correctly. "I was dumbfounded," he writes. "What were we to think of the great French Army and its highest chiefs?" He might have been thinking back to an observation he made after the First World War: "In all battles two things are usually required of the Commander-in-Chief: to make a good plan for his army and, secondly, to keep a strong reserve." The leaders of France had failed on both accounts.

Churchill was determined not to follow their example. "We will starve Germany out," he vowed to the French that day. "We will destroy her towns. We will burn her crops and forests."

In his memoirs, he would devote more than two hundred pages to depicting how French leaders let down their country by being divided, directionless, and demoralized. He concluded that the French had been "ruined" by a "completely defensive habit of mind." This became a major reason for his relentless prodding of his own generals and admirals during the war. "An effort must be made to shake off the mental and moral prostration to the will and initiative of the enemy from which we suffer," he ordered.

On the evening of June 17, Churchill ordered a statement broadcast on the BBC that began with, "The news from France is very bad." Paris had fallen to the Germans. The next day, the French government requested armistice talks. The military historian Walter Millis elegantly summarized the alarming military situation after Dunkirk: "Great Britain was left almost without ground defenses, while the occupation of nearly the whole Atlantic coast of Europe had opened innumerable unsealable gateways to the depredations of the U-boats." Indeed, the conditions that Hitler had laid out just thirteen months earlier had been reached: Poland had been taken, Belgium and Holland occupied, and France defeated. Now England stood alone in western Europe. Hitler planned to pummel and starve it.

Churchill warned his countrymen, in another theatrical conclusion:

The whole fury and might of the enemy must very soon be turned on us. Hitler knows that he will have to break us in this island or lose the war. If we can stand up to him all Europe may be free, and the life of the world may move forward into broad, sunlit uplands; but if we fail then the whole world, including the United States, and all that we have known and cared for, will sink into the abyss of a new dark age made more sinister, and perhaps more prolonged, by the lights of a perverted science. Let us therefore brace ourselves to our duty and so bear ourselves that if the British Commonwealth and Empire lasts for a thousand years men will still say, "This was their finest hour."

Roy Jenkins compares the significance of this speech with Lincoln's address at Gettysburg.

Orwell appreciated the role Churchill was playing that summer. "The reason why nearly everyone who was anti-Nazi supported Churchill from the collapse of France onwards," he wrote, "was that there was nobody else—i.e., nobody who was already well enough known to be able to step into power and who at the same time could be trusted not to surrender. . . . [W]hat was wanted was chiefly obstinacy, of which Churchill had plenty." Churchill appreciated this same quality in himself. The lesson of the first part of the war, he told the schoolboys of Harrow, was simple:

Never give in, never give in, never, never, never, never—in nothing, great or small, large or petty—never give in except to convictions of honour and good sense. Never yield to force; never yield to the apparently overwhelming might of the enemy.

Churchill vowed to his Cabinet that he would not flee England. Orwell privately told his diary something similar: "It is impossible even yet to decide what to do in the case of German conquest of England," he wrote in mid-June 1940. "The one thing I will not do is to clear out, at any rate not further than Ireland, supposing that to be feasible. If the fleet is intact and it appears that war is to be continued from America and the Dominions, then one must remain alive if possible, if necessary in the concentration camp. If the U.S.A. is going to submit to conquest as well, there is nothing to do for it but to die fighting, but one must above all die fighting and have the satisfaction of killing somebody else first." He dwelled again on this issue six days later. His wife and sister-in-law had urged him to flee to Canada "if the worst comes to the worst," he wrote in his diary, but he would not. "There are too many of these exiled 'anti-fascists' already. Better to die if necessary."

Difficult decisions loomed. Not long after the French armistice with the Germans, Churchill, fearing that the French fleet in Algeria could fall into German hands, ordered that it either surrender or be attacked. The French sailors fought back, briefly, and in less than one hour, some 1,297 were killed.

This hard-hearted assault on a recent ally shocked some of Churchill's admirals—but it demonstrated to the rest of the world the strength of British resolve. Among those who applauded it was Orwell, who wrote in his diary, "The frightful outburst of fury by the German radio (if rightly reported, actually calling on the English people to hang Churchill in Trafalgar Square) shows how right it was to make this move." Churchill cried when he had to explain to Parliament why he had ordered the attack on the Vichy French fleet.

"ACTION THIS DAY"

Even as he was rallying the nation and trying to bolster the French, Churchill also was working full time on another major task: waking the soporific British bureaucracy. His work in this area, while if anything underappreciated, arguably helped the war effort as much as his oratory did. One of the biggest problems facing the British internally when he took office was the lethargy of the government during the first nine months of the war. "Chamberlain [had] presided efficiently over the Cabinet," recalled Sir Ian Jacob. "Business was managed in an orderly fashion; but nothing much happened." One surprising sign of this official indolence is that Britain should have been revving up its industries as it mobilized for a large war, yet unemployment increased from 1.2 million in September 1939 to 1.5 million in February 1940.

Churchill, upon becoming prime minister, reacted to the "sedate, sincere, but routine" attitude of the Chamberlain government by firing a daily barrage of personal memos that shook both military leaders and senior civilians. The memos often were tagged with a bright red label demanding "Action This Day," a device Churchill first used at the height of the Dunkirk crisis, on May 29, 1940. His notes, wrote one aide, were "like the beam of a searchlight ceaselessly swinging round and penetrating into the remote recesses of the administration—so that everyone, however humble his rank or his function, felt that one day the beam might rest on him and light up what he was doing. In Whitehall the effect of this influence was immediate and dramatic. . . . A new sense of purpose and urgency was created as it came to be realized that a firm hand, guided by a strong will, was on the wheel." As another wartime aide remembered it, "All round Whitehall people sat up and took notice." They began working on nights and weekends—just as Churchill did.

Sometimes a new administration believes it can improve the performance of its bureaucracy simply by posing sharp questions. This was not the case with Churchill. Far more than an intelligent meddler, he had spent years educating himself on military issues. Even while on the outs, he sat on a secret government committee that tracked the issue of air defenses. As part of that work, he had visited the newly erected chain of radar stations on the south coast. He also had encouraged the navy to look into whether radar could be used to guide torpedoes at night. He had studied the rebuilding of the German air force. All this meant that when he stepped into the leadership of Britain at a crucial moment, the "mental field was well lit for me. I knew the various pieces and the moves on the board, and could understand anything I was told about the game." This knowledge enabled him to make judgments and take risks that other politicians might have shied from. He did not just push his people, he followed up with intelligent memoranda and orders that spurred subordinates accustomed to a slower pace and fewer questions.

Churchill's prodding of his generals and admirals at times was unpleasant, but it almost certainly was necessary. More than anything, he feared passivity of the sort he thought had undermined the French in May and June 1940. "His whole idea everywhere and at all times was 'Attack, attack, attack,'" said Sir Desmond Morton. After less than a month as prime minister, he emphasized to his generals that he believed that aggressive moves by British forces might make the Germans think less about how to attack and more about whether and where they might be attacked. It wasn't just his military commanders that he pushed. At one point during the war he found time to delve into domestic egg production, badgering the minister of agriculture. "I wish I could persuade you to try to overcome the difficulties instead of merely entrenching yourself behind them."

One of Churchill's themes throughout the war would be that aggressive moves by commanders must be assessed forgivingly. Later in the year he wrote to his top military officer that "any error towards the enemy and any evidence of a sincere desire to engage must always be generously judged."

He also understood, as many did not, that military moves that did not make sense on a tactical basis sometimes were nonetheless advantageous for strategic or political reasons. Churchill knew that in wartime it is almost always better for a military to do something—such as attack the Germans in Norway, as the British had done that spring—than to do nothing and so yield the initiative to the enemy. He was conscious that sometimes this bent for action would be difficult to justify in pure military terms. "You need not argue the value of bombing Germany," he once told his air commanders, "because I have my own opinion about that, namely, that it is not decisive, but better than doing nothing."

Churchill also perceived better than most the limitations of the military mind, especially the dangerous tendency to view operations in isolation from the larger strategic context. Early in the war, he had asked Chamberlain to sometimes hold meetings at which the generals and admirals were not present. "Much is being thrown upon the Chiefs of the Staffs which falls outside the professional sphere," he wrote. "I venture to represent to you that we ought sometimes to discuss the general position alone. I do not feel that we are getting to the root of the matter on many points."

From his time in service in World War I, and even more from his two turns at overseeing the British navy, Churchill had developed a delicate feel for the wiles of military bureaucracy. He urged subordinates to cut the numbers of officers in administrative jobs and move them to billets in which they could fight. In August 1940, when the need for pilots was absolutely crucial, he did a marvelous job of squeezing capable RAF officers out of desk jobs and into cockpits. "The tendency of every Station Commander is naturally to keep as much in his hands as possible," he skeptically advised an air force official. "The Admirals do exactly the same. Even when you have had a thorough search, if you look around a few weeks later you will see more fat has been gathered."

When his generals were able to plead genuine military necessity, he listened. In the first weeks of his premiership, in May and June 1940, when he was under intense pressure from the French to send more fighter aircraft to France and was being advised by some that the war would be decided there, he instead heeded the views of his air commanders and declined to do it. In retrospect, wrote Stephen Bungay, "This decision was undoubtedly correct. The fighters would have made no difference in France, but did make a big difference in Britain," as the Battle of Britain would show later that summer, during what would be the climactic period of Churchill's life.

CHAPTER 7

FIGHTING THE GERMANS, REACHING OUT TO THE AMERICANS

1940–1941

On August 8, 1940, Hermann Goering, commander of the Luftwaffe, the German air force, instructed it to commence "Operation Adler." He informed his subordinates that "within a short period you will wipe the British Air Force from the sky. Heil Hitler." British intelligence intercepted the order, which was passed up to Churchill.

Going into the fight, the Luftwaffe's commanders estimated their air campaign would require two to four weeks to succeed. This may appear hubristic now, but at the time it was consistent with the pattern of recent German walkovers in Poland, Holland, Belgium, and France. To many, Germany appeared unstoppable. Ambassador Kennedy cabled to the State Department his view that if the Germans had as many aircraft as claimed, they would shut down the Royal Air Force, after which he thought a British surrender "would be inevitable."

The aerial fighting filled the skies over southern England through the summer and early fall of 1940. German fighters crossed the English Channel in six minutes, and then, in full view of the British public, wheeled and dueled in the skies of southern England.

These were the months in which Churchill became England's symbolic rallying point. Orwell, watching this transformation, marveled at it. "Who would have believed seven years ago that Winston Churchill had any kind of political future before him?" Orwell wrote in his diary in August. As Britons faced the genuine prospect of invasion, even those who had denigrated Churchill for years rallied to his side. Few people had done more to keep Churchill out of the Cabinet in the mid-1930s than "T. J." Jones, who had been Prime Minister Baldwin's political counselor. He now saw the man he had disparaged for so long in a new light. "The coming of Winston to the top . . . [has] wrought a profound change," he wrote. "At last the country is awake and working." Later that summer, he added, "Winston is now the only speaker in Whitehall who reaches and moves everybody."

Not all were so contrite. Geoffrey Dawson, the resolutely pro-appeasement editor of the *Times,* later in 1940 wrote in a note of consolation to Neville Chamberlain, then close to death, "I shall always be an impenitent supporter of what is called the 'Munich policy.'" During the same season, Orwell argued with a young pacifist in the Café Royal, long a meeting place for writers and artists. The war would be over by Christmas, that youth assured Orwell, explaining, "There's obviously going to be a compromise peace." When Orwell commented that the Nazis would execute writers such as himself, the man, an aspiring artist, responded, "That would be just too bad."

Churchill's speeches from the time remain good reading seventy-five years after their delivery. Knowing them is essential to understanding the man and his role in history.

His address to the House of Commons on August 20, 1940, is remembered primarily for his powerful and accurate tribute to the fighter pilots of the Royal Air Force. "Never in the field of human conflict," he stated, "was so much owed by so many to so few." One Spitfire pilot, Hugh Dundas, later said, "I don't think we were conscious of making history until Mr. Churchill made his speech about 'the few.' We all puffed our chests out a bit then and thought how important we were but until then I don't think we'd thought about it."

Less well remembered in the same speech was Churchill's summary of the war, which is Orwell-like in its sobriety and its sparse accuracy in recounting the setbacks that had occurred during his first few months of leadership:

> Rather more than a quarter of a year has passed since the new Government came into power in this country. What a cataract of disaster has poured out upon us since then. The trustful Dutch overwhelmed; their beloved and respected Sovereign driven into exile; the peaceful city of Rotterdam the scene of a massacre as hideous and brutal as anything in the Thirty Years' War. Belgium invaded and beaten down; our own fine Expeditionary Force, which King Leopold called to his rescue, cut off and almost captured, escaping as it seemed only by a miracle and with the loss of all its equipment; our Ally, France, out; Italy in against us; all France in the power of the enemy, all its arsenals and vast masses of military materiel converted or convertible to the enemy's use; a puppet Government set up at Vichy which may at any moment be forced to become our foe; the whole Western seaboard of Europe from the North Cape to the Spanish frontier in German hands; all the ports, all the airfields on this immense front, employed against us as potential springboards of invasion.

Two nights later, central London was bombed for the first time. His catalog of disaster leads to a very sharp point: the possibility of German landings in England. Discussing invasion was not just a way to spur on the people. Churchill around this time was meditating on the prospect quite seriously. Among the questions he had to address was the possible role of British police in areas of the country occupied by Germans. Should they fight? Should they instead try to keep public order? If the latter, should they be told beforehand to cooperate with the Germans in order to do so? At this last thought, Churchill balked. "Should they fall into an area effectively occupied by the enemy," he instructed, "they may surrender and submit with the rest of the inhabitants, but must not in those circumstances give any aid to the enemy in maintaining order, or in any other way."

Near summer's end, the fear of a German invasion peaked when British reconnaissance aircraft detected a sudden increase in the assemblages of German invasion barges in Dutch, Belgian, and French ports. At 8:07 on the evening of September 7, 1940, the British high command transmitted the signal CROMWELL, the code word signifying that German landings on English soil were imminent. The novelist Evelyn Waugh, then serving with the Royal Marines in Africa, wrote to his wife that same month, advising her that if the Germans did land, to bide her time until the situation calmed and then to make her way to Quebec, Canada, where he would endeavor to find her. George Pellet, a member of a behind-the-lines sabotage unit, was told that his life expectancy following a German landing would be seven days.

But German tactics were shifting. Stymied in their effort to destroy Britain's air defenses, the commanders of the Luftwaffe turned to simply bombing the country—mainly the capital, and disproportionately its eastern end, where the poor and the workers tended to live, near the docks and factories. Burning London, Goering supposed, might destroy the will of the English people to fight on.

On the same night the CROMWELL signal was sent, the "Blitz" of London began, with 348 German bombers and 617 German fighters hitting the capital city. Flying toward England that afternoon, they formed a block in the air twenty miles wide and forty miles deep.

Some observers thought this changed approach would succeed. On the first night of the Blitz, Joseph Kennedy, walking down Piccadilly with a friend, said to him, "I'll bet you five to one any sum that Hitler will be in Buckingham Palace in two weeks." It was time, he advised the State Department, for the British to accept defeat.

Indeed, in the air-raid sirens, in the drone of the approaching bombers, and in the smoke, fire, and death they left behind them, "there was an imminent sense of apocalypse," summarizes the British historian and novelist Peter Ackroyd. The poet Edith Sitwell captured the feeling of the moment in a poem:

> Still falls the Rain—
> Dark as the world of man, black as our loss—
> Blind as the nineteen hundred and forty nails
> Upon the Cross

A fireman reported that the fires were so intense that "the heat blistered the car paint. It blistered the men's faces. . . . It hurt your eyes, hurt your nose. My chin was quite badly burnt and it blistered. As the roofs went in, so the sparks belched from the windows, as if blown by giant bellows."

The next day, September 8, Churchill visited the hardest hit area of the city, London's poor and crowded East End, where fires were still burning in bombed buildings. He began to weep at an air-raid shelter that had suffered a direct hit. Seeing him, an old woman said, "You see, he really cares, he's crying."

SEPTEMBER 15, 1940

After a week of this pounding, Churchill traveled to the headquarters of the 11th Fighter Group, the unit responsible for the defense of the air over London and southeastern England. This was not a random call—he knew from "Ultra" intelligence intercepts that almost all the German bombers based in France were to fly against London that day, and he knew from previous visits that summer that 11th Group's command post was the best location from which to monitor such a fight. Just two weeks earlier there had been a dogfight in the skies above it.

The day of Churchill's visit, September 15, would prove to be one of the fiercest days of aerial combat in the entire campaign. He would later recall the day as "the culminating date" of the Battle of Britain. It was a Sunday morning. At the 11th Group headquarters, located on the western fringe of London, he descended some fifty feet into the bunker containing the group's operations room and watched Air Vice Marshal Keith Park, commander of the fighter group, pace the room and issue orders, sending squadrons into combat. A giant display board, the width of the room, covered one wall, keeping track of each of the Fighter Group's twenty-five squadrons. A series of lights recorded the state of each unit—those on standby, those aloft, those that had sighted the enemy, and finally, at the top, red lights for those "Engaged"—that is, in action.

Light after light turned red. Soon Park had thrown all his assigned aircraft into the fight. This meant that soon all the squadrons would start landing to refuel. That would be a moment of great concern, because of the risk of the aircraft bunched on the ground being hit by German planes, which could cause intolerable losses. Park contacted his commander to request that he be allowed to use the three squadrons still in reserve. Close to two hundred German warplanes were in the air over southeastern England.

Churchill, unable to contain himself any longer, asked Park, "How many more have you got?" None, Park replied—"I am putting in my last." Park later wrote that at hearing this, Churchill looked "quite grave." He was indeed, because he realized, as he put it later, that "the odds were great; our margins small; the stakes infinite." For fifty minutes, there were no more British fighters available. Just four months earlier, Churchill had winced when he heard French leaders use a similar phrase about their lack of a reserve force. Their defeat had come not long after. As the Battle of Britain got under way, he had mused, "What a slender thread the greatest of things can hang by." Now he was seeing Britain's thread stretched almost to the breaking point.

But the British, unlike the French, would hold. The Spitfires and Hurricanes had to refuel, but the Germans had to as well—and they had to go much farther to do it. So another wave of raiders did not come, and the British fighters were not caught flat-footed on the ground while refueling. Yet thousands of German bombs dropped that day, including two that hit Buckingham Palace, likely by mistake. The RAF lost twenty-eight aircraft in the day's fighting but downed fifty-six German aircraft, for an impressive kill ratio of 2 to 1.

As Churchill departed the bunker, the "All Clear" sounded. Churchill went to the prime minister's official country residence, Chequers, walked straight to his room, and lay down to sleep for about four hours. This long spell was so unusual for him that his doctor, Charles Wilson, was notified. The next morning, Wilson asked him if he had been "all in" when he left the bunker. "When he did not answer, I asked him how Park was standing up to the strain," Wilson recalled. "He looking blankly at me; he had not thought about him. The fate of individuals no longer mattered. I suppose you come to think like that when you carry his burden of responsibility."

One of the buildings hit in the German bombing in mid-September was the palatial London town house, on Park Lane, of Lord Londonderry, the Nazi sympathizer. Colonel Raymond Lee, the American military attaché, strolled the few blocks over from the American embassy to gloat at the sight. He wrote in his diary: "A bomb had struck just across the street, blown down the wall, dug itself a deep hole, and done for every pane of glass in the vicinity. I could only wonder what that chump Londonderry thinks now of his friends, Hitler, Ribbentrop and Goering, with whom he was so chummy so short a time ago." Today a big Hilton hotel stands on the site.

After the war, Churchill would tell friends that if he could relive one year of his life, it would be 1940. Even in retrospect, it is impressive at how high his spirits—and energy level—were. When fears of a German invasion were highest, the "PM was very pleasant and as usual most refreshing and entertaining," General Sir Alan Brooke, who would become the prime minister's principal military advisor, noted in his diary. While carrying on his shoulders the fate of his nation, and indeed of Western civilization, he even managed to maintain a reserve of whimsy. During some of the darkest periods early in the war, when the United States had not yet entered and English cities were being burned by German bombs daily, and as the Germans expanded their reach into the wheat fields of Ukraine and the oil fields of northern Iraq, Churchill would distract himself and his guests by playing records ("martial airs, waltzes and the most vulgar kind of brass-band songs," his priggish aide Colville noted), by doing military drill with a hunting rifle, and by conversing with his pets. "While he brooded on these matters [of reversals in the Middle East and the questionable competence of British generals], he kept up a running conversation with the cat, cleaning its eyes with his napkin, offering it mutton and expressing regret that it could not have cream in war-time." He strolled through his garden in a purple dressing gown and a gray felt hat to visit his goldfish. He played with his daughter's dog, "a very engaging poodle." En route to one summit meeting he read a Horatio Hornblower novel; traveling to another, he spent a day with *Phineas Finn,*

Trollope's great novel of parliamentary ambition. While recovering from pneumonia, he finally read (or had read to him) *Pride and Prejudice.*

With hindsight, it is clear that the Germans were never as close to invading England, let alone conquering it, as it appeared they were in 1940. Achieving air superiority was an essential prerequisite to launching an invasion force, but the British were producing fighter aircraft faster than the Germans could destroy them. In addition, the British had put up a carefully considered, well-managed defense, while the German attack, while dashing, was a shambles, with unclear goals. When there is no coherent strategy, tactics, no matter how flashily executed, become meaningless.

Military historians have long recognized that technological innovation is close to useless without carefully constructed organizational support. It was the thoughtful organization of people and technology that gave the British the advantage in fighting the Luftwaffe. Stephen Bungay concludes in his definitive analysis of the Battle of Britain that the key to the battle was the extremely effective British early warning system. By combining radar, radio, and telephones, and having the effort managed by careful commanders, the British system enabled the RAF to seize the initiative. They gathered information, quickly moved it to the ready squadrons, and then directed those squadrons into the fight. This intelligent three-step approach, each involving very different tasks, was summarized well by Flight Lieutenant Charles MacLean, an air sector controller:

> The whole theory of fighter defence was created to avoid what they called "standing patrols." If you were guarding the country by having aeroplanes up all the time, you ran out of engine hours and you were on the ground when the attack occurred. So the RAF developed a system of reporting incoming raids. First, he used radar to plot the

aircraft as they were approaching Britain and then he used the Observer Corps to spot them when they'd crossed the coast. All the information was fed to a filter room and then to an operations room where you got a picture of the developing raids plotted on a table. That picture would be three or four minutes old but it was sufficiently up to date to get the fighters off when they were really needed.

Thus the characteristic image of the Battle of Britain that we have today is of young tousle-haired pilots lounging near their aircraft, not flying but ready to go aloft at a moment's notice. In historical retrospect, the British air defense system was the equivalent of a human-powered computer, a remarkable real-time information-processing system that worked so well in conserving British aerial resources—aircraft, pilots, and staff attention—that it was one reason the Royal Air Force actually grew more powerful with the passage of time in 1940. A second reason was that British aircraft factories finally swung into high gear.

The third reason that the British prevailed in the Battle of Britain was German incompetence in waging an aerial offensive. Contrary to the Teutonic reputation for martial skill, the Luftwaffe's approach was "astonishingly amateur," concluded Bungay, amounting to "little more than flying over England, dropping some bombs on various things to annoy people, and shooting down any fighters which came up as a result." It is no accident, Bungay adds, that the military service operating so incoherently was the only one of the German armed forces led by a Nazi politician, Goering, who before going into politics had been a pilot during World War I. Hitler supposedly liked to say that he had a conservative army, a reactionary navy, and a Nazi air force. That politicized air arm flew into English airspace unprepared for what it would encounter. Hans-Ekkehard Bob, who flew a Messerschmitt 109 fighter, recalled being surprised on a fogbound day: "I experienced a Spitfire formation all of a sudden coming up from behind, having a clear line of fire and I wondered how this was even possible. Having no visibility whatsoever, from above nor from below, how was it possible that an enemy formation was able to get into a firing position from behind?" The answer, of course, was the well-tuned British radar and early warning system.

The Germans in their days of pride also consistently overestimated the damage they were doing, believing in mid-August 1940 that the British had only 300 working fighters available. In fact, they had 1,438—which was twice as many as they had on hand just six weeks earlier. The kill ratio always favored the British, who lost a total of 1,547 aircraft while destroying 1,887 German ones. On top of that, because most of the aerial combat took place over England, British pilots could fly many missions in one day, with their aircraft reloaded with ammunition in under four minutes. And when they were shot down, they often could parachute to friendly soil and fly again, while parachuting Germans who survived became prisoners of war, and those who ditched in the frigid waters of the channel often were lost either to drowning or hypothermia. (For the same reasons, the RAF lost more bomber crew members during this period than it did fighter pilots—801 from Bomber Command versus 544 for Fighter Command.)

The British people also adjusted to being bombed. For example, a poll conducted for the government found that in mid-September 1940, 31 percent of Londoners reported having "no sleep" the previous night. By mid-October, only 5 percent reported such a total lack, and by mid-November, none did.

Even if the German army had landed on English soil, their bridgehead would have had to be supplied, in the fall of 1940, mainly by sea. German vessels then would have had to contend with the RAF in rare spots of good weather and with the foul autumnal weather of the North Sea at all other times. "The margin of victory was not narrow," Bungay concludes in his magisterial history of the Battle of Britain. "The Luftwaffe never came close."

But it is far easier to see all this now than it was during 1940. Because their troops and ships were not involved, Americans tend not to remember how agonizingly difficult the war was for the British before the Japanese attack on Pearl Harbor brought the United States into it. It is no accident that the American entry comes only at the end of the third volume of Churchill's six volumes of World War II memoirs. Dwight Eisenhower does not surface until about halfway through the fourth. Orwell caught this sober note about the time in his diary entry for October 19, 1940: "The unspeakable depression of lighting the fires every morning with papers of a year ago, and getting glimpses of optimistic headlines as they go up in smoke."

That same month, Churchill complained in a note to his foreign secretary that he was astonished by "this misleading Kennedy stuff." However, a few weeks later, FDR was elected to an unprecedented third term in office. This was a great relief to Churchill. It meant that American aid to Britain could be offered more openly, without as much worry about an isolationist backlash in the American Midwest. More locally, it also meant that FDR finally could get rid of Kennedy.

Kennedy, sent home, continued to spout off. "Democracy is finished in England," Kennedy confided to newspapermen when he was back in the United States. What's more, he added, it may also be washed up in the United States, so, he concluded, "There's no sense in our getting in."

Kennedy, who had toyed with running for president, then went to see Roosevelt at the president's house in Hyde Park, New York. FDR initially had thought of inviting Kennedy to stay the weekend, but after a private ten-minute conversation he changed his mind. He rolled out of the room and found his wife, Eleanor. "I never want to see that son of a bitch again as long as I live," he told her. "Take his resignation and get him out of there." When she protested that Kennedy had been invited at least for lunch, he instructed her to drive him around, give him a sandwich, and then put him aboard the afternoon train back to New York City. She later would recall that day as "the most dreadful four hours of my life."

Once back in New York, Kennedy met with Charles Lindbergh at the Waldorf Astoria Hotel. Lindbergh wrote in his diary, "He feels, as we do, that the British position is hopeless and that the best possible thing for them would be a negotiated peace in the near future." The main obstacles to such a settlement, Kennedy added, were Churchill and the prospect he held so dearly of an American entry into the war.

ENTER HOPKINS

Even as he led Britain in war, Churchill dedicated much of his time to wooing the Americans, and especially to countering the influence of Kennedy and other rightist isolationists.

He had problems with tone at first. In his early courtship of the Americans he was at times unctuous, as with the two sentences of a New Year's note he dispatched to FDR at the beginning of 1941:

> At this moment, when the New Year opens in storm, I feel it my duty on behalf of the British Government, and indeed of the whole British Empire, to tell you, Mr. President, how lively is our sense of gratitude and admiration for the memorable declaration which you made to the American people and to the lovers of freedom in all the continents on Sunday last. We cannot tell what lies before us, but with this trumpet-call we must march forward heartened and fortified, and with the confidence which you have expressed that in the end all will be well for the English-speaking peoples and those who share their ideals.

FDR wanted to know more about who Churchill really was, so in January 1941, he dispatched Harry Hopkins to London as his presidential envoy. A former social worker who was FDR's closest advisor, Hopkins's mission was to size up Churchill as a potential wartime ally. Hopkins had become so much a part of the life of the president that he moved into the White House, sleeping in the room that had been Abraham Lincoln's study, where Lincoln had signed the Emancipation Proclamation. Hopkins also was fond of backgammon, and card playing (poker, gin rummy, bridge). Despite his frail nature, he also enjoyed spending his days off at the racetrack, where he favored placing two-dollar bets on long-shot horses.

The choice of the cancer-ridden Hopkins, deathly thin, with just a few years to live, and deeply skeptical of aristocratic airs and lavish rhetoric, amounted to a challenge from Roosevelt to Churchill. One part of Hopkins's job in January 1941 was to determine if Churchill really was "unsteady" and "drunk half the time," as some in Washington maintained.

Hopkins used the new Pan American Clipper service, taking a flying boat from New York to Bermuda to the Azores, and finally to a landing on the Tagus River in Lisbon. From there he took a British Overseas Airways flight to Poole, England. He was greeted there by Brendan Bracken, who served as consigliere to Churchill, much as Hopkins did with FDR. This was an early signal that Hopkins's mission was understood. Despite his leftist background, he was not crossing the ocean to study social democracy or the improvement of soup kitchens. He was there to participate in a council of war on how to help England (and Churchill) survive.

Hopkins needed a day to recover from his travels. The next day, he was escorted into lunch with Churchill. "A rotund—smiling—red-faced, gentleman appeared—extended a fat but none the less convincing hand and wished me welcome to England," Hopkins reported to the president, writing his letters in longhand on Claridge Hotel stationery and sending them to the White House by courier. "A short black coat—striped trousers—a clear eye and a mush voice was the impression."

Over soup, cold beef, and salad, Hopkins frankly explained to the prime minister that the British, including Churchill, were not quite trusted back in the United States. "I told him there was a feeling in some quarters that he, Churchill, did not like America, Americans or Roosevelt," Hopkins reported to the president. "This set him off on a bitter tho fairly constrained attack on Ambassador Kennedy who he believes is responsible for the impression."

Churchill responded by telling Hopkins what he thought the Americans wanted to hear, rhapsodizing about pastoral England:

> We seek no treasure, we seek no territorial gains, we seek only the right of man to be free; we seek his rights to worship his god, to lead his life in his own way, secure from persecution. As the humble labourer returned from his work when the day is done, and sees the smoke curling upwards from his cottage home in the serene evening sky, we wish him to know that no rat-a-tat [here he rapped on the table] of the secret police upon his door will disturb his leisure or interrupt his rest.

It was classic Churchillian bluster.

Hopkins, a savvy political operator, knew when he was being fed a line. When Churchill asked what the president would think of those comments, Hopkins sounded like John Wayne in one of his 1930s cowboy movies. "Well, Mister Prime Minister, I don't think the president will give a damn for all that," Hopkins drawled. "You see, we're only interested in seeing that that Goddam sonofabitch Hitler gets licked." Churchill laughed loudly. It was exactly the right response, one that went straight to Churchill's innermost feelings and hopes.

The two men wound up talking for several hours. Hopkins reported to the president that he came away persuaded that the report that Churchill disliked Americans and Roosevelt was incorrect. "It just doesn't make sense," he wrote. It is not clear what he told FDR about Churchill's love of drink, but that phrase "clear eye" from the initial handshake probably helped address that question.

Except for Churchill, there was a pervasive condescension in the British attitude toward the Americans. Typical was the comment of Sir Alexander Cadogan, the senior diplomat at the Foreign Office, who after meeting Hopkins, wrote in his diary, "Seems simple and nice." This was wildly off the mark, and from a man whose profession involved assessing official foreign visitors.

For the next two years, Hopkins would be the key link between Churchill and Roosevelt, effectively the president's personal foreign minister. On that first trip to Britain, he wound up staying nearly a month, twice as long as planned. He spent twelve evenings with Churchill during that time. Weeks later, near the end of his visit, Hopkins dined with Churchill and his entourage at Glasgow's Station Hotel.

During the dinner, Hopkins stood and said, "I suppose you wish to know what I am going to say to President Roosevelt on my return." They did, very much indeed. Hopkins said he would use the Bible to recommend to the president the future course of the Anglo-American relationship. Then, in a near whisper, he recited from Ruth 1:16: "Whither thou goest, I will go; and where thou lodgest, I will lodge: thy people shall be my people, and thy God my God." (He did not quote the next verse, "Where thou diest, I will die.") Churchill responded with tears of gratitude.

At about the same time, the Americans firmly settled on a "Europe First" strategy: If the United States entered the war, the greater enemy would be Germany, not Japan, and the majority of resources would flow across the Atlantic. This was, for Churchill, probably the most significant American decision of World War II.

Emerging from the Pan Am aircraft back in New York, Hopkins told reporters, "One thing I can say is this: I don't think Hitler can lick these people." He had fixed much of the damage inflicted on the Anglo-American relationship by Ambassador Kennedy.

Yet there were still sleights of hand at play. In February 1941, Churchill assured the Americans that all that was needed was their resources—guns, tanks, airplanes, ships, food, fuel, and money. He memorably stated to the Americans, "Give us the tools, and we will finish the job." It was an appealing phrase—workmanlike, humble, and seemingly simple.

But this fine rhetoric was disingenuous. "What bravado Churchill was indulging in when he made his speech," U.S. military attaché Raymond Lee, by then a brigadier general, wrote in his diary. Lee was one of the most pro-British officials at the American embassy at the time. The historian Richard Toye concluded that Churchill almost certainly knew at the time that in order to end the war, not just America's vast wealth but its hordes of men would be needed. In fact, the British Joint Planning Staff concluded in June 1941, "The active belligerency of the United States has become essential for the successful prosecution and conclusion of the war." In other words, Churchill did not just need the tools, he needed the entire manpower and industrial might of the United States committed to the cause—and he knew it. But he could not say it.

CHAPTER 8

CHURCHILL, ORWELL, AND THE CLASS WAR IN BRITAIN

1941

George Orwell, watching the Battle of Britain and then the Blitz that followed, never believed the Luftwaffe could pound England into submission. "It does not seem probable that air bombing can settle a major war," he wrote.

In many respects, Orwell himself did not have a very good war. "They won't have me in the army, at any rate at present, because of my lungs," he told a friend. This was no surprise: In a 1938 medical examination, he was found to stand six foot three and to weigh just 159 pounds, and an X-ray slide showed shadows on his lungs. Despite that, and despite his neck wound, he remained a heavy smoker of strong hand-rolled cigarettes. He was again unlucky when he sought work at the Air Ministry's public relations office. Meanwhile, his wife was working at a government censorship office.

Had he enjoyed better health, Orwell probably would have made a great war correspondent, akin to a British version of Ernie Pyle, but with a stronger feel for combat, and more dedication to portraying the hard facts of war, instead of softening them, as Pyle sometimes did.

He felt he could and should contribute more to the war effort, but could not find a way of doing so. "It is a terrible thing to feel oneself useless and at the same time on every side to see halfwits and profascists filling important jobs," he lamented in a letter to a friend. One indication of his frustration is that he went around London one day ripping down pro-Soviet posters. "At any normal time," he confessed to his diary, "it is against my instincts to write on a wall or to interfere with what anyone else has written."

Significantly, the war seemed to knock fiction writing out of Orwell for several years. He published no novels from 1939, when the weak *Coming Up for Air* appeared, until *Animal Farm,* which he would begin late in 1943 and which would not appear in print until just as the war ended in Europe in 1945. Yet he, like Churchill, was energized by the war. In 1940 alone he produced more than one hundred pieces of journalism—articles, essays, and reviews. In one notable article, he took apart W. H. Auden for a line in the poem "Spain" about "the conscious acceptance of guilt in the necessary murder." Those last three words grated on Orwell. "Mr. Auden's brand of amoralism is only possible if you are the kind of person who is always somewhere else when the trigger is pulled," he wrote. "So much of left-wing thought is a kind of playing with fire by people who don't even know that fire is hot." Orwell almost certainly knew that Auden had departed for America in 1939.

Orwell took time on April 17, 1940, to write an illuminating and somewhat homey autobiographical note for an American book called *Twentieth Century Authors:*

Outside my work the thing I care most about is gardening, especially vegetable gardening. I like English cookery and English beer, French red wines, Spanish white wines, Indian tea, strong tobacco, coal fires, candlelight and comfortable chairs. I dislike big towns, noise, motor cars, the radio, tinned food, central heating and "modern furniture." . . . My health is wretched, but it has never prevented me from doing anything that I wanted to, except, so far, fight in the present war. . . . I am not at the moment writing a novel, chiefly owing to upsets caused by the war.

A few weeks later, he left the cottage behind and moved to London to be with his wife. In June, he joined the Home Guard, the local militias raised to fight on their home ground in the event of a German invasion. He quickly became a sergeant in the 5th London Battalion's C Company. He was dismayed when an officer lectured that they need not learn much tactically because in the event of a German invasion "our job, he said, was to die at our posts." He wrote in his diary that he was underwhelmed by the commanders in the Home Guard. "These wretched blimps, so obviously silly and senile, and so degenerate in everything except physical courage, are merely pathetic in themselves, and one would feel rather sorry for them if they were not hanging around our necks like millstones." His own lectures to his unit were more practical. Hand grenades, he noted, are "easier to throw downstairs than up." And bullets have a habit of ricocheting along walls, he warned.

Like many in mid-1940, Orwell thought it was "almost certain that England will be invaded within the next few days or weeks." Unlike many, but like Churchill, he enjoyed this time. His friend Cyril Connolly observed, "He felt enormously at home in the Blitz, among the bombs, the bravery, the rubble, the shortages, the homeless, the signs of revolutionary temper." His wife was similarly inclined. When the air-raid sirens began to wail, she would turn off the lights in their apartment and go to the window to watch the action. Orwell had always loved observing, and now there was much new and different to see and contemplate. He noted in his diary that he had seen no bomb crater deeper than about twelve feet, which made him think the German bombs were rather small, perhaps akin to the 15-centimeter shells he had seen used in Spain. He heard some grousing in an air-raid shelter about "hardness of the seats and the longness of the night, but no defeatist talk."

He was interested to see that dogs quickly learned to leave their walks in the park when they heard the wails of the air-raid sirens. His sole complaint was, "On nights when the raids are bad the deafening racket of the guns makes it difficult to work. It is a time in which it is hard to settle down to anything and even the writing of a silly newspaper article takes twice as long as usual."

His strongest piece of writing from this early part of the war is "The Lion and the Unicorn," an essay that can be read as a kind of song of the Battle of Britain. He worked on it from August to October 1940, during the height of that campaign. In it he contemplated the war from the viewpoint of a leftist patriot, dismayed by the behavior of British aristocrats and seeing the possibility of the war bringing a social upheaval.

His comments on Chamberlain just as easily could have come from Churchill. Orwell wrote that Chamberlain's

> opponents professed to see in him a dark and wily schemer, plotting to sell England to Hitler, but it is far likelier that he was merely a stupid old man doing his best according to his very dim lights. It is difficult otherwise to explain the contradictions of his policy, his failure to grasp any of the courses that were open to him. Like the mass of people, he did not want to pay the price either of peace or of war.

The opening phase of the war was a time of surprising optimism for Orwell. "This war, unless we are defeated, will wipe out most of the existing class privileges," he hoped. He would essentially be proven correct—many class privileges would indeed disappear after the war, though this would come not from a revolutionary break but from an orderly transfer of power to a postwar Labour government.

Churchill was the only Conservative Orwell seems to have admired.

He noted in an essay on the socialist and utopian writer H. G. Wells that Churchill had understood the Bolsheviks better than Wells had. Wells responded to Orwell with a furious note: "Read my early works, you shit!" The aging novelist took to dismissing Orwell as "that Trotskyite with big feet."

"Churchill's oratory is really good, in an old-fashioned way, though I don't like his delivery," Orwell wrote in his diary on April 28, 1941, following a speech by Churchill on the BBC. As for the rest, Orwell maintained a lingering distrust of the right. He wrote approvingly of a friend's statement that "with individual exceptions like Churchill the entire British aristocracy is utterly corrupt and lacking in the most ordinary patriotism."

The events of the Battle of Britain and then the Blitz carried class implications to which both Orwell and Churchill were sensitive. The poor suffered disproportionately from the German aerial attacks of 1940. Churchill's government had been slow to react to the impact the bombing had on them. The stations of the London Underground system were not at first opened for use as air-raid shelters, partly out of fear that those taking refuge would impede transportation and perhaps refuse to leave. Phil Piratin, a communist official in the neighborhood of Stepney, which was hit hard by the bombing, embarrassed officials by leading a group of East Enders to demand access to the shelter in the basement of one of the poshest of hotels, the Savoy. Churchill took notice of the newspaper articles about this, and asked his Cabinet why the Tube stations were not made available as air-raid shelters. "I was assured that this was most undesirable," he recalled. He disagreed, and soon the stations were opened for use.

The German bombing campaign, lasting from the fall of 1940 through the spring of 1941, had the effect of ennobling the poor in British eyes.

"Now the working class are 100 percent heroes," wrote Tom Harrisson, an anthropologist, who reviewed the literature of the Blitz in the middle of it. "Extravagant admiration is lavished without regard for modesty, dignity or accuracy."

Conversely, the rich came under suspicion, especially as many decamped from London to their country houses. "The lady in the Rolls-Royce car is more damaging to morale than a fleet of Goering's bombing planes," Orwell argued. Basil Stapleton, an RAF ace, recalled seeing a fireman's work impaired by a Rolls-Royce driving over the fire hose. He and his comrades blocked the car and, "with the help of some other people, we turned the Rolls-Royce over."

It was not only some British who were wary of the aristocracy. In Washington, General George C. Marshall, the chief of staff of the U.S. Army, worried aloud in July 1941 to an American reporter about whether the upper-class appeasers might undercut the entire war effort, and in the process trap any American troops he sent to Britain to prepare to invade Europe. "There is a possibility, so the State Department tells me, that the British may make peace with the Nazis," he said, according to an account written by the head of Army intelligence. He continued:

> Then where would my advance striking force be? I am very worried by some of the advices I have received from the State Department. The trouble seems to be that there is a section of British opinion which puts peace before the defeat. These are the people with the most to lose, the traditional ruling caste.

Churchill took pains to reassure visiting Americans that he would not tolerate such conciliatory moves toward the Germans. Later the same year, he told a congressman who represented the people of the Pennsylvania coalfields that "there is no sign of weakness in the nation nor would the working people for an instant tolerate any sign of weakness or indecision on the part of the governing class."

Moreover, it was not the gentlemanly army, nor the powerful navy, but the Royal Air Force that played the most significant role in 1940. The air force was a distinctly middle-class organization, carrying with it a whiff of gasoline and engine lubricants.

Both Orwell and Churchill noticed and commented on the middle-class nature of the RAF. Orwell observed that it was "hardly at all . . . within the ruling-class orbit."

Indeed, one historian has noted that there were jibes at the time that its members were "motor mechanics in uniforms," not unlike the nameless men who chauffeured the rich. Evelyn Waugh, always alert to class differences, has a character in one of his novels set during World War II bemoan the fact that a senior Royal Air Force officer has been allowed to join an elite dining club. This gaffe occurred, the character explains, because it came during the Battle of Britain, "when the Air Force was for a moment almost respectable. . . . My dear fellow, it's a nightmare for everyone." Aspects of the class system did manage to persist in the RAF. Members of some "auxiliary" units formed by the wealthy and titled of London amused themselves, recalled one pilot, Hugh Dundas, by referring to the regular RAF as "the coloured troops." Class differences also reached into the cockpit—RAF officers generally enjoyed the helpful privilege of flying the same aircraft every day, while sergeant pilots were assigned whatever machine was available.

Nonetheless, Orwell was struck by the class implications of the RAF's role in staving off a German invasion. "Because of, among other things, the need to raise a huge air force a serious breach has been made in the class system," he wrote. With the Battle of Britain just ended, he wrote in the conclusion of "The Lion and the Unicorn" that "the heirs of Nelson and of Cromwell are not in the House of Lords. They are in the fields and the streets, in the factories and the armed forces, in the four-ale bar and the suburban back garden and at present they still are kept under by a generation of ghosts."

Looking at the same question from a different perspective, Churchill noted to subordinates with some concern that the aristocracy had played a small role in the Battle of Britain. There had been, he observed, an "almost entire failure" of Eton, Harrow, and Winchester, where the nation's elite schooled its sons, to contribute pilots to the Royal Air Force. Of the three thousand pilots who flew fighters in the Battle of Britain, only about two hundred had attended Eton, Harrow, or other elite schools. That was a tiny figure compared with World War I, when Eton alone had contributed 5,768 men to the military, of whom 1,160 were killed and 1,467 were wounded. Churchill wrote, "They left it to the lower middle class"—that is, the offspring of hardworking teachers, bank clerks, Methodist shopkeepers, and low-ranking bureaucrats.

Of those "excellent sons" of the lower middle class, Churchill concluded, "They have saved this country; they have the right to rule it." In this sense, Margaret Thatcher, the daughter of a small-town grocer who had left school at the age of thirteen, clearly appears as Churchill's rightful political heir. As a rising young politician, she wore a silver lapel pin showing Churchill's profile. First elected to Parliament in 1959, she overlapped there with the decrepit Churchill for some five years, until he stepped down in 1964. She became prime minister in 1979, some thirty-nine years after the Battle of Britain.

Thatcher would remember Churchill well. Under her supervision, Churchill's wartime bunker was renovated and opened to the public for the first time. She also held a Churchillian view of the twentieth century. When she visited Czechoslovakia as prime minister, she specifically apologized for the actions of Neville Chamberlain. "We failed you in 1938 when a disastrous policy of appeasement allowed Hitler to extinguish your independence," she told the Federal Assembly in Prague. "Churchill was quick to repudiate the Munich Agreement, but we still remember it with shame."

Churchill, sensitive to class considerations in his conduct of the war, instructed his generals and admirals to be careful in how they governed the armed forces. Early on, he warned the navy to be "particularly careful that class prejudice does not enter into these decisions" about selection of cadets for officer training at the Royal Naval College in Dartmouth, England. "Unless some better reasons are given to me," he vowed, he would investigate the matter. The navy resisted this direction, so he did as promised and intervened directly. He even met with some of the candidates who had scored well on entrance examinations but had still been rejected. "I have seen the three candidates," he informed the navy's top officers. "It is quite true that A has a slightly cockney accent, and that the other two are the sons of a chief petty officer and an engineer in the merchant service. But the whole intention of competitive examination is to open the service to ability, irrespective of class or fortune." Concluding that an injustice had been done, he ordered that the three be admitted to officer training. This was a lot of effort for someone trying to run a war and stave off invasion.

In his interactions with navy personnel, he lived up to his rhetoric. While aboard HMS *Boadicea,* a navy warship, Churchill went missing from the bridge, where the top officers and senior civilian officials were gathered. "We lost him altogether for a time," a lieutenant aboard the ship wrote to his father, "and eventually found him on the stokers' mess deck, sitting on a mess table swapping yarns."

In another front of the class war, he squabbled for months with the British military establishment over the regimental insignia worn on uniforms. This would seem to be a trifling matter, but Churchill sensed—correctly—that again, it was actually an issue rooted in class distinctions. His generals told him that only the old-line army units associated with the aristocracy would receive special shoulder emblems. This was presented to the prime minister as an economical move, attributed variously to the shortage of wool used to make the insignias or the shortage of tailors to attach them. Churchill, dubious of those assertions and always willing to argue the details, learned from his Board of Trade that the amount of wool needed to provide the badges to all units, including *arriviste* ones officered by middle-class types, was relatively minor, just

85,000 yards out of a total of 8 million yards used every week. General Brooke, often small-minded, complained to his diary, "He has been behaving like a child in this connection and has been wasting a lot of our time."

But as the strategist Eliot Cohen has noted, such interventions in the trivia of military governance reflected Churchill's shrewd understanding of war leadership. It was a matter of keeping up the morale of an army that had been defeated repeatedly, so "the matter of distinctive patches and badges was no trivial matter." In wartime, as Napoleon observed, men will fight and sometimes die for bits of colored ribbon. "I should be glad," Churchill wrote to the civilian overseer of the army, "if you would also explain to me why the Guards [an elite unit] are to be specially favored in this matter. Has a special permission been granted to them, and if so, on what grounds? I should have thought that line regiments, and especially national regiments like the Welsh or the Scots, were even more anxious for the support to esprit de corps and the expression of individuality which the enjoyment of distinctive badges confers." This was more than just one aspect of Churchill's love of pageantry and bright colors. He understood that the middle-class officers and working-class soldiers fighting this war needed to be treated with more respect than they had been given in the past.

"England is the most class-ridden country under the sun," Orwell charged in "The Lion and the Unicorn." "It is a land of snobbery and privilege, ruled largely by the old and silly." Yet while condemning the ruling class, he went on in that essay to make an exception for the new prime minister. "Until the Churchill government called some sort of halt to the process, they have done the wrong thing with an unerring instinct ever since 1931."

Given his socialist stance, Orwell was himself surprised by how approving he was of Churchill through most of the war. "It is significant that in the moment of disaster the man best able to unite the nation was Churchill, a Conservative of aristocratic origins," he wrote later in the war.

But then again, Churchill to a surprising extent agreed with him on class issues. Orwell once described himself as "a Tory anarchist," while Churchill was an anarchic Tory, bolting from the party in 1904. He may have rejoined it in 1924, but Conservatives remained uncomfortable with him. He was never quite right to them.

Class issues always seemed to lurk in the background of the war, popping up in surprising places. Suspicion lingered among some Britishers that the aristocracy, with its widespread sympathy for fascism, was not completely to be trusted. William Joyce, who broadcast propaganda for the Nazis, was nicknamed by the British public "Lord Haw-Haw," even though he was not an aristocrat, and in fact had been born in Brooklyn, New York.

Both men became wary of their own classes, coming to see them as part of the problem. For Orwell, this turning had occurred when he was a young colonial police officer in Burma. Despite his background at Eton, Orwell for most of his adult life ate, drank, and dressed as if he were of the working class. One evening during World War II, he came home and absentmindedly ate the bowl of boiled eels his wife had left for the cat, while feeding the animal the shepherd's pie she had made for him. His friends and colleagues usually saw him wearing baggy corduroys, a worn tweed jacket over a dark flannel shirt, and unpolished shoes. "I never saw him wearing a suit or, in any weather, a hat," recalled one friend.

For Churchill, the suspicion of his own class came somewhat later, with his disappointment in the behavior of the ruling class in dealing with the rise of Hitler, and then with his frustration over the performance of the aristocratic elements of the military, such as many generals of the army and especially the leaders of the Royal Navy.

As Orwell understood, the Churchillian antics that alienated the aristocratic Tories boosted Churchill's standing with other classes. "For a popular leader in England it is a serious disability to be a gentleman, which Churchill . . . is not," he would write in 1943. Churchill was considered a pusher, a swashbuckler, a turncoat on two parties, and, perhaps worst of all, half American. One critic of Churchill pronounced him "half an alien and wholly undesirable."

When in 1940 Churchill was pressured by Halifax and others of the "old appeasers," as the historian Sir Max Hastings called them, to consider negotiations with Germany, it was the Labour members of the Cabinet, Clement Attlee and Arthur Greenwood, who backed him. Churchill would not forget this Labour support—at least until the war in Europe ended and he again allowed himself to engage in partisan politics, to his detriment.

Churchill's determined stance against any peace talks with Hitler also may have had a class element to it. Everyone knew that some prominent members of the aristocracy had been soft on Hitler, so Churchill's absolutist rhetoric may have contained an implicit promise to the middle and working classes, and even to the poor, that no sellout would occur on his watch. C. P. Snow, the son of a church organist, recalled in 1940 being reassured by listening to Churchill. "He was an aristocrat, but he would cheerfully have beggared his class and friends, and everyone else too, if that was the price of the country coming through. We believed it of him. The poor believed it, as his voice rolled out into the slum streets, those summer evenings of 1940."

Both Orwell and Churchill could be surprisingly tough-minded, even harsh, in their military judgments. This would be expected in Churchill, but it is a bit surprising to find Orwell mulling in his diary in March 1941 that England should let occupied France go hungry for political reasons. "The proper course would be to wait till France is on the verge of starvation and the Pétain government consequently rocking, and then hand over a really large supply of food in return for some substantial concession, e.g., surrender of important units of the French fleet. Any such policy totally unthinkable at present, of course." He concluded, "People don't have scruples when they are fighting for a cause they believe in."

He also hoped that the houses of the rich who had fled the wealthy western neighborhoods of London for their country homes would be requisitioned by the authorities to provide shelter for East Enders made homeless by German bombs, but was saddened to think that "the rich swine still have enough pull to prevent this from happening." This led him back to his view that eventually the poor would rise up against such behavior. "When you see how the wealthy are still behaving, in what is manifestly developing into a revolutionary war, you have to think of St. Petersburg in 1916." By the spring of 1941, however, he was beginning to adjust his thoughts about the prospects of an English revolution. "Looking back on the early part of this diary," he wrote on April 13, "I can see how my political predictions have been falsified, and yet, as it were, the revolutionary changes that I expected are happening, but in slow motion."

Orwell's experience as a policeman in Burma and a small unit leader in the Spanish Civil War seems to have made him an astute analyst of military actions, at least on the tactical level, seeing through wartime propaganda reports. On April 22, 1941, he wrote in his diary skeptically of optimistic reports about British military success in Greece. "The thing that most disturbs me is the repeated statement that we are inflicting enormous casualties, the Germans advance in close formation and are mown down in swathes, etc., etc. Just the same as was said during the Battle of France." Sure enough, two days later, the British-led Allied force began withdrawing from Greece, leaving behind twelve thousand men, some of them dead but most of them prisoners, as well as many tanks and other heavy equipment.

In August of the same year, he correctly predicted, "We are in for a long, dreary exhausting war, with everyone growing poorer all the time." At this point, without explanation, he stopped making entries in his diary for almost six months.

———————

Some of Churchill's senior military advisors blamed their own exhaustion on nothing so much as Churchill himself. But Churchill often knew better than they did how to deploy the assets of the British war machine. In April 1941, he ordered the Royal Navy's commander in the Mediterranean, Admiral Andrew B. Cunningham, to do something to impede the delivery of supplies to the Germans through Tripoli. Churchill suggested sinking a ship or two across the entrance to the city's harbor. "ABC" Cunningham, as he was known, rejected the idea. Churchill then said it would need to be bombarded by warships, telling Cunningham's superiors that unless the navy acted, it would be seen as "having let the side down." Cunningham protested that the raid might bring heavy losses of British sailors, and then unhappily steamed to Libya. To his surprise he was able to shell the port at dawn one morning for forty-two minutes without a single British ship or man being hit by enemy fire.

Cunningham followed up that casualty-free action with a cranky note to Churchill. "We have got away with it once, but only because the German Air Force were engaged elsewhere," he wrote. "Thus we achieved surprise. *It has taken the whole Mediterranean Fleet five days to accomplish what a heavy flight squadron working from Egypt could probably carry out in a few hours.* The fleet has also run considerable, and in my opinion unjustifiable, risks in this operation."

It was a cheeky note—and perhaps reckless for an admiral to seek to instruct the prime minister in the workings of land-based airpower. Churchill collected the relevant facts and fired back:

You should obtain accurate information because no judgement can be formed without it. The Chief of the Air Staff tells me that the same weight of bombs as you fired of shells into Tripoli in 42 minutes, viz., 530 tons, might have been dropped by one Wellington squadron from Malta in 10 1/2 weeks, or by one Stirling squadron from Egypt in about 30 weeks.

Churchill did not hold this exchange against Cunningham. He admired the admiral's fiery nature and, in keeping with his partiality for aggressive military leaders, two years later promoted him to be chief of the Royal Navy.

As the military officer who worked most closely with Churchill, General Alan Brooke, the chief of the Imperial General Staff, bore the brunt of Churchill's behavior. Brooke was a hardheaded Ulsterman of considerable military talent who, to his semicredit, rose halfway to the occasion of World War II. In his diaries he depicted Churchill not as the noble savior of the nation but as a drunken maunderer whose nocturnal ramblings during World War II did more to hurt the military effort than to help it.

He wrote in his diary in 1941 that at a late-night meeting, Churchill exhibited "the most awful outburst of temper, we were told that we did nothing but obstruct his intentions, we had no ideas of our own, and whenever he produced ideas we produced nothing but objections. . . . God knows where we would be without him, but God knows where we shall go with him."

The general, a devoted ornithologist, wrote in February 1942 that a meeting with Churchill "was a complete parrot house." Churchill was hard on his military leaders. Brooke complained that he would say petulant things like, "Have you not got a single general who can win battles, have none of them any ideas, must we continually lose battles in this way?"

Nor were admirals spared. Churchill, upset by a navy proposal early in the war to withdraw from the Mediterranean, obnoxiously reminded them, "Warships are meant to go under fire."

To Brooke's military eye, the case against Churchill amounted to the verdict that "planned strategy was not Winston's strong card." That conclusion was reached not in the heat and fatigue of the moment, but rather years later, as his considered postwar judgment. Churchill, he wrote in a note in his diaries, published many years later, "preferred to work by intuition and impulse. . . . His military plans and ideas varied from the most brilliant conceptions at one end to the wildest and most dangerous ideas at the other. To wean him away from these wilder plans required superhuman efforts and was never entirely successful in so far as he tended to return to these ideas again and again."

But all those charges, while accurate, are, when weighed in the balance, more or less irrelevant. Churchill was fond during the war of the phrase "the level of events," using it sometimes to question whether an official really understood the context within which he was working. Brooke in his judgments consistently failed to see that at the highest level of war, Churchill was a first-rate strategic thinker. The prime minister, unlike his general, excelled at assembling the pieces of the war as if they were a global jigsaw puzzle, connecting different theaters and peoples. Churchill was able to weigh operational and political obstacles, not just at one point, but continually over the course of several years. Churchill understood, as Brooke did not, that "it is not possible in a major war to divide military from political affairs." He wrote, "At the summit they are one. . . . Much of the literature of this tragic century is biased by the idea that in war only military considerations count and that soldiers are obstructed in their clear, professional view by the intrusion of politicians."

Churchill's best explanation of his approach to grand strategy was given in, of all places, his charming essay on his love of amateur painting. "Painting a picture is like fighting a battle," he explained. "The principle is the same. It is the same kind of problem as unfolding a long, sustained, interlocked argument. It is a proposition which, whether of few or numberless parts, is commanded by a single unity of conception."

Churchill tended to have more insight than his generals about the military unity of conception—that is, how to weave together airpower, sea power, and land power in ways that made the whole effort greater, and more intense, than the parts. Believing, for example, that his generals in Egypt were failing to use the navy to provide supporting fire to the army, and also to deliver supplies along the North African coast, he chided in a 1940 memorandum, "It is a crime to have amphibious power and leave it unused."

GERMANY ATTACKS RUSSIA

The German attack on the Russians on June 22, 1941, breaking the Nazi-Soviet pact of August 1939, provoked a lengthy meditation in Orwell's diary. Conventional thought and official military estimates in Britain were that Russia, like previous Nazi targets, would not last long against the triumphant German war machine. "People have visions of Stalin in a little shop in Putney, selling samovars and doing Caucasian dances," Orwell wrote. But he had more faith in the Soviets' staying power. "More sober estimates put it thus: 'If by October there is still a Russian army in being and fighting against Hitler, he [Hitler] is done for, probably this winter.'"

That night, Churchill welcomed Russia to the anti-Nazi alliance, saying about Hitler in a broadcast:

We shall fight him by land, we shall fight him by sea, we shall fight him in the air, until, with God's help, we have rid the earth of his shadow and liberated its peoples from his yoke. Any man or state who fights on against Nazidom will have our aid. Any man or state who marches with Hitler is our foe. . . . It follows, therefore, that we shall give whatever help we can to Russia and the Russian people.

Orwell, in his diary, applauded Churchill's speech as "very good."

Orwell also would be shocked by how quickly party-line communists sought to erase the memory of Stalin's treaty with Hitler, with no mention of it in official Russian histories. Instead, they began demanding that the United States and England open a "Second Front Now" to relieve German pressure on the Soviet Union. This ideological control of basic facts, of putting events in a kind of "memory hole," as he would call it, would become a major theme when he wrote *1984* seven years later.

ORWELL THE PROPAGANDIST

Orwell eventually found a way to support the war effort by joining the BBC's Overseas Service in August 1941. There, for more than two years, working on broadcasts to India, he engaged in the kind of propaganda that he spent much of his writing life denouncing. Here again, as with his decision as a young man to become a colonial policeman, Orwell put himself in an occupation that ran deeply against his grain.

Not surprisingly, Orwell found in it mainly discomfort, especially because part of his job was to put the best face on the war effort, not easy in 1941 and 1942. In January 1942, his broadcast asserted, "It is doubtful whether a fortress as strong as Singapore can be taken by storm." Of course, he was trying to rally support for the British cause in Asia, where India was threatened by Japan, and many people agreed with his analysis. But he was quite wrong, and the swift fall of the island fortress of Singapore just a few weeks later would be one of the worst defeats of the war. He did see fit later to salute Churchill for delivering the bad news himself, rather than leaving it to others.

After the failure of the Dieppe raid in August 1942, another of the war's most stinging setbacks, he struggled mightily to portray the operation as a draw, with "heavy casualties on both sides." This was not, in fact, the case. Dieppe had been a rout, and Orwell almost certainly knew that, or at least suspected it.

He had mixed success as a broadcaster, in part because of his damaged voice, in part because everything in his soul made him a poor choice to be a government mouthpiece. John Morris, the head of BBC's Japanese section, who worked near Orwell, recalled that "although he wrote so well, he was a poor and halting speaker; even in private conversation he expressed himself badly and would often fumble for the right word. His weekly broadcast talks were beautifully written, but he delivered them in a dull and monotonous voice."

Orwell's prose style indeed was as strong as ever. Here, for example, is part of a minor, almost forgotten 1943 commentary he wrote on *Macbeth:*

> *Hamlet* is the tragedy of a man who does not know how to commit a murder. *Macbeth* is the tragedy of a man who does. . . . *Macbeth* is the only one of Shakespeare's plays in which the villain and the hero are the same character.

The BBC liked Orwell more than he did it. "Good, sensitive, loyal work," stated his first yearly performance review. "He has strong convictions but is never too proud to accept guidance." He was recommended for a promotion and a raise.

Yet Orwell never fit into the BBC. At about the same time, he wrote in his diary, "Its atmosphere is something between a girls' school and a lunatic asylum, and all we are doing at present is useless, or slightly worse."

In his diary there are no complaints about heavy-handed editing or censorship of his thoughts. Rather, he was dismayed by the general incompetence of the organization, and the finding that it had far fewer listeners overseas than had been thought. This made him wonder about whether his work was quite useless. "The thing that strikes one about the

BBC . . . is not so much the moral squalor and the ultimate futility of what we are doing, as the feeling of frustration, the impossibility of getting anything done," he added three months later. "Nothing ever happens except continuous dithering."

The only time he enjoyed being in the BBC offices was in the early morning, when the cleaning women swept the halls, singing songs in unison. "A huge army of them arrives all at the same time, they sit in the reception hall waiting for their brooms to be issued to them and making as much noise as a parrot house, and then they have wonderful choruses, all singing together as they sweep the passages. The place has a quite different atmosphere at this time from what it has later in the day."

His only break during his time at the BBC was a vacation in Worcestershire, where he fished the river Severn. In his early novel *Coming Up for Air,* the narrator says something that may have been autobiographical: "When I look back through my life I can't honestly say that anything I've done has given me quite such a kick as fishing. Everything else has been a bit of a flop in comparison, even women." Orwell indeed loved fishing, but may not have been very good at it—during his two weeks on the Severn, he caught almost nothing for five days, and mainly dace, a small fish, when he did.

Perhaps most significantly, Orwell's tenure at the BBC intensified his distrust of state control of information. "All propaganda is lies, even when one is telling the truth," he wrote in 1942, fashioning a paradox that would become central to *1984.* More sardonically, he named the torture chamber in that novel "Room 101," after the conference room at the BBC's building in London at 55 Portland Place, where he sat through meetings, deadly bored.

He also must have suspected that his talks on Shakespeare and Gerard Manley Hopkins, no matter how insightful, were not really contributing much to the war effort.

He was beginning to mull the nature of the postwar world. This was, of course, informed by what he had seen of Hitler and Stalin, and also by his experience in Spain. Early in the war, well before the United States entered it, he was worried about the world that would emerge from the conflict. He suggested in the spring of 1941 that totalitarianism might spread around the world.

> And it is important to realise that its control of thought is not only negative, but positive. It not only forbids you to express—even to think—certain thoughts, but it dictates what you shall think, it creates an ideology for you, it tries to govern your emotional life. . . .

From such frightening meditations, his two most powerful books would emerge.

While he was contemplating leaving the BBC, Orwell met David Astor, the third child of Nancy and Waldorf Astor. David was distant from his overbearing mother, who once stated that her five children by Waldorf were "conceived without pleasure and born without pain." One descendant recalled that she enjoyed driving children to tears. She had a strong independent streak, and became the first female member of Parliament. When young David was at Oxford, he rejected both her faith in Christian Science and her support for appeasement.

Generally more liberal than most of his family, Astor was working at the *Observer* newspaper, which was owned by his father, and was looking for good writers to spruce it up. The previous editor had resigned over disagreements with the Astors about Churchill's handling of the war. Astor did enliven the newspaper, doubling its circulation during his first decade of controlling it.

"As soon as I met him I liked him enormously," Astor recalled of Orwell. "I'd liked all that I'd read of him, but he was not at all a well-known name. He was more of an essayist and was doing something in the BBC, but he wasn't an established figure." Astor considered taking on Orwell as a war correspondent, but a medical examination found Orwell's health "unfit for service overseas due to condition of chest." Instead, Orwell, after finally leaving the BBC, wound up writing book reviews regularly for the *Observer* for several years. His friendship with the aristocratic Astor—unusual for Orwell—would last the remainder of his life, and would contribute to his most important work. Astor would help him find a place in which to write *1984*. A few years later, he would secure a burial plot for him.

CHAPTER 9

ENTER THE AMERICANS

1941–1942

When the Japanese raided Pearl Harbor on December 7, 1941, Churchill's near-ecstatic response was that the world war was won.

Characteristically, the reaction of his chief military aide, General Brooke, was more blinkered. The general complained to his diary that it meant that the previous forty-eight hours of his staff's work were "wasted!!"

"That," concluded Roy Jenkins, "was the difference between a fine staff officer and a world statesman."

For Churchill, the bombing of Pearl Harbor brought a joy that he could hardly disguise, even when writing about it at a distance of eight years. The unrestrained passage in his memoirs can be read as a kind of hosanna:

England would live; Britain would live; the Commonwealth of Nations and the Empire would live. . . . We should not be wiped out. Our history would not come to an end. We might not even have to die as individuals. Hitler's fate was sealed. Mussolini's fate was sealed. As for the Japanese, they would be ground to powder. All the rest was merely the proper application of overwhelming force.

Indeed, at this point in the war, Churchill had achieved his two major strategic tasks: to keep Britain going in the war and to bring the United States into it. The mission he had described to his son while shaving eighteen months earlier had been accomplished.

Even so, he faced much hard work in handling the American account over the next four years. His next step was to make sure the United States government stuck to the Europe First strategy of making the defeat of Hitler the foremost war aim. He needed to do this without being seen as overbearing.

Churchill's speech to the joint session of the U.S. Congress on December 26, 1941, was brilliant in several respects. Just going to Capitol Hill to speak was a canny move. Neville Chamberlain, had he been in office, likely would not have done so, and if he had, probably would have struck the American legislators as a combination of a stuffy valet and an unfunny version of Charlie Chaplin.

Churchill's post–Pearl Harbor address to Congress was a work of political genius. Its structure was artistic, with four sections that could be titled:

I
We
They
Us Against Them

Churchill began by spending several hundred words introducing himself to Congress—and to America. The first three paragraphs of the speech begin with the word "I." He portrayed himself almost as one of them, invoking his half-American background. "I cannot help reflecting that if my father had been American and my mother British . . . I might have got here on my own"—that is, by vote rather than by invitation.

He then spoke indirectly to the American distaste for aristocrats. "I am a child of the House of Commons. I was brought up in my father's house to believe in democracy." He then laid it on thicker, quoting Lincoln. "I have always steered confidently towards the Gettysburg ideal of 'government of the people by the people for the people.'"

Introductions concluded, he turned the spotlight to the new wartime alliance, in an almost poetic fashion. He moved here from "I" to "We." He welcomed the United States to the war, and praised the atmosphere of confidence he found in Washington. "We in Britain had the same feeling in our darkest days," he said, gently alluding to the fact that the British had been at war for sixteen months. "We, too, were sure in the end all would be well."

That first "we" referred to the British, of course. Then, two sentences later, his next reference to a collective pronoun referred to the British and Americans together: "The forces ranged against us are enormous. They are bitter, they are ruthless." Hereafter, when he said "our side," he meant both nations. They had been bonded in his speech. "We both of us have much to learn in the cruel art of war. . . . We have indeed to be thankful that so much time has been granted to us. . . . We are doing the noblest work in the world. . . . We are the masters of our fate. . . . As long as we have faith in our cause and an unconquerable will-power, salvation will not be denied us."

Next came a quick review of the state of the war at land and sea. In the course of this, Churchill managed with some sleight of hand to link the future of the British Empire to the future of freedom, a connection that many Americans would not make. "It is a fact that the British Empire, which many thought eighteen months ago was broken and ruined, is now incomparably stronger, and is growing stronger with every month. Lastly, if you will forgive me for saying it, to me the best tiding of all is that the United States, united as never before, have drawn the sword for freedom."

He concluded this section with an aria about the foolishness of Japan going to war simultaneously against the United Kingdom and the United States. "What kind of people do they think we are?" he asked. It was a very American sort of question—*Do they know who they are messing with?* In it, he again had made the American and British peoples one. "Is it possible they do not realize that we shall never cease to persevere against them until they have been taught a lesson which they and the world will never forget?" That line got a standing ovation. In his memoirs, he would happily note that these rhetorical questions won "the loudest response." All in all, this was more than a speech, it was the diplomatic equivalent of a marriage proposal.

That night, Churchill got out of bed to open a window in his room at the White House. He suddenly felt short of breath, telling his doctor, who was travelling with him, that he had "a dull pain over my heart. It went down my left arm." The doctor knew that the prime minister had suffered some sort of mild heart attack, but minimized the event to Churchill, whom he felt already had enough on his mind.

As indeed he did. Within a week, Churchill was acting as if his proposal to the Americans had been accepted and the partnership consummated. In a note to his Cabinet, he reported that at one point he found it necessary to defer to American views, explaining, "We are no longer single, but married." A man who never waited on anyone took care to push FDR's wheelchair himself when they went to their evening cocktails, which were mixed by the president. This was much more than a mere summit meeting. Churchill stayed two full weeks at the White House. He dined with Roosevelt and Harry Hopkins on thirteen of those fourteen nights.

Cozying up to the American president was never as natural as Churchill made it look, either at the time or in his subsequent memoirs. Earlier in his career, he had sometimes sounded rather anti-American, at least in private. In 1928, after President Calvin Coolidge spoke about the need for European war debts to be repaid to the United States, Churchill ranted to friends about the Americans. "This evening, Winston talked very freely about the USA," a houseguest, Henry James Scrymgeour-Wedderburn, the future Earl of Dundee, recorded in his diary. "He thinks they are arrogant, fundamentally hostile to us, and that they wish to dominate world politics."

Churchill wrote to his wife, "My blood boiled too at Coolidge's proclamation. Why can't they let us alone? They have exacted every penny owing from Europe; they say they are not going to help; surely they might leave us to manage our own affairs." The same day, Clementine, who was staying at a country house, wrote back to caution him about rumors that he would be moved from chancellor of the exchequer to become foreign secretary. She wrote presciently, "I think it would be a good idea if you went to the Foreign Office—But I am afraid your known hostility to America might stand in the way—You would have to try & understand & master America and make her like you."

In the 1940s, he would do exactly as his wise wife had advised. Perhaps the truest line in his memoirs is his comment about working with Roosevelt: "My own relations with him had been most carefully fostered by me."

It was unnatural for Churchill to fawn, but he did so because he had to. It was a wartime necessity, but back home, his peers noticed and shuddered with distaste. "We crawl too much to the Americans," charged the king's brother-in-law. "Recent telegrams of the PM to FDR have been almost nauseating in their sentimental and subservient flattery."

Orwell's reaction to Pearl Harbor was markedly more skeptical about the Americans. While Londoners were becoming more pro-Russian, he observed, "There is no corresponding increase in pro-American sentiment—the contrary." The reason for this, he explained, was that "our new alliance has simply brought out the immense amount of anti-American feeling that exists in the ordinary lowbrow middle class."

Whatever the cause, in dealing with America, Orwell switched roles with Churchill. He became the fact-free romantic and Churchill the hard-bitten realist.

"The civilisation of nineteenth century America was capitalist civilisation as its best," Orwell once argued. In his view, the America of the early 1800s had been a kind of libertarian paradise for the workingman. "The State hardly existed, the churches were weak and spoke with many voices, and land was to be had for the taking. If you disliked your job you simply hit the boss in the eye and moved further west." Of course, Orwell's fondness for the wild days of American history was very much the perspective of a white male. The freedom and opportunities available to blacks, Native Americans, and women were far less than advertised in his assessment.

Early in his career, in the mid-1930s, Orwell had contemplated writing a biography of Mark Twain, but could not find a publisher interested in the project. Churchill also contemplated a book on an American theme in his youth—a history of the American Civil War. As a young man on his first lecture tour in America, he was introduced on the stage by Mark Twain.

Among Orwell's favorite authors were three Americans—Twain, Walt Whitman, and Jack London. Orwell does not seem to have been much influenced by the scathing portrayal of the nineteenth-century United States by another of his favorite writers, Charles Dickens. *Martin Chuzzlewit*, a novel based upon Dickens's tour of the United States in 1842, depicted America as a nation of "dollars, demagogues, and bar-rooms," violent and deeply hypocritical, prating about honor, freedom, and liberty while enslaving millions.

Orwell did not seem much interested in the United States of his own time. "He exhibited a curious blind spot" about America, observed the writer Christopher Hitchens, who generally was a worshipper at Orwell's altar. "He never visited the United States and showed little curiosity about it. . . . America, in other words, is the grand exception to Orwell's prescience about the century in which he lived."

British anti-Americanism would only increase as hordes of U.S. Army soldiers poured into the country. Sixty-six convoys delivered 681,000

American men to the island in 1943. "More and more Americans were to be seen in the streets," recalled one female Londoner. "They called to each other with strange Red Indian war cries and organized baseball games in the Green Park." The American military presence in Britain would peak in May 1944, on the eve of D-Day, at a staggering 1.6 million.

Orwell was occasionally better attuned to British politics than Churchill was, and that seems to have been the case early in 1942. The prime minister returned from his successful American visit to find the House of Commons in some turmoil, its members wondering aloud if some changes were needed in war leadership. It was a hard moment for Churchill, because much of the war news had been bad, and he suspected worse was coming. After more than two years of war, the British had suffered a series of sobering setbacks. British Expeditionary Forces, or BEF, had been ousted from the European continent in the west (France and Belgium), in the north (Norway), in the southeast (Greece), and also had been expelled from Dakar in Africa. The rueful joke around London was that BEF really stood for "Back Every Fortnight." British forces also were reeling under Japanese attacks in East Asia.

Churchill challenged the House of Commons to debate the war and then vote on whether it had confidence in his leadership. "We have had a great deal of bad news lately from the Far East, and I think it highly probable, for reasons which I shall presently explain, that we shall have a great deal more," he began preemptively. "Wrapped up in this bad news will be many tales of blunders and shortcomings, both in foresight and action. No one will pretend for a moment that disasters like these occur without there having been faults and shortcomings." He invited his opponents to do their worst, using remarkably casual language: "No one need be mealy-mouthed in debate, and no one should be chicken-hearted in voting."

Three days of debate followed, some of it quite harsh. "It is no use the Prime Minister getting up and saying that he is satisfied with his team and that if there have been mistakes he alone is to blame," scoffed Herbert Williams, a Conservative, on day one. "He is the only person in this country who is satisfied with his own team."

Thomas Sexton, a Labour member, echoed the point. "The people of this country are bewildered. It is no good blinking the fact. They are bewildered by reason of the various hopes which have been held out to them during this war—hopes of Norway, hopes of Greece, hopes of Crete and hopes of Malaya."

Another member accused Churchill of running a "one-man government" who ruled "with a combination of what might be called despotism and paternalism."

Near its end, Edward Turnour, an old Chamberlainite, warned that the vote was essentially meaningless. "There is a very great degree of disquiet in this House at the present time, and nothing that can be done in the way of a vote will alter that disquiet," he said. "Only one thing will do that—facts and results more favourable to our cause than those which have occurred in the last few months."

When it was over, Churchill stood and addressed the House again:

I offer no apologies, I offer no excuses, I make no promises.

In no way have I mitigated the sense of danger and impending misfortunes of a minor character and of a severe character which still hang over us, but at the same time I avow my confidence, never stronger than at this moment, that we shall bring this conflict to an end in a manner agreeable to the interests of our country, and in a manner agreeable to the future of the world.

I have finished.

At that point he swept his arms down, his palms facing outward, "to receive the stigmata," commented Harold Nicolson. Churchill then told the House, "Let every man act now in accordance with what he thinks is his duty in harmony with his heart and conscience." He won that vote 464 to 1.

In mid-February 1942, Singapore did indeed fall. The end was swift and disturbing. Singapore was a great symbol, the bastion of British imperial strength in Southeast Asia, but the British commander surrendered to an inferior Japanese force after only one week of fighting. Some 85,000 Allied prisoners of war were taken. The event, Churchill later lamented, was "the worst disaster and largest capitulation of British history."

Orwell admired Churchill, but thought the defeat so disturbing that he doubted that Churchill could last as prime minister. "Up to the fall of Singapore it would have been true to say that the mass of people liked Churchill while disliking the rest of his Government, but in recent months his popularity has slumped heavily. In addition he has the right-wing Tories against him (the Tories on the whole have always hated Churchill, though they had to pipe down for a long period)," he wrote. He concluded, "I wouldn't give Churchill many more months in power."

Orwell, after long feeling mired at the BBC, steeled himself to leave. He had felt busy but unproductive there:

I now make entries in this diary much more seldom than I used to, for the reason that I literally have not any spare time. And yet I am doing nothing that is not futility and have less and less to show for the time I waste. It seems to be the same with everyone—the most fearful feeling of frustration, of just footling around doing imbecile things, . . . things which in fact don't help or in any way affect the war effort, but which are considered necessary by the huge bureaucratic machine in which we are all caught up.

Even his effort to grow his own food misfired, because he had expec[]
there would be a potato shortage. Instead, the British potato crop o[]
1942, he noted in the same dour diary entry, "is enormous." His own
plantings had been for naught.

Orwell knew he should be doing something other than the BBC job,
but did not quite know what that was. Yet his life was not entirely sour.
His nephew Henry Dakin, who came to stay with him and Eileen for
three months, remembered being taken by Orwell to see Charlie Chaplin's *The Gold Rush*, which had been edited and rereleased as a sound
film. "He guffawed with laughter, more than anyone else in the place,"
Dakin said.

The normal routine at the house was that both Orwell and Eileen
would have breakfast and then head off to work. In the evenings, he usually would go to his room and write. "Eileen's appearance was rather un-
kempt, but she was extremely nice looking and very pleasant," Dakin
recalled. "They led a pleasant life together and were always amiable to
each other and very amiable towards me."

Dakin noted that she seemed to always wear a black coat, even while
cooking and eating. She may have been deeply depressed during this
period. Lettice Cooper, who knew her at work, said that after Eileen's
brother was killed at Dunkirk, "she used to say that she didn't mind
whether she lived or died. She said that all the time."

During the war, the Orwells gave up living at their country cottage.
Both were employed in wartime London, and so lived through hundreds
of Luftwaffe raids. They moved from one apartment to another, partly
due to bomb damage to some buildings, partly because better housing
became available as more wealthy people moved to the country. At one
point, after they moved to Abbey Road in St. John's Wood, some friends
gave them a celebratory dinner with a good chicken and a valued bottle
of claret. As they sat down to eat, a bomb exploded close by. "We were
lifted out of our seats by the blast," recalled the host, Mark Benney, who

see that the wine bottle was whole, as were all the diners.
provided a class-based interpretation of their survival: "If
one of those working-class hovels round the corner we'd be
as mutton now!"

While maintaining his position at home, Churchill also had to continue to cultivate his relationship with the Americans as the war unfolded. Sometimes great achievements are underrated because the person doing them makes them look easier than they really were. Churchill's handling of America during World War II may be such a case. The Anglo-American alliance is easy to take for granted in retrospect, but it was conducted on a vast and lethal minefield of issues that needed unearthing and defusing. The Americans disliked Churchill's appetite for nibbling at the edges of German power in the Mediterranean and North Africa, a strategy Churchill rightly defended as necessary, at least in 1942 and 1943, to draw German forces away from the Russian front. Churchill, for his part, disdained American anticolonialism and saw part of his task with the Americans as "bringing them into touch with political issues on which they had strong opinions and little experience," such as the future of the British Empire—especially India. Churchill had embraced de Gaulle; FDR remained wary of him. Churchill was flabbergasted that many Americans considered China as important a nation as Britain. After that first visit to Roosevelt, he wrote, "If I can epitomise in one word the lesson I learned in the United States, it was 'China.'"

The Western Allies' view of the Russian role in the war would prove especially vexing. FDR thought he could manage Stalin in a way the British could not, telling Churchill, "I know you will not mind my being brutally frank when I tell you that I think I can personally handle Stalin better than either your Foreign Office or my State Department. Stalin hates the guts of all your top people." In this FDR greatly overestimated his abilities. Stalin was an implacable master of control, not only in the conduct of the war, but in shaping the postwar world. When both the Americans and British were taken aback by Stalin's cold, suspicious attitude, Churchill counseled Roosevelt, "The Soviet machine is quite convinced it can get everything by bullying." It was a comment that could have come from Orwell.

Churchill frequently bit his tongue. In April 1942, FDR sent him some advice on how to handle India. Churchill drafted a blistering response that began, "I am greatly concerned to receive your message." He went on to threaten to step down from the premiership over the issue. Then he put aside that angry draft and wrote a new message that instead started, "I have read with earnest attention your masterly document." That change feels almost electric, psychologically charged.

Despite being a dedicated anti-imperialist, Orwell sided with Churchill on the question of American advice on India, writing in his diary, "One trouble at the moment is the tactless utterances of Americans who for years have been blabbing about 'Indian freedom' and British imperialism, and have suddenly had their eyes opened to the fact that the Indian intelligentsia don't want independence, i.e., responsibility."

The relationship between president and prime minister was cemented during Churchill's second wartime visit to Washington, which came six months after the first, when he had addressed Congress. On the morning of Sunday, June 21, 1942, Churchill, who was staying at the White House, awoke in his bedroom, just across the hall from the one where Harry Hopkins lived. The prime minister read the newspapers in bed, had some breakfast there, and then strolled downstairs to see Roosevelt in his office.

As Churchill and Roosevelt began talking, a pink telegram was brought in and passed to the president, who scanned it and then, without a word, handed it to Churchill. It read, "Tobruk has surrendered, with twenty-five thousand men taken prisoners." It was a physical blow for Churchill. At first he did not believe it. Just the night before he had received a telegram from Cairo assuring him that the defenses of the fortress, facing the Germans near the border between Libya and Egypt, were in good order. It was well stocked, with three months of supplies, including a huge reservoir of gasoline. There appeared to be no compelling reason for its commander to have surrendered so swiftly.

Churchill asked for confirmation of the defeat. When it arrived, he winced. As at Singapore five months earlier, besieged Allied defenders had capitulated to an inferior number of enemy attackers.

Churchill was anguished, and likely wept, though he does not precisely say that in his memoirs. Rather, he states, "I did not attempt to hide from the President the shock I had received. It was a bitter moment. Defeat is one thing; disgrace is another."

The Americans noticed that he made no excuses. "He said it was just plain bad leadership," Secretary of War Henry Stimson wrote in his diary. "Rommel had out-generaled them and had out-fought them and had supplied his troops with better weapons."

"What can we do to help?" asked FDR, sitting at his desk.

Churchill seized the moment. "Give us as many Sherman tanks as you can spare, and ship them to the Middle East as quickly as possible."

General George C. Marshall, chief of the U.S. Army, was summoned. He noted that providing the tanks would mean recalling them from his 1st Armored Division, which had just received them. "It is a terrible thing to take the weapons out of a soldier's hands," Marshall said, according to Churchill's account. But, he continued, "if the British need is so great they must have them." Marshall volunteered that he also could find and ship a hundred self-propelled 105-millimeter artillery pieces, which resemble lighter versions of tanks. Some three hundred tanks, along with the guns, were soon on their way. More important, Churchill gained the emotional upper hand in the discussion of whether the U.S. military would lead an invasion of North Africa in 1942, a move both Marshall and Dwight Eisenhower vigorously opposed as a distraction from landing somewhere in France.

That afternoon, Churchill called his doctor to his room. "Tobruk has fallen," he said. "I am ashamed. I cannot understand why Tobruk gave in. More than 30,000 of our men put their hands up. If they won't fight—" He stopped and fell into a chair.

Churchill's lasting gratitude for the help the Americans gave him at that moment is evident in his memoirs. He returns to it not once but twice in the same volume. But equally powerful was the pain he felt over this second surrender of 1942.

Churchill's growing affection for the Americans was not entirely shared in Britain by other members of his class, either on the left or right. The pro-Soviet spy ring of Anthony Blunt, Kim Philby, Donald Maclean, and Guy Burgess was motivated in part by distaste for the United States and its culture. Philby, in his own memoir, relates that Burgess delighted in publicly taking "hefty sideswipes at the American way of life in general."

Anti-Americanism was, if anything, even more intense on the English right. "It is always best and safest to count on nothing from the Americans but words," Neville Chamberlain had stated in December 1937. When Lord Halifax was sent by Churchill to become the British ambassador to Washington, Lord Linlithgow, the viceroy of India, wrote him a note of sympathy about "the heavy labour of toadying to your pack of pole-squatting parvenus."

One good definition of a snob is someone who, encountering an awkward social situation, quickly assumes the other person is at fault. Nicolson personified this. On a visit to America before the war, he found the natives well meaning but pitiful: "Most of them feel kindly but are so ignorant and stupid that they do not understand my point of view." Nor did he trust their tendency toward openness. "There is something about the smarminess of Americans which makes me see red . . . the eternal superficiality of the American race." These doubts persisted into the war.

In November 1943, he wrote to his wife, "We are far more advanced. I despair sometimes about the Americans."

There also was a suspicion that the Americans, for all their easy grins, did not share a major British wartime goal, the preservation of the British Empire. "The President was no friend of the British Empire," noted Harold Macmillan, who would become prime minister in 1957. "This anti-colonialism was a strong part of Roosevelt's make-up, but he seemed to have very crude ideas as to how independence could be gradually introduced in the great colonial empires without disorder." One of Roosevelt's notions that the British deemed crude was his view that Vietnam should become independent. History might be different had FDR's advocacy of Vietnamese independence not been rebuffed by the British and French.

Condescension would lead many British officials to underestimate the growing power of the United States, and then to be shocked and angry when, in 1944, the Americans began acting as the dominant partner in the relationship.

All these prejudices meant that the initial Anglo-American meetings were like many first dates—a heady mix of enthusiasm, ignorance, and fumbling awkwardness. "President's entourage very Jewish," noted the diplomat Oliver Harvey. He also found American society to be surprisingly backward, judging it "a hundred years behind us in social evolution."

Harvey, an advisor to Anthony Eden, the British foreign minister for most of World War II, was not just being a snob. He was appalled by America's racism, and disliked the U.S. military's insistence on following American rules of segregation while posted to England. "It is rather a scandal that the Americans should thus export their internal problem. We don't want to see lynching begin in England. I can't bear the typical Southern attitude toward the negroes. It is a great ulcer on the American civilisation and makes nonsense of half their claims." This, of course, had been a theme of British Tories for more than a century, going back to the writer Samuel Johnson's piercing question about American revolutionaries: "How is it that we hear the loudest yelps for liberty among the drivers of negroes?"

When shipped off to Washington in 1941, Lord Halifax had a similar reaction. He believed that he was unpopular with Americans not because he was associated with the failed policy of appeasement, but because of the sway over the public held by "some section of the press affected by Jewish influence." He soon came to think of the Americans as "a mass of little children—a little crude, very warm-hearted and mainly governed by emotion."

There also was something in the British makeup, especially the determined insouciance of the aristocracy, that must have driven Americans up a wall. Anthony Eden once noted that during the Battle of Britain, fierce air battles frequently would take place over his country home, "sometimes while we were playing tennis." Once a Messerschmitt crashed into the woods behind the house. He doesn't record whether that incident stopped play. Sixteen years later, Eden's own extreme misreading of the Americans would contribute to the Suez Crisis, which destroyed his premiership and further reduced British standing in the world.

CHAPTER 10

GRIM VISIONS OF THE POSTWAR WORLD

1943

A t this point, Orwell, still a minor figure in British life, stood on the verge of greatness. Churchill, meanwhile, began crashing downward from the pinnacle of power as he began to face the grim realities of the postwar world.

Facing both men was the rise of the Americans, who made an initial poor impression in the war, leading the British to underrate them. The indiscipline of the American troops worried their more seasoned British counterparts. "Where we mounted a ceremonial guard each night, they leaned on their rifles, chewed gum, smoked cigarettes and generally adopted a most unsoldierly-like attitude," recalled a British NCO.

Orwell also winced at the Americans' appearance. Late in 1942, he wrote of seeing U.S. Army soldiers in the streets of London. "They wear on their faces a look of settled discontent." It was not a visage he liked.

At the highest levels also, the U.S. military underwhelmed the British. General George C. Marshall and his staff arrived badly unprepared at the

Casablanca conference of January 1943, at which major decisions would be made that would shape the next year of the war, such as the move to invade Sicily and then perhaps the Italian mainland. Roosevelt had instructed Marshall to bring only five advisors, with the result that, as Marshall confessed to his biographer, "Our staff preparation was most incomplete." The British, by contrast, reveling in the nearly forgotten delights of Morocco's sunshine, eggs, and oranges, brought aboard the 6,000-ton HMS *Bulolo* an entire shipload of well-educated, quick-minded officers. Those officers had with them rough drafts of a variety of war plans, and also the ability to churn out position papers on any war-related topic that arose in the leaders' discussions. The Americans found that "every time they brought up a subject the British had a paper ready," complained Admiral Ernest King, the crusty chief of the U.S. Navy whose service dated back to the Spanish-American War. The Americans were often unable to respond intelligently. For example, they had among them no expert on transatlantic shipping, and when they told the British that their working assumption was that they would be required to carry 3.6 million tons of supplies to Britain annually, the British informed them that the figure actually was 7 million tons.

Churchill, in contrast to the Americans, was as usual steeped in the details. When his own top planners insisted that an invasion of Sicily could not be launched before August 30, 1943, he spent most of an afternoon combing through their assumptions. He concluded that the assault actually could take place weeks earlier, in late June or early July. Time would prove him correct, with British and American soldiers landing on Sicily's southern beaches at dawn on July 10, 1943.

The British were unimpressed with the thinking the Americans did present. "Marshall has got practically no strategic vision, his thoughts revolve around the creation of forces, and not on their employment," General Brooke, Churchill's military advisor, wrote in his diary during the Casablanca meetings. "He arrived here without a single real strategic concept, he has initiated nothing in the policy for the future conduct of the war. His part has been that of somewhat clumsy criticism of the plans we put forward."

The Americans came to Casablanca determined to discuss the timing and preparation of the cross-channel attack into northern Europe, which they hoped to see take place in 1943. They departed with nothing of the sort, having instead agreed at the meetings to a Mediterranean-oriented strategy, at least for that year. This more cautious approach was, perhaps, what FDR privately had wanted all along, and so may have been the reason he had constrained Marshall on bringing an adequate number of advisors and planners. In fact, Churchill had told his advisors that he believed FDR favored the Mediterranean plan. Roosevelt was less enthusiastic than Marshall about crossing the channel in 1943, worrying that it was too risky, that American forces needed more combat experience, and that a year's delay would also reduce German ground forces and even more so German airpower. Marshall, despite his advocacy of landing in France in 1943, had told Roosevelt that General Mark Clark, who had been closer to the action in Africa, agreed with the British that "there must be a long period of training before any attempt is made to land against determined resistance." Roosevelt also may have welcomed the diversion of resources to the Pacific war that was allowed by that delay in invading Europe.

The Americans learned from their mistakes, and quickly. Marshall, for his part, when he got back to Washington from Casablanca, ordered a reorganization of his planning staff. "We lost our shirts," one of his planners, Brigadier General Albert Wedemeyer, unhappily reported to his immediate superior in Washington. He continued:

We came, we listened, and we were conquered. . . . They swarmed down on us like locusts, with a plentiful supply of planners and various other assistants, with prepared plans to insure that they not only accomplished their purpose but did so in stride and with fair promise of continuing in the role of directing strategy for the whole course of this war.

That awkward first large-scale wartime planning session set up the Americans for years of condescension from the British. "The Americans are still amateurish in their approach," the British diplomat Oliver Harvey wrote in August 1943. "If the Western war is to be won quickly, it must be run by our strategy and our people."

What is striking is how little attention General Brooke paid to the Americans in 1942 and 1943. In his diary he noted the names of all British officials with whom he met, and most of the French as well. But aside from Eisenhower and Walter Bedell Smith, who became familiar to him by their presence, his dinner companions are listed simply as "some American officers" and such, as if they were like the children who should be seen and not heard. This was not an accident. Brooke "did not get on with the Americans," noted Churchill's doctor.

When Brooke did focus on the American military in his diaries, it usually was with a tinge of contempt. "I am afraid the American troops will take a great deal more training before they will be any use," he sighed to his diary in February 1943. This was around the time the U.S. Army first fought the Germans, at Kasserine Pass in Tunisia, with notably poor results. "We say the Americans run away the moment a shot is fired," Harold Nicolson chuckled in his diary. Even Churchill was given pause by the shambling American showing at Kasserine. "The IId American Army Corps sustained a heavy defeat, and apparently was deprived of about half its important weapons without inflicting any serious loss upon the enemy," he reported to the king. But he concluded on a note of informed optimism: "They are brave but not seasoned troops, who will not hesitate to learn from defeat, and who will improve themselves by suffering until all their strongest martial qualities have come to the front." As late as May 1943, Brooke would insist to the Americans that D-Day-type landings could not take place in France "until 1945 or 1946."

Nor did Brooke always grasp how crucial it was to keep Russia in the war. He complained to his diary about shipping a few hundred tanks and fighter aircraft to Stalin. "Personally I consider it absolute madness," he wrote about the transfers to Russia. He did not appreciate that any equipment that encouraged Russia to stay in the fight was worth its weight in gold. Indeed, a commonality among Churchill's critical subordinates is that they tended toward small-mindedness. They did not understand the war as well as he did. Thus, in October 1942, while the crucial Battle of Stalingrad raged, and when it was essential to encourage Russia, the Foreign Office's Sir Alexander Cadogan crowed in his diary, "Succeeded in retaining in draft reply a nasty cut at the Russians."

From Casablanca, Churchill headed to Egypt. He continued to enjoy himself in the midst of war. Breakfasting at the British embassy in Cairo at 7:30 one morning, preparing for a bout of war planning, he rejected a proffered cup of tea and asked instead for a tumbler of white wine, which he drained in one gulp. When his hostess diplomatically expressed surprise, he reassured her that this was his third drink of the day, having that morning already consumed two glasses of whisky and soda. Churchill's self-indulgence, maintained even during the stresses of war, is a work of art in itself. He customarily wore underwear made of pale pink silk.

He could be a picky eater—his servants knew never to put before him a variety of loathed foods, among them sausages, cabbage, corned beef, and rice pudding. One wartime aide counted him going through about sixteen cigars a day. "It was astonishing to me that anyone could smoke so much and drink so much and keep perfectly well," Eleanor Roosevelt recalled.

A NEW WORLD
EMERGES IN TEHRAN

In November 1943, some ten months after the Casablanca summit, the three major Allied war leaders—Churchill, Roosevelt, and Stalin—

actually met for the first time. (The only other time would be at Yalta, as the war was drawing to a close.) Though the Tehran conference is little remembered today by Americans, the meetings there would have a huge influence on both Churchill and Orwell. The prime minister would be flung by it into a long dark mood. The novelist and journalist would be provoked by it to write his first great work of fiction.

For Churchill, the Tehran sessions were a startling time. He would devote almost as much space in his memoirs to it as he did the later session at Yalta. The Tehran conference—the run-up, the talks, the dinners, and the consequences—dominates the fifth volume of his World War II memoirs. In that volume, he claimed that he considered the Tehran meeting a smashing success, at least in military terms. He wrote, "Surveying the whole military scene, as we separated in an atmosphere of friendship and unity of immediate purpose, I personally was well content." This is an Orwellian sentence, in our contemporary sense of using language to conceal rather than to reveal.

In fact, Churchill was profoundly disturbed by the Tehran meeting. He arrived suffering from a painful sore throat. Things went downhill from there. After the first session of the talks, his doctor asked him if there was something wrong. "A bloody lot has gone wrong," Churchill snarled. It was the first time Roosevelt began to act as if he held the senior role in the partnership. It was in Iran that Churchill realized that his dream of dominating a long-term Anglo-American alliance would not come to fruition.

In his memoirs, Churchill disclosed two moments that particularly distressed him. First, President Roosevelt declined to meet with him privately, despite having done just that with Stalin. The Russian leader's demeanor was the opposite of Churchill's. At formal meetings of the three, he appeared relaxed, smoking and happily doodling with a thick red pencil.

Second, Stalin indulged in macabre humor at a small dinner party of the three summiteers and just seven other officials, offering the thought that fifty thousand German officers would need to be executed at the end of the war. Churchill was outraged by the suggestion, and responded, "The British Parliament and public will never tolerate mass executions. . . . The Soviets must be under no delusion on this point."

Stalin then mused more on the subject of the mass liquidation of the German General Staff. Churchill again denounced it, saying he would rather be shot himself than to "sully my own and my country's honour with such infamy." Roosevelt, probably seeking to reduce the tension with humor, however ill conceived, proposed that as a compromise, only forty-nine thousand German officers would need to be executed.

At this point, FDR's son, Elliott Roosevelt, who had joined the dinner without being officially invited, arose from his seat at the table. It was not his place to speak, but he did so, and in a particularly startling manner. He rejected Churchill's argument and instead endorsed Stalin's bloodthirsty plan. According to the account offered by Churchill, the debauched, scandal-plagued young American—who was not unlike Churchill's own troubled son, Randolph—added that he was certain the U.S. Army would support the idea. The younger Roosevelt had twice been a guest of Churchill's in England, and apparently by 1943 thought that he was familiar enough to speak at the tables of the great.

Churchill could suffer this intrusion no longer. "I got up and left the table, walking off into the next room, which was in semi-darkness," he recounted. Elliott Roosevelt, in his own pedestrian memoir, adds that Churchill, as he passed, said to him, "Do you know what you are saying? How can you dare say such a thing?"

A moment later, Churchill, standing in the shadows of the adjoining room, felt two hands clap his shoulders from behind. It was Stalin, his dinner host, who had come to reassure the prime minister that he was "only playing." Churchill, of course, understood well that mass murder was not just a matter of jokes with the Russian leader. The prime minister had been informed six months earlier that Stalin in the spring of 1940 almost certainly had ordered the execution of twenty thousand Polish officers in the Katyn Forest near Smolensk. That knowledge was made more excruciating by the fact that neither Churchill nor Roosevelt was in a position to denounce Stalin for that atrocity, and that both, in fact, would suppress efforts during the war to investigate the massacre.

Further complicating Churchill's emotions that evening was the fact that earlier the same day, he had presented Stalin with a ceremonial sword to commemorate Russian resistance at Stalingrad the previous year, the battle that arguably was the turning point of the entire war. This gift inspired the novelist Evelyn Waugh, who was appalled that the West would ally with a monster such as Stalin, to mockingly dub his series of novels about World War II "*The Sword of Honour* trilogy." In a synopsis he wrote for the beginning of *Unconditional Surrender* (published in the United States as *The End of the Battle*), he writes of his hero: "He believes that the just cause of going to war has been forfeited in the Russian alliance."

Churchill saw the decline of Britain illuminated at Tehran. It was, he saw, a major moment in world history. Some of his closest advisors were not as perceptive. Sir Alexander Cadogan wrote in his diary while in Tehran that he was "bored by this Conference—have little to do and am wasting my time."

Churchill flew out of Tehran in a black mood, anguished by the passing of British supremacy in the world. After that conference, his personality seemed to change. The dynamo of 1940 became the sluggard of 1944—increasingly forgetful, less eloquent, and often terribly tired, napping more often and sleeping in late many mornings. One evening at his country house, he sat by the fire, drank his soup, and confessed to General Brooke that neither he nor Roosevelt were the men they used to be. "He said he could still always sleep well, eat well and especially drink well! but that he no longer jumped out of bed the way he used to, and felt as if he would be quite content to spend the whole day in bed. I have never yet heard him admit that he was beginning to fail."

Churchill began to think of the Tehran summit in terms of animals. Soon after it, he told his old chum Violet Bonham Carter that in meeting

with Stalin and Roosevelt in the Iranian capital, he realized how insignif-
icant his country was in comparison with those of his confreres. "On the
one hand the big Russian bear with its paws outstretched—on the other
the great American Elephant—& between them the poor little British
donkey—who is the only one who knows the right way home."

Of course, many people also thought of Churchill in terms of animals.
Early in the war, Colville, his aide, noted that when he brought the morning dispatches to Churchill, he found the prime minister, pink, bald, and
plump, "lying in bed, looking just like a rather nice pig, clad in a silk
vest." Lady Diana Cooper thought that in the zippered overalls Churchill
often wore during the war, "he looks exactly like the good little pig building his house with bricks." His doctor, seeing him swim in Florida in
January 1942, wrote, "Winston basks half-submerged in the water like a
hippopotamus in a swamp."

Orwell was on the same track. The Tehran conference would be central
to Orwell's understanding of his time, influencing both his great novels,
Animal Farm and *1984.* The former is an allegory about the present, the
latter a portrait of a dystopian future. Both have some roots in what he
saw happen at Tehran: the world being cut up by leaders of the emerging
superpowers. Hence, in *1984,* the world consists of three totalitarian
superstates: Oceania, Eastasia, and Eurasia. England, meanwhile, was
being reduced to the "Airstrip One" of *1984.*

As the Tehran conference was concluding, Orwell finally began to
take the steps that would make him a great writer. He left the Home
Guard in November of that year. This ostensibly was for medical reasons,
but it was also a good time to leave the guard because it had become clear
that a German invasion was out of the question. The tide of war was
turning, and Allied forces were assembling and preparing for the following year's landings in France. At the same time, Orwell left the BBC,

explaining in a polite letter of resignation that "I feel that by going back to my normal work of writing and journalism I could be more useful than I am at present." He would be proved absolutely correct in this assessment. In the following six years, he would write his two great novels and some of his best political and cultural commentaries.

He would in that time also begin writing a column called "As I Please" for the *Tribune,* a minor weekly newspaper whose socialist politics were closer to his than those of David Astor's *Observer.* For his inaugural column, which ran in December 1943, he chose to offer a mocking look at American soldiers. "Even if you steer clear of Piccadilly with its seething swarms of drunks and whores, it is difficult to go anywhere in London without having the feeling that Britain is now Occupied Territory. The general consensus of opinion seems to be that the only American soldiers with decent manners are the Negroes." Most important, he began writing *Animal Farm.*

CHAPTER 11

ANIMAL FARM

1943–1945

There is no record that Churchill ever read *Animal Farm*, Orwell's great tale of how farm animals revolt against their human masters, only to be enslaved by the local pigs. He well might have, given that he enjoyed *1984* several years later. But he easily could have arrived on his own at the same conclusions about Russia's leaders. Talking to Malcolm Muggeridge about Stalin in 1950, Churchill lamented, "What a pity he has turned out to be such a swine!"

Churchill also would have found the book solidly in his cultural milieu. The tradition of fables featuring talking animals is ancient, dating back at least to Aesop, but it appears to have flourished particularly during the height of the British Empire, in the late nineteenth and early twentieth century, the time of Churchill's youth and early adulthood.

Rudyard Kipling led the way with two volumes of *The Jungle Books* in the 1890s. It is not surprising that Churchill admired Kipling and his works. "He had a great influence on me," he observed in 1944. It is a bit more unexpected to find that Orwell, whose *Burmese Days* was a fierce denunciation of the effects of British imperialism, also appreciated the empire's poet laureate. "Rudyard Kipling was the only popular writer of this century who was not at the same time a thoroughly bad writer," he wrote in 1936, soon after Kipling's death. "It was still possible to be an imperialist and a gentleman, and of Kipling's personal decency there can be no doubt."

There was much more to come in this peculiarly British genre. *The Tale of Peter Rabbit* appeared in 1902, the year between the death of Queen Victoria and the birth of Orwell, and was enormously popular, selling millions of copies and leading to a series of sequels. That book has its own macabre streak, one that Orwell might appreciate. "'Now my dears,' said old Mrs. Rabbit one morning, 'you may go into the fields or down the lane, but don't go into Mr. McGregor's garden: your Father had an accident there; he was put in a pie by Mrs. McGregor.'" It may not be entirely an accident that the head of the local British community in *Burmese Days* is named "Mr. Macgregor."

A. A. Milne's sentimental tales about "Winnie the Pooh" and his animal friends came in the 1920s, and again were hugely popular. But among all this anthropomorphic fiction, few books were so entirely immersed in the upper-middle-class Edwardian world as was Kenneth Grahame's *The Wind in the Willows,* published in 1908. This classic of children's literature begins with "the Mole" assiduously doing the spring cleaning of "his little home," which features images of Garibaldi, Queen Victoria, and a print of Sir Joshua Reynolds's 1776 painting of *The Infant Samuel,* which was heavily reproduced in nineteenth-century Britain. But even an Edwardian mole has his limits. Tiring of his cleaning tasks and lured by the day's warm weather, he flings his brush to the floor and exclaims, "Bother!" The Mole sets outside to explore the spring day and soon befriends "the Water Rat," who tells him, "I like your clothes awfully old chap. . . . I'm going to get a black velvet smoking-suit myself some day, as soon as I can afford it." The story ends with the Mole and the Rat, along with their friends the Badger and the Toad, attacking and reclaiming Toad's home, which has been occupied by weasels, stoats, and ferrets.

This book, with its memorable account of the joys of "messing around in boats" in the upper Thames Valley, must have evoked for Orwell his own youth in the same area, first as a child in Henley-on-Thames and later a few miles to the east as a student at Eton, which borders the river, where he spent much time while at school. Throughout his life he loved the natural world. He observed it closely, and reveled in working in it, farming, hunting, and fishing. "A toad has about the most beautiful eye of any living creature," he wrote during the first spring after the end of World War II. "It is like gold, or more exactly it is like the gold-coloured semi-precious stone which one sometimes sees in signet rings." His eye for the natural world even invigorated his political writing. The Labour politician Clement Attlee was not just a cold fish, he was to Orwell "a recently dead fish before it has had time to stiffen."

Then, of course, there is *The Story of Doctor Dolittle*. Hugh Lofting was a military engineer in the Irish Guards during World War I, vainly looking for signs of humanity on the front lines. *Doctor Dolittle* began as a series of letters home to his children. In a world where men lived like animals, in trenches or burrowing underground, where they were surrounded by rats and infested by lice, where they were slaughtered by the thousands, were they not simply talking animals? The children's story was published just two years after the end of the Great War.

All these authors were in the air for Orwell when he set about to write one of the most memorable books ever to feature talkative beasts.

ORWELL'S CAUTIONARY TALE

Orwell gave *Animal Farm* the subtitle *A Fairy Story*. It is that, but his is an adult tale of *dis*enchantment, of political violence and betrayal of ideals. Like Peter Rabbit's father, utopia runs into trouble as it ambles down the garden path. The story is set on Manor Farm, in Willingdon, in East

Sussex, between Hastings and Brighton on the southeastern English coast. The farm is run by Mr. Jones, an old drunk who is neglectful of his animals. He goes off to drink at the Red Lion—perhaps not coincidentally, in *Wind in the Willows,* the destination of Toad when he runs away.

Upset at the fruits of their labor being taken from them even as they are maltreated, the animals begin to grumble. After they are left unfed for an entire weekend, they run Jones off the land, along with his farmhands. The animals' first action afterward is to give the hams hanging in the kitchen a decent burial. They are led by a Stalin-like figure, Napoleon the pig, who at first cooperates with his Trotsky-like rival, Snowball. Then, in a scene reminiscent of the battle at the climax of *Wind in the Willows,* an attempt is made by humans to retake the farm, but the farm animals rally and rout them.

Trusting and plodding, most of the animals are slow to notice how quickly they are exploited by the new porcine regime. "The pigs did not actually work, but directed and supervised the others," sending the other animals out to harvest the hay, and then drinking all the milk gathered that morning. Snowball teaches the animals the maxim: "Four legs good, two legs bad." The sheep like the phrase so much that they would bleat it for hours, "never growing tired of it." The pigs soon also reserve the eating of apples for themselves alone, telling the others it is necessary in order to carry out their supervisory duties. Orwell wrote in his diary that he considered this scene to be "the turning point of the story." He explained to a friend that "had the animals stood up to the pigs when they kept the apples for themselves it would have been all right."

Snowball and Napoleon split on the issue of whether to build a windmill, provoking Napoleon to introduce a new element—nine enormous dogs who work solely for him. The dogs chase Snowball off the farm and then return to Napoleon. "It was noticed," the anonymous narrator relates ominously, "that they wagged their tails to him in the same way as the other dogs had been used to do with Mr. Jones." Napoleon soon announces an end to public debate. When "four young porkers" squeal in disapproval, Napoleon's dogs respond with menacing growls.

The pigs then move out of the sty and into Mr. Jones's farmhouse. They also begin to sell eggs to humans, causing a short rebellion led by three young pullets. The chickens and their followers are starved into submission, with nine deaths. Then the four pigs who had protested are accused of secretly collaborating in sabotaging the farm with the fugitive Snowball. Once they finish confessing, the dogs tear out their throats. "And so the tale of confessions and executions went on, until there was a pile of corpses lying before Napoleon's feet and the air was heavy with the smell of blood."

The pigs discover a case of whisky in the farmhouse cellar and carry on into the night singing. The pigs then begin brewing beer, while cutting the rations of the other animals, except for the guard dogs.

Years pass, and the pigs begin walking on their hind legs. At that, the sheep change their chant, making it, "Four legs good, two legs better!" Napoleon carries a whip in his trotter. By the end of the book, in its most famous line, the members of the farm are advised, "All animals are equal, but some are more equal than others." It is, effectively, the epitaph for the animals' revolution.

In a move that goes to the heart of Orwell's concerns about the modern state, the pigs begin revising their history. The fugitive Snowball is accused of not having been a hero at all, but a coward and a tool of the humans. Orwell had been mulling this tendency for years. "The peculiarity of the totalitarian state is that though it controls thought, it does not fix it," in the sense of making it unchangeable, he had written in 1941. "It sets up unquestionable dogmas, and it alters them from day to day."

In such a regime, reality is whatever the state holds it to be that given day. The accepted facts change and become simply a function of power. So, in *Animal Farm*, the pigs steadily revise the rules of the farm to their own advantage, and along with it their accounts of the history of the farm. To Orwell, such behavior, controlling the past as well as the present and future, was an essential aspect of total state control. He later would conclude, "Totalitarianism demands, in fact, the continuous alteration of the past, and in the long run probably demands a disbelief in the very existence of objective truth." That thought would become one of the core themes of his final book. It is not just the future that belongs to the all powerful, but also the past.

In the book's final scene, the pigs are inside the house playing cards and drinking with the humans with whom they do business. Napoleon and one of the men are cheating in the game. The other farm animals stand outside, gazing in through a window. "The creatures outside looked from pig to man, and from man to pig, and from pig to man again; but already it was impossible to say which was which."

It is a cautionary tale, Stalinism reflected through a fun-house mirror. "Of course I intended it primarily as a satire on the Russian revolution," Orwell told his friend Dwight Macdonald. "But I did mean it to have a wider application in so much that I meant that that kind of revolution (violent conspiratorial revolution, led by unconsciously power-hungry people) can only lead to a change of masters."

While Orwell was writing *Animal Farm,* he read aloud his work to his wife in bed at night. That may be one reason the tale unwinds so well. *Animal Farm* also works purely as a fable: the smart pigs who spend much of their time reading, the dogs who know how to read but don't care to, the self-regarding cat who hypocritically votes on both sides of the issue of whether all two-legged creatures are the enemy—an issue that irked the birds of the farm. Rereading it, one must wonder how much it influenced E. B. White, who in 1949, four years after *Animal Farm* was published and became a global bestseller, began writing *Charlotte's Web,* about a much kinder, gentler pig named Wilbur, and his friendship with a wise spider named Charlotte.

These two tales featuring talking swine rank among the bestselling books of all time—along with Lofting's *Doctor Dolittle.*

In the years before he wrote *Animal Farm,* Orwell had repeatedly seen how ferocious the Soviet regime could be. Trotsky himself had been assassinated in Mexico in August 1940 by a Spanish communist trained by the NKVD, the Soviet secret police. That attack, committed with a mountaineer's ice ax, with the handle sawed down to make it less bulky, followed an unsuccessful assault on Trotsky with rifles and a bomb three months earlier by another group of Russian-supervised veterans of the Spanish Civil War.

A Russian defector, Walter Krivitsky, had died in mysterious circumstances in February 1941 in a hotel room in Washington, D.C., where he had been providing information to American officials—including the fact that one British journalist in Spain had been working there for the NKVD and had been ordered to assassinate Franco. He did not know the name of that journalist, but after the collapse of the Soviet Union, secret police archives were opened and confirmed that it was Kim Philby. Before becoming a British intelligence official, Philby had worked as a war correspondent for the *Times* of London during the Spanish Civil War, and again in France in 1940 as the Germans attacked.

In Spain, Philby had operated for two years under the guise of being profascist. But by the time he actually met Franco, the NKVD's interest had turned, with the Soviets more focused on suppressing Spain's anti-communist left, including POUM and its members, such as George Orwell.

Krivitsky, the dead Soviet defector, had fled after one of his close friends, Ignace Reiss, was killed by Soviet agents in Switzerland. The NKVD for years had also been conducting a campaign of kidnapping and murder against White Russian émigrés in France. Even nowadays, notes historian Christopher Andrew, people tend to fail "to recognize the priority given to assassination" in Soviet foreign policy in the late 1930s.

Orwell found it surprisingly difficult to get *Animal Farm* published, in part because of the intervention of Soviet moles. He had warned Victor Gollancz, the left-wing publisher who had issued Orwell's books from 1933 to 1939, from *Down and Out* to *Coming Up for Air,* that Gollancz would not like it and would not publish it. Nonsense, replied Gollancz, who had turned down Orwell only once, declining to publish *Homage to Catalonia.* But after reading the new manuscript, he quickly returned it with a note that Orwell had indeed been correct. He wrote to Orwell's literary agent, "I could not possibly publish . . . a general attack of this nature."

At least four other British publishers also rejected the book, including T. S. Eliot, then an editor at Faber, who found the story too Trotskyite for his tastes. He also found that the pigs were "far more intelligent than the other animals and therefore the best qualified to run the farm." One house, Jonathan Cape, was inclined to publish the book, but decided against doing so after being warned off by Peter Smollett, then head of the Russian section at the British Ministry of Information, who expressed concern that the book might damage Anglo-Soviet relations. Smollett was revealed years later to have been a Soviet agent, recruited by Kim Philby.

Orwell was staggered by all these rejections. "I'm having hell and all to find a publisher for it though normally I have no difficulty in publishing my stuff and in any case all publishers are now clamouring for manuscripts," he wrote in a letter to a friend in May 1944. American editors were equally unsympathetic, with five rejecting the book before Harcourt Brace bought the U.S. rights in December 1945 for 250 pounds, and then only after the book had proved a success in England.

Orwell finished writing *Animal Farm* in February 1944, but it would not be published until August 1945. He spent part of the intervening period writing his column for the *Tribune.* He and his wife also adopted a child, Richard, in June 1944. The baby, born in Newcastle in May, was just three weeks old and had no clothes. Orwell's wife had worried that she wouldn't love the child, a friend recalled, but "in the end Eileen was very happy having him, loving him, and very proud of him." When she had to appear before a judge later to make the adoption permanent, she dressed neatly and even bought a yellow hat for the occasion.

Not long after the adoption, their apartment was made uninhabitable by the nearby explosion of a V-1 "flying bomb," the Nazi's early version of a cruise missile. They moved once more, to Islington. Though fashionable now, the setting of novels such as Zoë Heller's *Notes on a Scandal* and Nick Hornby's *About a Boy,* it was in 1944, comments one biographer, quite run down, "the kind of marginal area Orwell loved . . . a lower-middle-class enclave into working-class territory."

In February 1945, Orwell went to the continent to cover the closing phase of World War II in Europe for the *Observer.* David Astor recalled, "He wanted to go into Germany with the first troops that went in because he was aware that, although he'd written a lot about dictatorships, he'd never been in a country that was under a dictatorship."

It was not a wise venture to undertake. Orwell still was not a healthy man. In late March, he checked himself into a hospital in Cologne. There he occupied himself with writing "Notes for My Literary Executor," notable because in it he dismissed two of his early novels as "silly potboilers." While hospitalized, he received news that his wife needed an operation to remove uterine tumors. On March 29, 1945, before she was wheeled into the operating room, she wrote him a note reassuring him that her hospital room was pleasant, with a view of a garden. The next day, he received a telex informing him that Eileen had died while under anesthetic. Her funeral was held on April 3. That may be why Orwell would set the opening of *1984* on April 4, 1984—the beginning of his dismal new life.

After the funeral, he left their son in the care of a friend and returned to his journalism in Europe. He actually seems to have produced very little while there, which is understandable. "I don't think he felt he saw anything that was particularly useful," Astor said. He wrote to the novel-

When the Royal Navy was the symbol of global British power, young boys were photographed in sailor suits. To the right, Winston Churchill at the age of seven, already looking imperious. At bottom, Eric Blair ("George Orwell") at age three.

In 1895, Churchill was a second lieutenant in the Fourth Queen's Own Hussars.

Churchill in 1911 as first lord of the admiralty.

Churchill (on the right) after being taken prisoner by
the Boers in South Africa in November 1899.

George Orwell (back row, first on left) with the Eton wall game, similar to rugby union, in 1921.

George Orwell at age seventeen.

Wigan Pier as it might have appeared to Orwell. Two children talking to an unemployed man on a street corner in Wigan, published 1939.

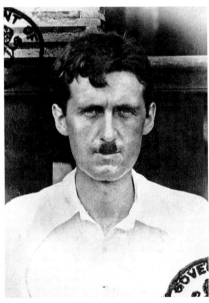

George Orwell's passport photo from his time in Burma.

Orwell (back row, third from left) at a police mess in Burma, 1923.

Prime Minister Neville Chamberlain with Hitler in Munich, September 1938. He would return to London to declare that he had secured "peace for our time."

Members of the Partido Obrero de Unificación Marxista (POUM) militia guard at the headquarters of the POUM in Barcelona in the midst of the Spanish Civil War, 1936. Orwell stands at the very back.

Orwell writing in Morocco during a recuperative stay there in the winter of 1938–1939.

Churchill, now prime minister of Great Britain, inspects
bomb damage in the dockyards of Malta, 1943.

Orwell (back row, far right) with the Home Guard during World War II.

Between 1941 and 1943, Orwell
worked as a talks producer
for the BBC's Eastern Service
producing commentary meant
to support the war effort.

Churchill waves to a crowd
in London on May 8, 1945,
declaring that the war with
Germany had been won.

Above, Churchill confers with President Franklin D. Roosevelt at the Casablanca Conference, 1943. Below, Churchill sits with Roosevelt and Joseph Stalin during the Tehran Conference, held later the same year. Churchill left Tehran distraught, as he realized that the U.S. and the Soviet Union were elbowing Britain aside. The conference also was a major inspiration for Orwell's *Animal Farm*.

Churchill in America: Above, with his family in a limousine in 1946. Below, notably aging at a meeting at the White House with President Harry Truman in 1952.

Churchill and Orwell as contemporary figures: Above, more than half a century after his death, Churchill's portrait appears on a political poster urging Britain to remain in the European Union. Below, a 2014 protest against a military coup in Thailand invokes Orwell's most famous book.

In Germany in 2013, a protester holds a sign with a drawing of Orwell during a day of nationwide demonstrations against eavesdropping in that country by the U.S. National Security Agency.

Two writers (and smokers): Above, Orwell at his desk. Below, Churchill at his seat in the Cabinet Room in the prime minister's residence at 10 Downing Street, London.

ist Anthony Powell from Paris on April 13: "Eileen is dead. She died very suddenly and unexpectedly on March 29th during an operation which was not supposed to be very serious. I was over here and had no expectation of anything going wrong. . . . I didn't see the final findings of the inquest and indeed don't want to, because it doesn't bring her back." His silence at this time is likely an indication of his pain. George Woodcock, a Canadian anarchist and poet who befriended Orwell in the 1940s, wrote, "He only once mentioned to me his first wife Eileen."

Animal Farm appeared in Britain's bookstores five months after Eileen's death, and just three days after the end of World War II. It was published by Fredric Warburg. The reaction was entirely unlike that given any earlier book by Orwell. "We printed as many copies as we had paper for, that is, 5,000 copies, and they were sold within a month or two," said Warburg. "And then we scrounged around and got more paper and we printed and printed and printed. And it's never stopped selling since."

For the first time in his life, Orwell found himself a literary and financial success. He was able to repay, through a friend, the anonymous benefactor who had sent him three hundred pounds in 1938 to enable him to spend a winter in Morocco resting his lungs. In a note accompanying the first installment of the repayment, he was apologetic. "It's a terribly long time afterwards to start repaying, but until this year I was really unable to," he wrote. "Just latterly I have started making money."

But he was hardly cheerful. Not long after *Animal Farm* appeared, Orwell purchased a pistol from a friend, telling him that he feared a communist attempt to kill him. Two experts on Orwell, John Rodden and John Rossi, write that his fear was more real than he might have known. The post–Cold War examination of the Soviet archives has revealed that he had been listed for execution in Spain if captured. That said, outside of Spain, most of those murdered by Soviet secret police were Soviet defectors or anticommunist Russians, so there may have been at least a bit of paranoia in Orwell's thinking.

Newly widowed, Orwell began withdrawing from the world, spending as much time as possible on the far, almost roadless northern end of the remote island of Jura, off the west coast of Scotland. But he also knew he was lonely, and on his visits to London proposed marriage to a variety of young women, often barely knowing them. He knew he was ill, and wanted to ensure there was someone to care for his son, Richard, after he was gone. One friend, Celia Kirwan, gently rejected his proposal, but kept seeing him. In another encounter, he invited to tea Anne Popham, a neighbor he barely knew. She recalled that he asked her to sit on the bed, embraced her, and said, "You're very attractive. . . . Do you think you could care for me?" She found the awkward approach "embarrassing" and left as quickly as she could disengage herself.

"POLITICS AND THE ENGLISH LANGUAGE"

Orwell also was thinking about the destruction of language, which would be a major theme of his next (and last) book, *1984.* In about December 1945, after the publication of *Animal Farm,* and as he was mulling *1984,* he finished what is probably his best-known essay, "Politics and the English Language."

Orwell usually wrote as an observer, but here he is a prescriber, laying down rules and offering advice. A careful writer, he instructs, should ask himself about every sentence a series of questions, such as what he is trying to say and what words will best express it. He should be especially careful about using stale, worn-out imagery that fails to really evoke an image in the reader's mind.

He summarizes his points succinctly, offering six "elementary" rules:

   i. Never use a metaphor, simile, or other figure of speech
      which you are used to seeing in print.
  ii. Never use a long word where a short one will do.
 iii. If it is possible to cut a word out, always cut it out.
 iv. Never use the passive where you can use the active.
  v. Never use a foreign phrase, a scientific word, or a jargon
     word if you can think of an everyday English equivalent.
 vi. Break any of these rules sooner than say anything outright
    barbarous.

Any writer today would do well to post those rules on the wall of his or her work space.

Less noted about the essay is that it isn't simply against bad writing, it is suspicious of what motivates such prose. He argues that writing that is obscure, dull, and Latinate is made that way for a purpose—generally, in order to disguise what is really happening. "Political language . . . is designed to make its lies sound truthful and murder respectable, and to give an appearance of solidity to pure wind." So, he writes memorably, in one of his best passages anywhere:

> Defenceless villages are bombarded from the air, the inhabitants driven out into the countryside, the cattle machine-gunned, the huts set on fire with incendiary bullets: this is called *pacification*. Millions of peasants are robbed of their farms and sent trudging along the roads with no more than they can carry: this is called *transfer of population* or *rectification of frontiers*. People are imprisoned for years without trial, or shot in the back of the neck or sent to die of scurvy in Arctic lumber camps: this is called *elimination of unreliable elements*.

That paragraph serves well as a short history of Orwell's time. This is Orwell at the height of his powers.

Churchill felt much the same way. He also had made his living by words, and was sensitive to their ill use. "The man who cannot say what he has to say in good English cannot have very much to say that is worth listening to," he once commented.

Like Orwell, Churchill maintained a lifelong vigil against bad prose. "He waged continual war against verbosity in official documents, especially Foreign Office telegrams," recalled a wartime aide, Sir John Martin. He once gave a copy of Fowler's *Modern English Usage* as a Christmas present to a member of the Royal Family, probably the young Princess Elizabeth, soon to become queen. He complained to his foreign minister about British diplomats repeatedly misspelling "inadmissible." When Anthony Eden proposed early in the war that local militias be called "Local Defense Volunteers," Churchill changed the name to the simpler and more solid term, Home Guard. Likewise, Churchill objected to the minister of food's dutiful plan for wartime "Communal Feeding Centers," disliking both the wordiness and the tinge of socialism. They were rebranded as "British Restaurants."

Even while overseeing a sprawling war of survival, Churchill paused to coach subordinates on writing. He found time on August 19, 1940, in the midst of the Battle of Britain, to issue a directive on brevity. "The aim should be reports which set out the main points in a series of short, crisp paragraphs," he began. Then, in a passage that could have been lifted from an Orwell essay, he offered some examples of offending verbosity:

Let us have an end of such phrases as these: 'It is also of importance to bear in the mind the following considerations . . . ,' or 'Consideration should be given to the possibility of carrying into effect . . .' Most of these woolly phrases are mere padding, which can be left out altogether, or replaced by a single word. Let us not shrink from using the short expressive phrase, even if it is conversational. . . .

He even ventured to advise FDR on writing, telling him in February 1944 that "it is nearly always better to cut out adverbs, and adjectives too." In writing his memoirs, he would continue to be sensitive to clumsy language. At one point, while quoting a wartime memo about fighting in the Sahara, he apologizes to the reader for using the word "depotable" in it. "This was the wretched word used at the time for 'undrinkable.'" For this, he adds, "I am sorry."

CHAPTER 12

CHURCHILL (AND BRITAIN) IN DECLINE AND TRIUMPH

1944–1945

I n the final phase of the war, both Churchill and Orwell were losing strength.

Churchill went through an entire lunch with the songwriter and showman Irving Berlin believing he was talking to the historian and philosopher Isaiah Berlin, then serving at the British embassy in Washington, D.C. Irving Berlin was visiting London at the time to put on his show *This Is the Army.* The prime minister discussed the state of the war and the reelection prospects of President Roosevelt with the composer of such hits as "White Christmas," "Puttin' on the Ritz," and "God Bless America." Irving Berlin began to suspect there was an identity problem when the prime minister addressed him as "professor" and then grew taciturn. After the composer left, Churchill was dismissive: "Berlin's just like most bureaucrats. Wonderful on paper but disappointing when you meet them face to face."

It was at about this time that Orwell noticed Churchill's weakened state. "Churchill, if one can judge by his voice, is aging a great deal," he wrote in April 1944, as D-Day neared.

Churchill's oratory went into abeyance. David Cannadine's volume of "the great speeches" of Churchill contains nothing from the period after February 1942 until his comments on the deaths of Lloyd George and FDR in the spring of 1945. That is a gap of three years. Churchill's first appearance before Congress in December 1941 had been electrifying; his second speech, seventeen months later, was dutiful, thorough, and unremarkable.

In the second half of the American participation in the war, in 1944–45, there was nowhere for the Anglo-American alliance to go but down. Churchill had grasped this at Tehran, and that would set the tone for his view of the last two years of the war.

Three tensions strained his relationship with his allies. The Americans were irked by Churchill's reluctance to open a second front in Europe. Roosevelt seemed to put off Churchill in 1944, sometimes taking his time in responding to the prime minister's messages. This was, of course, in part because he was a sick man. Duff Cooper, the former minister of information and later British ambassador to Paris, complained to his wife in a letter in April 1944 that British policy was "handcuffed to an obstinate old cripple"—that is, President Roosevelt. But it was also because a distance was growing between them. The Americans simply did not need the British as much anymore. They were going to win the war and own the world, in effect.

Churchill also knew that Britain was declining. He had engaged in some rhetorical sleight of hand when he vowed, "I have not become the King's First Minister in order to preside over the liquidation of the British Empire." He almost certainly knew that Great Britain would emerge from the war a shadow of what it once had been.

Churchill's antics were also beginning to wear thin. By 1944, General Brooke was heartily sick of the prime minister. In January of that year, he wrote, "My God how tired I am of working for him." A month later, he jotted, "I often doubt whether I am going mad or whether he is really sane." In March, "He has lost all balance and is in a very dangerous mood." The same month, "I feel like a man chained to the chariot of a lunatic!!"

In June 1944, after the D-Day landings in Normandy, Brooke wrote, "We had a long and painful evening of it listening to Winston's strategic ravings." He denounced Churchill in his diary as "a complete amateur of strategy [who]. . . . swamps himself in details he should never look at and as a result fails ever to see a strategic problem in its true perspective." His bottom line on Churchill was, "Never have I admired and despised a man simultaneously to the same extent."

Brooke was perhaps most exasperated after a meeting on July 6, 1944, when London was being hit by a wave of Germany's V-1s, with, as noted earlier, the Orwells' apartment one of the casualties.

> He was very tired as a result of his speech in the House concerning the flying bombs, he had tried to recuperate with drink. As a result he was in a maudlin, bad tempered, drunken mood, ready to take offence at anything, suspicious of everybody, and in a highly vindictive mood against the Americans. In fact so vindictive that his whole outlook on strategy was warped. I began by having a bad row with him. He began to abuse Monty because operations were not going faster, and apparently Eisenhower had said that he was over cautious. I flared up and asked him if he could not trust his generals for 5 minutes instead of continuously abusing them and belittling them. He said that he never did such a thing. . . . He then put forward a series of puerile proposals. . . .

Much of what Brooke wrote in his diary, and what others would charge after the war—often in response to Churchill's self-centered World War II memoirs—was accurate. Churchill displayed many faults as a war leader. He neglected logistics. He failed to appreciate the role of naval aviation and several other major aspects of the war. Like many in Britain, he continued to see aircraft carriers as the eyes of the fleet, outliers to help direct cruisers and battleships, rather than as the new striking arm of the fleet, replacing battleships. He underestimated the impact that German submarines would play in the war. Like his generals, he underrated the military power of Japan while overvaluing the staying power of the British military in Asia, especially at the stronghold in Singapore. Generally, wrote one of his researchers, "it is not unfair to say that Churchill suffered from a number of misconceptions, if not delusions, about the Far East which affected his decisions as a statesman and his writing as a historian."

Early in the war, he had persisted in believing that victory might be achieved mainly by bombing Germany, rather than by invading it, probably because he could offer no other plausible theory of how Britain, before the American entry, might prevail. "When I look around to see how we can win the war I see that there is only one sure path," he wrote in July 1940, ". . . and that is an absolutely devastating, exterminating attack by very heavy bombers from this country upon the Nazi homeland. We must be able to overwhelm them by this means without which I do not see a way through."

He frequently was diverted by military raids and indirect attacks, often to the detriment of the main goal. "Winston adored funny operations," commented his intelligence advisor, Sir Desmond Morton. He overestimated the gains to be had by invading Italy. He was the major driver behind the landing at Anzio, southwest of Rome, one of the worst quagmires of the war for the Allies. Relying too much on his experience of World War I, he failed to appreciate how much the mechanization of military power during World War II devalued the role of foot soldiers and elevated the importance of artillery and tanks. That blind spot probably also led him to underestimate how militarily effective the Americans would be in 1944–45. This likely caused him to drag his feet on landing in France while pushing for more attacks on the periphery of the Axis.

Yet, on the big things, he was more often right than wrong. He certainly was more right than most of his subordinates, which is why there was such value in his continual questioning of them. Looking back on the war's strategic quandaries, Churchill mused, "It is always right to probe." He was correct, profoundly so. His persistent interrogation of subordinates amounted to "a continuous audit of the military's judgment," wrote Eliot Cohen, the American strategist and historian. Other wartime leaders would do well to imitate his inquisitive approach. They should not look for consensus, and instead should examine differences between advisors, asking them for the reasons for their different views. This is a way of discovering the assumptions that subordinates may have made without realizing it. If meetings are not contentious, they probably are not productive—especially planning sessions. This is often unpleasant, especially for the advisors, but it is the best way to develop strategy and to uncover one's weaknesses before the enemy does. The essence of strategy is making hard choices, deciding between what Dwight Eisenhower once called the essential versus the important. Churchill excelled at that task.

Summarizing Churchill's strategic thinking, Cohen concluded, "He saw war policy in terms of large building blocks which together created a structure of victory. Very few people can or do think in this fashion." Most striking, Cohen added, was Churchill's sense of strategic timing— first buying time to build up the British military and await the American entrance into the war, then agreeing to invade Europe in 1944.

To Churchill's credit, he understood that he needed someone like General Brooke to argue with him. It was, after all, Churchill who first noticed Brooke, promoted him to lead the British military, and kept him there for years. When Brooke's critical diaries were first published, Churchill's doctor asked him if he had ever thought of firing the general. "Never," Churchill responded, then paused, and repeated the word "with complete conviction."

During the war, Churchill once told General Ismay, his military assistant, that he had come to believe that Brooke hated him. "I know he does. I can see it in his eyes," he said.

Ismay responded, "The CIGS [Chief Imperial General Staff] doesn't hate you! He loves you! But he will never tell you he agrees when he doesn't." This was, of course, essential to doing his duty.

At this, Churchill teared up. "Dear Brooke!"

As American power rose, so did British resentment of the newcomers. Enoch Powell is remembered now as an anti-immigration reactionary politician of the 1960s, but he had two disparate and successful careers before that. Before World War II, he had been one of the most brilliant classicists of his time, noted especially for his work on Thucydides. Then, during the war, he became an extremely successful military intelligence officer, rising from enlisted private to brigadier. At the same time, he became strongly anti-American. In February 1943, he wrote to his parents, "I see growing on the horizon the greater peril than Germany or Japan ever were . . . our terrible enemy, America." At one point during the war he was trained in field security by Malcolm Muggeridge, who himself was then serving as a sergeant-instructor, and who later became a friend of Orwell's, seeing him frequently in the months when Orwell lay dying.

Orwell reported on the growing anti-Americanism he saw in England. "There has been an obvious growth of animosity against America, and this now extends to people who were previously pro-American, such as the literary intelligentsia," he wrote. Leftists, he added, were beginning to understand "that the USA is potentially imperialist and politically a long way behind Britain. A favourite saying nowadays is that whereas Chamberlain appeased Germany, Churchill appeases America."

At the end of 1944, the *Economist* magazine picked up that line, accusing Churchill of pursuing a "policy of appeasement" with the United States. In March 1945, as victory in Europe loomed, Churchill's aide John Colville wrote in his diary, "The Americans have become very unpopular in England."

Likewise, Americans were chafed by Churchill's reluctance to invade France and defeat the Germans directly. As Ralph Ingersoll, then a left-leaning journalist, put it, "The cynics felt that from 1942 on, the British were spending Russian lives and American dollars and getting a profitable banker's percentage on both. So what's the hurry?"

AMERICA OVERTAKES BRITAIN

But the British deceived themselves by dwelling on American shortcomings, because it blinded them to the astonishing pace at which the Americans were improving. By the end of 1943, the British forces had been fighting for four years. They were tired. Their nation was running out of soldiers. American forces were then just coming into their own.

Early in 1943, Churchill had told General Brooke that he, a British general, would be the supreme commander of the Allied invasion of Europe. But by August of the same year, Churchill had come to recognize that the force that defeated the Germans on the western front would be predominantly American, and so conceded to FDR that the commander be American. "We shall be able to match the American expedition with a nearly equal force of British divisions, but after the initial assault the build-up must be entirely American, as I am completely at the end of man-power resources," he wrote a few weeks later.

At the beginning of 1944 came the quagmire of Anzio, the Churchill-inspired but American-led beach landing southwest of Rome. It quickly stalled, providing more opportunity for the Allies to engage in another round of assigning blame. The Americans noted the fatigue of British troops (rightly so). The British in turn pointed at the cautiousness and incompetence of the American commanders, John Lucas and Mark Clark (again, rightly), and at the cowardice of American troops (in that case, quite wrongly). In fact, if anyone was primarily to blame, it was Churchill, who had cooked up the idea of leapfrogging up the Italian coast to catch the Germans off guard. It is a testament to Eisenhower's skills, energy, and patience that the failure at Anzio did not sour Allied relationships even more.

The Americans were coming across the Atlantic with a torrent of men, machines, and energy. By mid-1944, they were surpassing the British in combat effectiveness. The Americans notably were mechanizing their forces, making them far more mobile than Britain's foot-bound soldiers. In France in 1944, when British field marshal Bernard Montgomery doubted U.S. Army general Lawton Collins's logistical plans, saying that a corps (that is, a group of usually three divisions, totaling around fifty thousand men) couldn't be supplied using just one road, Collins cheekily replied, "Well, Monty, maybe you British can't, but we can."

The British were surpassed by the Americans in part because they overestimated their own technological prowess while underestimating American agility. British industry was faltering, with one cause being the British aristocracy's disdain for applied science. For a long time, Orwell observed, Britain had been "ruled by narrow-minded, profoundly incurious people" who thought of science as "faintly disreputable," and even "despised" it.

Churchill also sensed this fault. In December 1944, Churchill wrote to his minister of production about penicillin, then a new miracle drug. "It is discouraging to find out that, although this is a British discovery, the Americans are already so far ahead of us, not only in output but in technique." Yet even Churchill, for all his appreciation of radar, nuclear weapons, and other gizmos of his time, tended to neglect British science in his historical works. In his writings, observed the historian Ronald

Lewin, "The Industrial Revolution might hardly have happened. Nor, compared with the soldiers and statesmen, do the scientists receive honourable mention. Newton, Faraday, Rutherford and their peers are either passed by in silence or thrown a few desultory words."

Churchill was hardly alone among historians in this neglect. When academics come from the aristocracy, they often reflect the biases of that small group. British historians have tended over the years to resent the social upheaval wrought by the Industrial Revolution. George Trevelyan, one of the most influential scholars of his time—he was born two years after Churchill, and like him was the son of a prominent British politician—came near to depicting science and technology as anti-British, an odd view for the nation that just decades earlier had led the way in the Industrial Revolution. "Already in the middle years of the nineteenth century, industrial change was creating the mass vulgarity which was destined ere long to swamp that high standard of literary culture with the advent of the new journalism, the decay of the countryside, and the mechanization of life," he wrote in *English Social History*. "Scientific education, when at last it came, inevitably displaced humanism."

The historian Correlli Barnett found that as a result of such attitudes among elites, sluggishness in the practical application of innovative science became a pervasive problem in twentieth-century Britain. Examining the production of British tanks during World War II, he concluded that their mechanical failings were "largely the fault of commercial firms incompetent at design, development, and manufacture," with the tanks victims of "over-hasty, botched piecemeal development instead of thorough-going preliminary design and testing; exactly the same calamitous pattern as with the new models of British cars after the war." This was one reason, he notes, that the United States built more tanks for Britain from 1939 to 1944 than Britain made for itself. This dismaying pattern was repeated with a variety of other products—trucks, radar equipment, radios, and indeed in virtually every area of technology except jet propulsion, where the British continued to excel. But even in that area, to make jet engines, the British had to turn to America for fabrication of turbine blades and impellers that would not fail under pressure.

Some academics have challenged Barnett's argument, but not very persuasively. For example, the historian David Edgerton in a 1991 essay denounced Barnett—but failed to address his basic point, which is that the British decline in aerospace, automobiles, and information technology that became incontrovertibly evident in the 1950s was already manifesting itself during the war a decade earlier.

The American gains were human as well as technological. The combat effectiveness of the American soldier improved during the war far more than that of his British counterpart. Bernard Lewis, later a prominent historian of the Middle East, but in World War II a British military intelligence officer, said that he had two dominant impressions of the American military. First was that they arrogantly refused to study British combat experience and so insisted on making their own mistakes. Second, and more significant, he said, "was the speed with which they recognized these mistakes, and devised and applied the means to correct them. This was beyond anything in our experience." One reason for believing the British had little to teach, noted Raymond Lee, the American military attaché, was the cocky feeling of Americans that, as of early 1942, "the British have not been successful, so far, in the war; why should they advise us?" As for their technical abilities, Lee was contemptuous: "The British really are not a mechanically inclined race and will use any excuse to avoid dealing with something new. This, of course, is not only true of tanks and planes, but of every other instrument we let them have."

British generals were forced to pay more attention to the Americans in the months after D-Day, when they were without troop reserves and the Americans were fielding combat forces that grew to be three times the size of the British presence. The Americans began demanding a greater voice in war decisions, and on occasion simply made them on their own without consulting the British.

CHURCHILL "DRAGOONED"

Typically, in 1944, as the war neared its end, Orwell sat back to review his journalism during the conflict. "The first thing I have to admit is that up to at any rate the end of 1942 I was grossly wrong in my analysis of the situation," he wrote. "I over-emphasised the anti-Fascist character of the war, exaggerated the social changes that were actually occurring, and underrated the enormous strength of the forces of reaction." He could not know as he wrote that sentiment that just seven months later a Labour government would take power and begin implementing some of the sweeping social changes that he supported.

Churchill was no longer capable of such intellectual flexibility, in part because he was tired, but also because he was feeling hemmed in by the Americans. By the late summer of 1944, as the Allied armies charged toward Germany, the Yanks sometimes took a new stance, politely taking note of British advice and then disregarding it. "Up to July 1944, England had a considerable say in things," Churchill would observe a decade later. "After that I was conscious that it was America who made the big decisions."

Churchill learned this the hard way that summer when the Americans repeatedly slapped aside his determined opposition to Operation Dragoon, a plan to invade southern France and drive northeast to join the armies landed at Normandy. Earlier in the war, he had been right about using indirection, because the most important reason for attacking the Nazi periphery had been to give the Russians reasons to stay in the war. But by mid-1944, the Allies were strong enough to attack into the heart of Europe. The time for peripheral actions now had passed.

Churchill long had favored getting to the facts of the matter because they tended to support his strategic views. But now the facts were against him, and he seemingly did not know what to do.

He introduced the subject in his memoirs by saying the issue of the southern France operation "occasioned the first important divergence on high strategy between ourselves and our American friends." He disliked the plan in part because it depended on drawing Allied troops away from northern Italy. This was irrational on his part, because the Italian front was stalemated. Even if German lines were broken, the Allies as they moved north would face other Germans dug formidably into the passes of the Alps. In fact, Stalin had made just that point eight months earlier at the Tehran conference, when almost his first statement was an emphatic recommendation against such a plan. In the Soviet view, he said, Italy was not "a suitable place from which to attempt to attack Germany proper; the Alps constituted an almost insuperable barrier." Of course, Stalin may also have preferred not to have Allied troops moving into parts of eastern Europe that he coveted—and soon would occupy and subdue.

Churchill campaigned long and hard against the southern France operation, writing to both Roosevelt and the president's advisors. "There is no doubt," he argued, "that an advance up the Rhone Valley begun at the end of August could easily be blocked and stemmed." A few weeks later, he cabled to FDR again. "I beg you" to call it off, he wrote. He also went to work on Eisenhower, predicting that Dragoon would prove a fiasco akin to the landings at Anzio, where Allied forces were stalled for months on the Italian coast earlier in 1944. "Ike said no, continued saying no all afternoon, and ended saying no in every form of the English language at his command," Ike's aide-de-camp wrote in his diary. Churchill then went on to accuse the Americans of having a "bullying" attitude and threatened to step down as prime minister over the Dragoon issue.

He never would admit that the operation in southern France was successful. It promised to be an important flanking attack against the Germans, complicating their military situations in both France and Italy. In fact, when the landings were made, in mid-August 1944, the Americans faced remarkably little opposition, precisely because the Germans were busy elsewhere. Within a month, the Americans chased retreating German forces from the French Riviera almost to the intersection of the borders of France, Switzerland, and Germany, and then linked up with Patton's army. Churchill, like Montgomery, perhaps had yet to take on board just how fast the mechanized U.S. Army could advance.

Unlike his supple-minded self of earlier in the war, he remained petulant and quibbling. "So far [it] has had the opposite effects for which its designers intended it," he insisted, wrongly, after the landings.

Even in his memoirs, writing years later, he refused to face the facts of the matter. He asserted that even if the operation opened up ports such as Marseilles, "they would be too late to help. This in fact was what happened, and indeed already seemed likely to happen early in 1944."

Actually, as the historians Williamson Murray and Allan Millett would observe in their magisterial history of World War II, "The Americans were right." This was mainly, they note, because the capture of the big southern ports of Marseilles and Toulon "proved a logistic godsend to the supply of U.S. forces fighting on the German frontier in fall and winter 1944–45, especially since the Allies could not use the port of Antwerp until December." The harbor facilities of Marseilles were relatively undamaged, as was the rail network leading to it, which had not been saturated with bombs in preparation for D-Day, unlike the railroads of northern France. One quarter of all Allied supplies in western Europe in 1944–45 would come through southern France and then move quickly to the front on railways in good shape. By December 1944, the Allies were moving 501,000 long tons of cargo a month through Marseilles and nearby ports, twice the total tonnage of the northern French ports. Of course, Churchill tended to be weak on logistical calculations, perhaps one reason that Antwerp remained in German hands for so long.

Churchill's peevishness over Dragoon also may have carried an opportunity cost. The summer of 1944 was a time when his great mind could have dwelled on the larger pieces of the postwar world. For example, was there anything more to be done to counter the likely Russian takeover of eastern Europe? In particular, could anything be done to help the Poles?

These were questions worthy of his powers. But perhaps they were so overwhelming, or so intractable, that he chose instead to focus his energies on the secondary issue of whether to land in southern France.

As the outlines of the postwar world began to be seen, Churchill grew gloomier, falling into one of his dark moods that he famously called the "Black Dog." He told his old friend Violet Bonham Carter over lunch in August 1944 that he had concluded that "a terrible world lies ahead of us." She reflected in her diary that night, "W. gave me the impression of being a very tired man. . . . Above all I didn't feel the exultation in approaching victory I had expected."

A few weeks later, he ominously told his doctor, "I do not believe in this brave new world."

The man who once delved so deeply into the details of the war now sometimes seemed bored by it. At the Quebec summit meeting in September 1944, he was in his bath while one of his aides was trying to brief him on the plans for zones of occupation in Germany. He was surprised to see the prime minister slide under the water occasionally, making himself "deaf to certain passages."

The British often reacted to their overshadowing by sulking. General Brooke's unhappy reaction in the fall of 1944 was to argue that the Allied effort was hampered by "two main factors . . . a) American strategy and b) American organization." This was not just peevish, it was an inaccurate assessment of the realities of the battlefield. To resolve the problems he saw, his recommendation was that "we must take the control out of Eisenhower's hands." Even to believe such a move possible was an indication that Brooke simply did not understand the balance of power between the two countries. Another sign of how little Brooke understood the Americans is a note about Eisenhower he wrote around this time to himself. Success in the Allied offensive into Germany, he thought, "is all dependent on how well Monty can handle him." Brooke seems to have been entirely unaware that Eisenhower loathed Montgomery, distrusted his military judgment, resented his failure to open the essential Belgian port of Antwerp, felt he did not understand how the Americans were operating, and soon would seriously contemplate removing him—a move that was within Eisenhower's powers. In the end, it was Ike who handled Monty, not the other way around.

Such acidity was not uncommon in the weeks and months after D-Day. In October 1944, Lieutenant General Sir Henry Pownall, a senior British officer in Asia, wrote in his diary that the United States was "a very raw, immature and uneducated nation with no code of manners." Interestingly, Pownall later helped Churchill write the six volumes of war memoirs, but does not appear to have had much influence over the memoirs' account of the Anglo-American relationship.

By the beginning of 1945, Brooke, Churchill's top military advisor, found him "looking very old, very meandering in his thoughts and watery about the eyes." Churchill was indeed exhausted, in mind and body.

The old order was ending. In February, Churchill saw Roosevelt for the last time, aboard the USS *Quincy* in the harbor of Alexandria, Egypt, following the Yalta summit. "I felt he had a slender contact with life," Churchill wrote. Two months later, FDR was dead.

Inexplicably, Churchill, who had traveled so often and freely during the war, decided against attending Roosevelt's funeral, citing the press of government business. This is simply not credible, given Churchill's wartime globe-trotting. He seems to have thought that, after five years of his kowtowing to the Americans, it was time for them to come to him. "I think it would be a good thing that President Truman should come over here," he wrote in his note to the king explaining why he had decided against the voyage. Then, despite his claim of urgent government business, he went off for a country weekend and danced a Viennese waltz with his daughter so heartily that he grew dizzy, said "Stop," and staggered to a chair. One member of Parliament who saw Churchill around this time said he seemed "remarkably unmoved" by FDR's death.

Churchill's doctor, Charles Wilson, suspected that all along Churchill had, in fact, been a bit bored by FDR. "The cast of Roosevelt's mind—I am thinking of his preoccupation with social problems and the rights of the common man—struck no sparks in Winston's mind. The war was all they had in common." Wilson thought Churchill was more intrigued by Stalin, "a type Winston had not met before; he interested him, notwithstanding his deliberate rudeness and his rough speech. . . . The man had caught his imagination." Churchill told Wilson in 1947 that Roosevelt was "a man who hadn't any ideas at all."

Roy Jenkins, in his biography of Churchill, arrived at a similar conclusion. "It is more probable that the emotional link between Churchill and Roosevelt was never as close as was commonly thought," he observed. "It was more a partnership of circumstance and convenience than a friendship of individuals."

That assessment may sell their relationship a bit short. It was not a usual friendship, and should not be judged in those terms. Rather, it was a surprisingly close attachment between two world leaders during years of crisis. They must have recognized something akin in each other. What happens when two colossal monologists meet? It may be that they stop and pay attention to each other. As Robert Sherwood, Harry Hopkins's biographer, put it, "Churchill was one of the few people to whom Roosevelt cared to listen, and vice versa."

Some in Churchill's circle came to believe that, in fact, the prime minister underestimated the president and so wound up being played by him. Sir Desmond Morton, a longtime Churchill advisor, believed that Churchill's half-American background may have "blinded him to Roosevelt's aim to overthrow the British Empire—in which he succeeded."

That view is historically uninformed. The British Empire had been in decline for many decades before FDR appeared on the scene. Britain had lost its industrial dominance by the end of the nineteenth century, had been depleted of manpower by the fighting of World War I, and then was drained of its remaining money by World War II.

Moreover, its industries were slowly strangling themselves. Managed by family members more interested in reaping dividends than investing in new machinery and other gear, "British firms were unable to adopt modern, best-practice technology," concluded business historian Alfred D. Chandler Jr. As a consequence, Britain's brilliant university research generally did not make the transition into factories. Britain had led the first Industrial Revolution of coal and steam power, but generally sat out the "Second Industrial Revolution" of the late nineteenth and early twentieth centuries, built around oil, chemicals, metals, electricity, electronics, and light machinery, such as automobiles. By the end of the 1940s, it would have neither an empire nor an economy capable of competing with those of other major powers. As Correlli Barnett put it, the reality was that by the time World War II ended, the British "had already written the broad scenario for Britain's postwar descent to the place of fifth in the free world as an industrial power, with manufacturing output only two fifths of West Germany's." Interestingly, Barnett was the keeper of the Churchill Archives at Cambridge University from 1977 to 1995.

The only thing that energized Churchill at this point in the war was visiting the front. In March 1945, he was excited to stand on a bridge over the Rhine in Germany. General William Simpson, a low-key Texan who has been unfairly forgotten among senior American commanders in the war, was alarmed. "Prime Minister, there are snipers in front of you, they are shelling both sides of the bridge, and now they have started shelling the road behind you. I cannot accept the responsibility of your being here, and must ask you to come away." Churchill reacted petulantly, clinging to a broken girder of the bridge and looking back at Simpson angrily. But after allowing himself that pout, he relented and left the vulnerable spot quietly. As such episodes indicate, there was in Churchill, observed Violet Bonham Carter, an "eternal childhood." One must also wonder if Churchill somehow recognized that there was little left for him to do on Earth, and that being killed on the front lines as the war ended would be a fine way to exit the world's stage.

CHURCHILL STUMBLES
AS THE WAR ENDS

Just how far had Churchill declined? Quite a lot, by the time he had to be pulled from that bridge. This was confirmed by his last major speech of the European war, delivered on May 13, 1945. He was at his worst. It had been exactly five years since he had delivered his magnificent "blood, toil, tears and sweat" speech. He was no longer capable of scaling the oratorical heights he had reached in that earlier address.

In the May 1945 speech, he began, "After various episodes had occurred it became clear last week that so far things have worked out pretty well." He sounded almost distracted.

Then, at this most historic of occasions, he digressed into an unneeded swipe at the neutral Irish government of President Éamon de Valera. "With a restraint and poise to which, I say, history will find few parallels, His Majesty's Government has never laid a violent hand upon them [the Irish], though at times it would have been quite easy and quite natural, and we left the de Valera government to frolic with the Germans and later with the Japanese representatives to their hearts' content."

Throughout the war, one of Churchill's strengths had been to rise to the occasion, morally and emotionally, but on this momentous occasion he failed utterly to do that. His bitter aside at a small neutral neighbor that had been violently oppressed by England was hardly the stuff of a great English leader's speech celebrating a European victory that would determine the future of the world. His rambling words suggest that he was improvising. In fact, Churchill privately might have had reason to thank de Valera. The British had wanted early in the war to base submarine-hunting aircraft and ships in Ireland. Some historians calculate that if the Irish government had played its hand better, it might have been able to persuade Churchill to give Ireland control of Northern Ireland in exchange for the Irish permitting the bases and then entering the war on the side of Britain. In this instance, Churchill probably may have been angry that de Valera, respecting diplomatic niceties, two weeks earlier had extended the condolences of the Irish government to Germany upon the death of Hitler.

As he neared the conclusion of this odd speech and looked to the future, Churchill regained some balance. In one passage that sounds a bit like George Orwell, he warned, "On the continent of Europe we have yet to make sure that the simple and honourable purposes for which we entered the war are not brushed aside or overlooked in the months following our success, and that the words 'freedom,' 'democracy' and 'liberation' are not distorted from their true meaning as we have understood them." He soon would return to this theme in the speeches in London and Missouri in which he warned of an "iron curtain" dividing Europe, behind which people had to fear "the policeman's knock."

The digression about Ireland also showed how Churchill's mind-set was changing as the end of the war loomed. He seemed to feel that once again he could give free rein to his divisive instincts. The following month, warning of the dangers of the Labour Party taking power, he indulged in more extravagant rhetoric. "No Socialist Government conducting the entire life and industry of the country could afford to allow free, sharp, or violently worded expressions of public discontent. They would have to fall back on some form of Gestapo." This was an unexpected and foolish way to discuss the Labour Party leaders with whom he had spent the war in a coalition government, and, in fact, had helped make him prime minister in 1940 by refusing to support Neville Chamberlain in such a government. They had been better to him than many Tories had. In this election, Muggeridge wrote, Churchill "discarded the role of national leadership, which he had so richly earned, in favour of party leadership, for which he was ill-fitted, and which ill-became him."

Even so, Orwell thought that Churchill would prevail in the election. "I have predicted all along that the Conservatives will win by a small majority," he wrote a few weeks before the vote, "and I still stick to this, though not quite so confidently as before, because the tide is obviously running very strongly in the other direction. It is even conceivable that Labour may win the election against the will of its leaders."

THE TEARS OF WINSTON CHURCHILL

For Churchill, the war would end, as it began, with tears. In May 1945, with Hitler dead and Germany subdued, Churchill shook hands with each member of his War Cabinet. "He thanked us all very nicely and with tears in his eyes for all we had done in the war, and all the endless work we had put in 'from El Alamein to where we are now,'" wrote Brooke.

When Churchill in May 1940 had offered blood, toil, tears, and sweat, he certainly gave the last three himself. Probably no modern world leader has wept in public as frequently as Churchill did while prime minister. This is especially noteworthy because it occurred, Simon Schama noted, in "a culture which looked on such demonstrations of emotion as dreadfully bad form." He cried often—not just at somber ceremonies, or moments of personal grief, but in conversation and in public speeches. It was, arguably, an essential element of his style of leadership, spectacularly un-British and so all the more striking in a British leader. Of course, it also reflected his odd lack of a boundary between the public and private realms.

Once, returning to Britain from a convalescence from pneumonia in Morocco, Churchill hardly had taken his seat in his beloved House of Commons "when two large tears began to trickle down his cheeks." He could even move himself to tears while dictating a speech. "For minutes he might walk up and down trying out sentences to himself," recalled one of his secretaries. "Sometimes his voice would become thick with emotion, and occasionally a tear would run down his cheek." Once, in explaining to General Brooke just how stressful it was to be a wartime prime minister, Churchill began crying. "Tears streamed down his face," Brooke noted.

His tendency to cry in public was perhaps a sign of the strain he was under. Even so, it was not a political weakness, but a strength. The people of England suffered during the war. Some 67,000 British civilians were killed during the war by bombs and missiles and the fires and collapses they caused, in what was genuinely a "home front." Looking at Churchill, Britons could see their leader was a man of feeling. This was not a given in a nation with such huge distance and distrust between the classes.

That said, many of Churchill's tears may have been shed mainly for himself, or for his own ends. Churchill understood that if he was not moved, those around him would not be. "The orator is the embodiment of the passions of the multitude," he asserted in an early unpublished essay called "The Scaffolding of Rhetoric," written in 1897. "Before he can move their tears his own must flow. To convince them he must himself believe."

What did all those teardrops mean? Sir Desmond Morton, who was close to Churchill during the war but later became a harsh critic, came to believe that the man loved power far more than people, and in fact was almost entirely lacking in empathy. "Winston simply never had any idea of the trouble others took on his behalf," he wrote. "Winston was always quite unable to enter the mind of anyone else." Another sometime ally and aide, Robert Boothby, came to a similar conclusion, writing, "'Thou shalt have none other gods but me' has always been the first, and most significant, of his Commandments." But, he added, that was not entirely a bad trait for Churchill to have. "No man without an element of ruthlessness in his character could have stood up to Hitler."

To deepen the paradox, Churchill's essential selfishness may have been a necessary vice for a wartime leader. A man with more empathy might have been crushed by the emotions and pressures of waging global war year after year.

TWO VISIONS OF
DEATH IN POTSDAM

In July 1945, Churchill left London to attend the last summit conference of the war, at Potsdam, Germany. There the Americans informed the British that they had just tested the atom bomb successfully. Churchill, awed, began to meditate aloud on how the new weapon might alter the end of the war, and even help contain the Russians. Brooke, typically, dismissed the news as just more "American exaggerations." He worried in his diary that Churchill would be carried away by the implications of this new nuclear age. "I shudder to feel that he is allowing the half-baked results of one experiment to warp the whole of his diplomatic perspective!" This was the view of a conventional man unable to discern the long-range meaning of sudden changes. Churchill's talent was that he could do just that.

On the same day of the American nuclear explosion, July 16, Churchill traveled into Berlin to see Hitler's bunker, including the room in which the Führer died. Eight days later, he dreamed that he himself was lying in a morgue. He told his doctor, "I saw it—it was very vivid—my dead body under a white sheet on a table in an empty room. I recognized my bare feet projecting from under the sheet."

The premonitory dream was accurate. The next day, Churchill suffered a political death, as he and his party lost the national election in a landslide. It was a stunning repudiation to be forced out of office even before World War II had ended in the Pacific. "Churchill stood for the British Empire, for British independence and for an 'anti-Socialist' vision of Britain," concludes the historian John Charmley. "By July 1945 the first of these was on the skids, the second was dependent solely upon America and the third had just vanished in a Labour election victory."

And so, for the first time in six years, Churchill had to look for a place to live in London. It was a devastating turnabout for someone who had just led his nation to a great victory: Britain stood unconquered, and was still a democracy. That stands even now as a memorable double triumph. As historian Williamson Murray concluded, "Through Churchill's stewardship, Britain had survived with her values largely intact, a monumental achievement considering her situation in June 1940."

CHAPTER 13

CHURCHILL'S REVENGE

THE WAR MEMOIRS

Wounded and angered by the 1945 election, Churchill, like Orwell, retreated to the countryside. But he did not go to the Inner Hebrides. Instead, he holed up at his country house in the soft green hills south of London to write his account of the war. Over the next eight years, he and his team of researchers and writers would produce a barrage of 1.9 million words, printed on 4,823 pages in six volumes. In them he would claim center stage in the greatest conflict the world has ever endured. And unlike so many political memoirists, he would give full rein to his powerful emotions, which is one reason the books were readable—and are still read.

That is not to say that they are entirely accurate. In fact, whole books have been written detailing his errors, exaggerations, and omissions. Yet the memoirs remain compelling for several reasons. They are, foremost, the only account of World War II by one of its major leaders. In them, Churchill takes a stance reminiscent of an ancient Greek king relating his own central role in a Homeric war. "I was now well content with the main decisions which the Admiralty were taking," he recalls at one point,

avoiding *lèse-majesté* only by using the first person singular. He sometimes employed that regal voice during the war, writing once to the Royal
Navy, "I am much disquieted by these facts" about British losses to
U-boat attacks. His prose even acquires a Homeric tinge on occasion, as
when he describes General Bedell Smith, Eisenhower's chief of staff,
arriving "quick-winged from Eisenhower's headquarters."

But there is a major tension between the events of the war and his account of them. Churchill's performance during the war was triumphant,
and he was, of course, ultimately victorious. Yet when he sat down to
write his memoirs, it was with the growing realization that Britain was no
longer an empire, and probably not even a great power. It was tired, relatively poor, and being battered in economic competition. Its best hope lay
in the unpalatable role of taking a backseat to the pole-sitting parvenus,
clumsy politicians, and overweening generals of the nouveau riche United
States, and trying to guide them toward the path of wisdom.

VOLUME I: THE GATHERING STORM

Historians may challenge the accuracy of the memoirs, and they should.
It is important to know, for example, that Churchill had no memory of
having met Franklin Roosevelt at a London dinner in 1918, but claims in
The Gathering Storm that at that meeting, "I had been struck by his mag-
nificent presence." (FDR had quite a different memory, once buttering up
Joe Kennedy by telling him that he, Roosevelt, had "always disliked him
[Churchill] since the time I went to England in 1918. He acted like a
stinker at a dinner I attended, lording it all over us.")

The Churchill memoirs may not be traditional history, but they are
memorable reading. Especially in the earlier volumes, Churchill's distinctive voice cuts through the fog of war. He can compress an image into a
small phrase, as when he refers to "the scaly wings" of defeat that flapped
over Germany in the interwar period. He writes with a great sense of

rhythm, sometimes so much so that his prose can have the reassuring tone of an adult reading aloud to a loved child: "The Rhine, the broad, deep, swift-flowing Rhine, once held and fortified by the French Army, would be a barrier and shield behind which France could dwell and breathe for generations. Very different were the sentiments and views of the English-speaking world." His stylistic errors are those of excess. He floridly writes that during the 1930s, the British were content with "frothing pious platitudes while foemen forge[d] their arms." He never deploys one word where two will provide some mellifluous alliteration, writing, for example, that the prewar era provided "a picture of British fatuity and fecklessness."

But most of the time, Churchill's writing hand is sure and solid, especially in the first and most personal of the six volumes. Hitler's rise was aided by "the truculent and transient figure of the commercial magnate, [Alfred] Hugenberg." The Germany of the 1930s would be "led by a handful of triumphant desperadoes."

He takes his time in unrolling the scroll of his saga. Where a formal historian might simply state that German industry went on a war footing in 1936, Churchill paints the picture, writing: "The German munition plants were working at high pressure. The wheels revolved and the hammers descended day and night in Germany, making its whole industry an arsenal and welding all its population into one disciplined war machine."

He sketches his principal figures well. As prime minister, Neville Chamberlain "was alert, business-like, opinionated, and self-confident in a very high degree. . . . His all-pervading hope was to go down to history as the Great Peacemaker; and for this he was prepared to strive continually in the teeth of facts, and face great risks for himself and his country." Adolf Hitler, who shattered those ambitions, is depicted as "the demon-genius sprung from the abyss of poverty, inflamed by defeat, devoured by hatred and revenge, and convulsed by his design to make the German race master of Europe or maybe the world."

He has a feel for description, injecting it with a powerful physicality.

He does not simply write that for the first time since the age of William the Conqueror, England faced invasion. Rather, he writes, "It was nearly a thousand years since Britain had seen the fires of a foreign camp on English soil."

He depicts the British UXB squads—soldiers specializing in climbing into holes to defuse unexploded German bombs—as wearing faces different from those of other men. "They were gaunt, they were haggard, their faces had a bluish look, with bright gleaming eyes and exceptional compression of the lips. . . . In writing about our hard times, we are apt to overuse the word 'grim.' It should have been reserved for the U.X.B. disposal squads."

As a writer, Churchill also had an advantage that few historians can hope to possess. That is, he knew in his bones what events had felt like, and so can bring his reader into the room. For example, there is his account, previously discussed in chapter 4, of his lunch in 1937 with von Ribbentrop, then the German ambassador in London. He concludes his recollection of the man by recalling that he subsequently attended one other lunch with the diplomat. That time was, he drily observes, "the last time I saw Herr von Ribbentrop before he was hanged."

Also unlike historians, he often writes emotionally, especially in the first two volumes, the best of the six. The Polish participation in the Nazi dismembering of Czechoslovakia in 1939—a shameful role now largely forgotten—he calls a "hyena" act.

VOLUME II: THEIR FINEST HOUR

The seven months of 1940 in which he was prime minister, from May of that year on, were the climax of Winston Churchill's life, as we've seen. The first volume is probably better written, but the story in the second is equally compelling, and even more intense. Arguably, during 1940, Churchill saved Britain. Indisputably, he led the effort to halt Nazi domination of Europe. It was a time when Germany was allied with Italy and Japan and at peace with Russia. "Nothing surpasses 1940," he writes in this volume. He titled it *Their Finest Hour,* but, of course, it also was his.

Though he never says it in so many words, he was shocked almost speechless by the fall of France, and was especially appalled by the behavior of its leaders. Yet the worst was still to come. "The Battle of France was lost," he writes at the end of this volume. "The Battle of Britain was won. The Battle of the Atlantic had now to be fought." In one of the more memorable expressions of personal emotion in the memoirs, he states, "The only thing that ever really frightened me during the war was the U-boat peril"—that transatlantic shipping might be wiped out by German submarines, bringing Britain to its knees by starving it of food, energy, and munitions. His fear was most acute when, in one convoy from Canada of thirty-four ships late in 1940, a full twenty were sent to the bottom.

VOLUME III: THE GRAND ALLIANCE AND VOLUME IV: THE HINGE OF FATE

After the first two installments, the writing becomes less personal and more bureaucratic. The production of the war memoirs was a team effort in which Churchill oversaw a collaborative process. His underlings gathered documents, took his dictation, and drafted sections for him. The result was a work in which he is part author, part subject, part coach, and part editor. David Reynolds, a Cambridge historian who wrote a fine book on how the memoirs were produced, concluded that Churchill "was running a large, well-funded research group on par with the barons of modern science. He did not do all the work personally, but he set its parameters, guided its direction, and sustained its momentum."

As a result of this process, the memoirs gradually acquire the feel of semiofficialness to them, of obligatory recitation and committee drafting, such as, "South of the British sector the French XIXth Corps occupied the Djebel Fkirine, while in the north the U.S. IId Corps, attacking on the 23rd, made steady progress toward Mateur." This is, of course, to be expected in a work of more than four thousand pages.

Sometimes the writing team wandered into simple sloppiness. The chapter on the early American victories in the Pacific concludes with a salute to the U.S. Navy and Air Force—but the latter service isn't mentioned in that chapter. On one page he gives the date of his second speech to Congress as May 19, 1943. Six paragraphs later, he lists it as May 20.

Some of the slippage is to be expected. There is a psychological power to his narrative of the first years of the war that cannot be sustained. In 1940, Churchill's back had been to the wall. He had been working to keep Britain alive and for his own survival. He had staved off naysayers and pushed the British war machine into high gear. In the later years of the war, from 1942 on, he simply had to keep that machine working, and also to try to steer the Americans in the directions he considered best.

That said, some of the mistakes made by the memoir-writing factory were dreadful. Most egregiously, chapter XIV of volume IV provides a brisk account of the key "American Naval Victories." It is fine history, but it was not truly Churchill's. Thus the chapter heading carries a peculiar punctuation mark: "Chapter XIV. American Naval Victories*." That asterisk has to do not with the nature of those victories in the Pacific in 1943, but with the provenance of Churchill's account of them. "Very little of 'American Naval Victories' was Churchill's work," notes Reynolds. "He rewrote the opening and sharpened some phrases but otherwise relied on the draft from Gordon Allen, who in turn had largely paraphrased volume 4 of Samuel Eliot Morison's history of U.S. naval operations in World War II." This proved troublesome because Morison's naval history, though written with official cooperation, was not a government publication, and was, in fact, under copyright, unlike the U.S. Army's history of the war, which was official and thus carried no copyright.

Morison himself stumbled across this borrowing. Before Churchill's chapter appeared in book form, it was excerpted in the *New York Times.* Reading the newspaper in October 1950, Morison was astonished to find his own thoughts and conclusions published under Churchill's name. Morison had, for example, written: "The Battle of Coral Sea will be ever memorable as the first purely carrier-against-carrier naval battle in which all losses were inflicted by air action and no ship on either side sighted a surface enemy." Churchill's account stated of Coral Sea: "Nothing like it ever had been seen before. It was the first battle at sea in which surface ships never exchanged a shot."

Morison called his lawyer, who in turn contacted Churchill's American publishers. The result of their exchange was that odd asterisk at the top of that chapter, hastily added as a veiled acknowledgment of debt. At the bottom of the page, the reader is instructed to "*See S.E. Morison, *Coral Sea, Midway, and Submarine Actions.*" A sentence also was added to the acknowledgments of the book, in which Churchill noted, "I wish to acknowledge my debt to Captain Samuel Eliot Morison, U.S.N.R., whose books on naval operations give a clear presentation of the actions of the United States Fleet." This allusion to the work of another historian was, Reynolds adds, "unique in Churchill's volumes, but it was essential to head off an embarrassing charge of plagiarism." Morison graciously let the matter end there, never making it public.

In one last hurrah, at the end of volume III, Churchill remembers himself triumphantly addressing three thousand British and American troops in the immense Roman amphitheater in Carthage, near Tunis. "The whole audience clapped and cheered as doubtless their predecessors of two thousand years ago had done as they watched gladiatorial combat."

VOLUME V: CLOSING THE RING AND VOLUME VI: TRIUMPH AND TRAGEDY

Not all war leaders are astute analysts of their wars. They know what they did but not necessarily why things happened, or how the pieces of the war came together. Churchill, by contrast, was very good at this task, on the grandest scale. He was fascinated by how war works, and probably more than any other leader of the twentieth century he understood the mysterious art of creating what he calls in volume V "a general harmony of war effort by making everything fit together."

That trait animates Churchill's account of the massive, complex preparations for D-Day, which provides the climax to the war in the West, and so to his memoirs. It is the last time in the books that his heart really seems to be in his narrative. Even then, the emotional intensity is only a fraction of that of 1939–41, reflecting again that by the time of the run-up to D-Day, the Americans were dominant.

The questions in early 1944 ranged from the strategic (How to handle de Gaulle?) to the operational (How to prevent German U-boats from sinking the cross-channel troop convoys?) to the personal (Would Churchill and King George travel to witness the Allied entry?). As he told the House of Commons on the day of the landings, "This vast operation is undoubtedly the most complicated and difficult that has ever occurred. It involves tides, wind, waves, visibility, both from the air and the sea standpoint, and the combined employment of land, air and sea forces in the highest degree of intimacy and in contact with conditions which could not and cannot be fully foreseen."

The power of the books then falls off considerably. In mid-1950, Malcolm Muggeridge, then overseeing the serialization of Churchill's fifth volume in the *Daily Telegraph,* went out to Churchill's country house, Chartwell, to discuss some minor production problems. He found the great man uneasy. Muggeridge wrote in his diary that he quickly came to understand the much greater underlying difficulty:

> What has happened about his Memoirs, and why he was so troubled, is that in truth he has lost interest in them and has simply been stringing together masses of documents which he had written in the war. The Americans, who have paid a huge sum of money for the serial and book rights, have protested. In the course of conversation about them it slipped out that certain chapters had not been written by him at all, and I suspect he is doing extremely little.

In the sixth volume, covering the end of the war in Europe, but not the end in the Pacific, there is an unusual shift: Churchill becomes less the author and more the subject. Much of this last volume was drafted by the team that had supported him for years in producing the memoirs. By the time it was being finished, he was preoccupied again, taking a mediocre second turn as prime minister, starting in October 1951. On top of that, while in office, he suffered a minor stroke in February 1952 and a fairly severe one in June 1953.

What would emerge as volume VI "was still Churchill's book," concludes Reynolds, the historian of the memoirs. "He may not have written most of the words, but he decisively set its tone and determined when—and even whether—it would be published."

In particular, Churchill needed to tread more carefully in his sharp critique of General Eisenhower's handling of the end of the war in Europe, because, by the time the book appeared, Ike had become president. Churchill told an aide that he had to omit part of what he wrote: "He could no longer tell in full the story of how the United States, to please the Russians, gave away vast tracts of territory they had occupied and how suspicious they were of his pleas for caution." The result is not a bad book, but one quite different from its five predecessors. It relies more on contemporary documents, using brief running commentary to string them together. Often the official missives are separated by just a sentence, such as "I telegraphed to Stalin on the same day" or "On the same day came the following."

Aside from the excitement of the run-up to D-Day, the tone of the volume is increasingly bleak. The biggest surprise of this final book is its pervasive sadness. Paradoxically, the coming of victory was for Churchill "a most unhappy time." Churchill had seen the future, and feared it.

The truth of the matter is that Churchill was off his game at the end of the war and after. The plain facts of British decline were becoming harder to ignore. Churchill's oratory of this period "seemed in danger of degenerating into mere windy bombast," writes Simon Schama.

Yet as a whole, the six volumes of the memoirs succeeded brilliantly. They appeared roughly annually from 1948 to 1953–54, with the last appearing in the U.S. five months before the British edition appeared in April 1954. By the time the last one was published, Churchill had succeeded in putting his view of the war front and center, and in putting himself in the center of that view. No one can ever consider the history of World War II without referring to Churchill's account.

CHAPTER 14

ORWELL IN TRIUMPH AND DECLINE

1945–1950

L ike Churchill, Orwell would emerge from the war a partially broken man. Orwell's deterioration would prove more evident than Churchill's, and more devastating. The writer would grow increasingly ill as he labored on his last book, which would prove his most durable.

What's more, the tubercular socialist would grow even more pessimistic than the aging former prime minister. Churchill spent the postwar years looking back in triumph. Orwell at the same time looked forward in horror.

"Spring is here, even in London N.1, and they can't stop you from enjoying it," he wrote in April 1946. "The atom bombs are piling up in the factories, the police are prowling through the cities, the lies are streaming from the loudspeakers, but the earth is still going round the sun, and neither the dictators, nor the bureaucrats, deeply as they disapprove of the process, are able to prevent it." He liked this "unofficial" aspect of nature.

Orwell began thinking about his last book as World War II ground to a close. In 1946, as he began writing it, London was "a battered, grey and tired-looking place," wrote his friend Tosco Fyvel. Bread rationing had been avoided in Britain throughout the war, but was imposed in 1946 in order to help stave off starvation in Europe, especially in Germany. In May of that year, he recorded:

> For anyone outside the armed forces, life since the armistice has been physically as unpleasant as it was during the war, perhaps more so, because the effects of certain shortages are cumulative. The clothing shortage, for instance, becomes less and less tolerable as our clothes become more and more completely worn out, and during last winter the fuel situation was worse than it had been at any time during the war.

Animal Farm had been a political play on the tradition of fables. Orwell's next work of fiction would be a political twist on another genre—the horror story. His monster was not a product born of nineteenth-century science, as was Frankenstein, or of twentieth-century weaponry, as would be Godzilla, but rather of twentieth-century politics, which produced the all-intrusive state, sometimes vicious but almost always more clumsy than clever.

Orwell, like Churchill, would spend the immediate postwar period warning of the great dangers that still existed despite the defeat of the Nazis. Churchill spoke in his Iron Curtain speech in March 1946 of a world in which "the power of the State is exercised without restraint, either by dictators or by compact oligarchies operating through a privileged party and a political police." He believed that "a shadow has fallen upon the scenes so lately lighted by the Allied victory. . . . From Stettin in the Baltic to Trieste in the Adriatic, an iron curtain has descended across the Continent."

Orwell also saw that curtain's shadow lengthening westward. He had seen the future and he wanted to warn that it did not work, at least for people like him who cherished individual privacy and freedom of speech. He had been thinking on the subject of oppression in postwar Europe for several years, warning in 1941, "This is the age of the totalitarian state, which does not and probably cannot allow the individual any freedom whatever. When one mentions totalitarianism one thinks immediately of Germany, Russia, Italy, but I think one must face the risk that this phenomenon is going to be world-wide." Not only would the all-powerful state forbid people to express certain thoughts, he worried, it would take an additional step and tell them what to think.

Fearing distraction, and perhaps becoming more of an introvert, Orwell stayed as much as possible on the island of Jura, to try to finish the book. It was "just the most remote place you could find almost in the British isles," said his friend David Astor, who found him the house. "I never imagined that he'd stay there. I only suggested that he go there for a short holiday because he obviously needed a holiday." He added that "for a person in delicate health it was a crazy place to go."

On the cold, storm-raked island where Orwell took refuge, the nearest telephone was twenty-seven miles to the south, over a bad road that in parts was not much better than a moorland track. On July 21, 1946, which should be high summer, it was "cold enough to make one want a fire in every room." The following January, the wind was "so violent that it was difficult to stay on one's feet."

He had not moved there to entertain people, as one household visitor learned. "He was sort of in a self-destructive mood and used to grumble. He had this wound in this throat [from being shot in Spain] which used to whistle, and there was this dismal whistling sound as he went about, and this droopy moustache. And instead of this very lively and entertaining mind, there was this miserable, hostile old bugger that we just had to put up with." Living was hand to mouth, not for lack of money, but because of rationing. He asked a friend coming from London for a visit to bring flour. "We are nearly always short of bread and flour here since the rationing," he explained.

Orwell's reckless streak still surfaced on occasion. In August 1947, he decided, despite his continuing poor health, to spend another winter on Jura. "Part of the winter may be pretty bleak and one is sometimes cut off from the mainland for a week or two, but it doesn't matter so long as you have flour in hand to make scones," he assured a friend.

The same month, he took his son and some visitors, including his nephew Henry Dakin, on a motorboat excursion that led them through the famous Corryvreckan whirlpools at the northern end of the island. Orwell airily reassured his guests that he had read up on the dangers of this maelstrom, one of the largest in European waters. He had badly underestimated the power of the sea. "We were flung this way and that way," recalled Dakin. "There was a cracking noise, and the engine came straight off its mountings and disappeared into the sea." They rowed to a cliff, only to have the boat overturn as Dakin pulled it up. The little group sat on a rocky island, soaked and disconsolate, except for Orwell, who went off to explore and study the puffin population. Two hours later, they were picked up by a passing lobster boat. The next day, Orwell went fishing in two nearby lochs and caught twelve trout.

For most of his time on Jura, Orwell was a gravely ill man. He told his landlord, a friend, that he hoped he would be able to finish writing the book before he died. In May 1947, he wrote in a note to his publisher, "I have made a fairly good start on the book and I think I must have written nearly a third of the rough draft. I have not got as far as I had hoped to do by this time, because I have really been in most wretched health this year since about January (my chest as usual) and can't quite shake it off." He never really did, as is shown by some of his diary entries over the next two years:

—September 5, 1947: "Unwell (chest), hardly went outside."
—October 13, 1947: "Unwell, did not go out."
—September 16, 1948: "Very unwell, temperature about 101 each evening."

—October 13, 1948: "Pain in side very bad. Sea calm."

—For December 19, 1948, there is a notation entered not long after he finished revising the book. After a lapse of twelve days he wrote in it, "Have not been well enough to enter up diary."

Two weeks later he was taken to a sanatorium for TB victims, and eventually was moved to a London hospital, where his doctor was Andrew Morland, who also had treated D. H. Lawrence. He lay slowly dying as *1984* went to press. It would be his last book, published in June 1949, the same month that *Their Finest Hour,* the second volume of Churchill's memoirs, appeared in Britain. Time was running out on Orwell, who had less than seven months to live.

1984

The hero of *1984* is a miserable middle-aged Englishman named Winston Smith. He resides in an apartment building, Victory Mansions, that resembles the one Orwell lived in during World War II, just off Abbey Road. About three blocks to the southwest of Orwell's high-rise was the small two-story recording studio that in the 1960s would be made famous by the Beatles making their records there, starting in 1963, and eventually naming one of their albums for it.

The novel begins with a matter-of-fact but disturbing statement: "It was a bright cold day in April, and the clocks were striking thirteen." That is, by the end of the sentence, the reader is being taken into a world that is different, and probably gone very wrong. Orwell being Orwell, the second paragraph begins with the sentence, "The hallway smelt of boiled cabbage and old rag mats." The ominous sense is then confirmed at the end of that paragraph, when the hero—identified twice, each time as "Winston"—passes posters captioned "BIG BROTHER IS WATCHING YOU," emphatically capitalized in the text.

By the end of the book's first page, it is clear that the author knows what he wants to say and how to say it. We are introduced to a world in which objective reality does not exist, or at least is deemed to be illegal by the all-seeing state. There is universal surveillance, conducted by "the Thought Police" using "telescreens" that simultaneously transmit and receive, and are delicate enough to sense an accelerating heartbeat. "It was even conceivable that they watched everybody all the time," Orwell writes, foreseeing today's electronically omniscient state. Winston gazes out the window of his apartment and sees, a kilometer away, looming on the building of the Ministry of Truth, the three slogans of the Party:

WAR IS PEACE
FREEDOM IS SLAVERY
IGNORANCE IS STRENGTH

The author goes on to describe the other government departments: the Ministry of Peace, "which concerned itself with war," the Ministry of Plenty, and the Ministry of Love, responsible for police functions. This last one "was the really frightening one. There were no windows in it at all." These are the arms of the monster in Orwell's modern horror story.

Despite his name, the character of Winston has far more in common with his creator than he did with Churchill. Like Orwell, Winston smokes cigarettes made with cheap, foul tobacco, and at about age forty wheezes when he bends over to pick up something. And like Orwell, he remembers his father "vaguely." Of course, the author being Orwell, much of the unpleasantness of the world presented in the book is conveyed through odor. Winston's workplace cafeteria reeks of "a sourish, composite smell of bad gin and bad coffee and metallic stew and dirty clothes."

For Winston, as for the author, the most significant act in life is not to speak out or to be published, but simply to observe accurately the world around him. Collecting the facts is a revolutionary act. Insisting on the right to do so is perhaps the most subversive action possible. Underscoring the connection, Winston does this and then writes emphatically in his diary, "DOWN WITH BIG BROTHER." He is especially provoked by the Party's insistence that only it could determine what was real and what was not. "The Party told you to reject the evidence of your eyes and ears," he thinks at one point. "It was their final, most essential command." But Winston, dangerously, is beginning to think for himself, writing in his diary, "Freedom is the freedom to say that two plus two make four. If that is granted, all else follows."

Winston does not know it, and Orwell does not say so, but he is clearly reasoning in the tradition of that most British of philosophies, the empiricism of John Locke and David Hume. Most specifically, the totalitarian state has driven him to begin thinking like John Stuart Mill, the intellectual heir to Locke and Hume.

One of Mill's best-known works, *On Liberty*, published in 1859, is a meditation on how individual freedom might be maintained as the power of the state grows. That prescient essay begins with Mill stating that his subject is "the nature and limits of the power which can be legitimately exercised by society over the individual." This, he continues, is "a question seldom stated, and hardly ever discussed in general terms, but which . . . is likely soon to make itself recognised as the vital question of the future." At the very core of liberty is the domain of the individual, "the inward domain of consciousness . . . liberty of conscience . . . liberty of thought and feeling."

In *1984,* Mill's question has indeed become vital. The interior realm is under attack by the state. Orwell makes the philosophical connection explicit later in the novel, writing that the society of Big Brother has failed to achieve gains in productivity because "scientific and technical progress depended on the empirical habit of thought, which could not survive in a strictly regimented society." A society in which technological progress could coexist with the surveillance state was beyond Orwell's ken.

Winston realizes he is becoming a dissident, likely to be discovered and hunted down by the state. "He was a lonely ghost uttering a truth that nobody would ever hear," Orwell writes. "But so long as he uttered it, in some obscure way the continuity was not broken. It was not by making yourself heard but by staying sane that you carried on the human heritage." In that passage, Orwell presages the dissidents such as Solzhenitsyn, Sakharov, and Amalrik, who in testifying about the facts they perceived, helped bring down the Soviet Union just a few years after the real year 1984. In both worlds—the imaginary one of *1984* and the real Soviet Union—it was a moral victory simply to question the official presentation of truth and posit an alternative by documenting observable reality. The state in both cases knew this and regarded such an act as seditious.

Winston's occupation in the novel is rewriting history. He loathes it, and his rebellion is spurred by his repugnance for the entire enterprise. Early in the book he muses, "If the Party could thrust its hand into the past and say of this or that event, it never happened—that, surely, was more terrifying than mere torture and death." He labors in a cubicle, where his neighbor is a woman whose job is to delete from all records "the names of people who had been vaporized and were therefore considered never to have existed. There was a certain fitness in this, since her own husband had been vaporized a couple of years earlier." He works on a machine called a "speakwrite," a name that might bring to mind the 1980s software for word processing named WordPerfect. At the edge of his desk is the "memory hole," into which documents containing discarded facts are dropped.

The one glimmer of hope Orwell sees is in the proletarians. Winston writes in his diary, "If there is hope, it lies in the proles." This is the theme of the book, especially its first half. Winston mulls the phrase repeatedly, not quite understanding it, thinking of it more as a matter of faith. Orwell never really explains the thought in this book, but he did so in 1942 in an essay in which he meditated on some "visions of a totalitarian future." In it, he explained why he thought the working class would be most resistant to an intrusive right-wing state:

> To win over the working class permanently, the Fascists would have to raise the general standard of living, which they are unable and probably unwilling to do. The struggle of the working class is like the growth of a plant. The plant is blind and stupid, but it knows enough to keep pushing upward towards the light, and it will do this in the face of endless discouragements.

Orwell depicts the proletarians as essentially uncontrollable. The state does not try to control them as much as it simply distracts them. "Heavy physical work, the care of home and children, petty quarrels with neighbours, films, football, beer, and, above all, gambling, filled up the horizon of minds," Winston thinks. "They were beneath suspicion." But they have retained human feeling, loyal neither to party nor country, but "to one another." This seems to be the essence of the hope Winston and his creator place upon them. But neither of them seems to know how this might lead them to the source of escape from the nightmare world of *1984*. Thomas Pynchon, a modern novelist sympathetic to Orwell, noted, "Winston Smith doesn't seem to know any proles himself."

The second half of the book is dominated by Winston's clumsy love affair with a woman named Julia. Orwell was never very adept at writing about women in general and about sex in particular. At times he seems to consider sexual intercourse an act that men perform and to which women merely submit. Winston and Julia first start to make love after entering a secluded grove during a walk in the countryside. "He had pulled her down on the ground, she was utterly unresisting, he could do what he liked with her," he writes. Smith falters, but rejuvenates after Julia tells him how much she enjoys sex.

For the doomed lovers, sexual intercourse is the ultimate form of rebellion against the state. "Their embrace had been a battle, the climax a victory. It was a blow struck against the Party. It was a political act." At first this may seem an early form of hippie-ism, but it may be more than that. Orwell is correct that there is something chaste, and chastening, about totalitarian states. Consider the harsh public image of Mao Zedong's wife, or, more recently, the sexualized rebellion of the Russian punk rock band Pussy Riot against Vladimir Putin's oligarchical state. Even so, Orwell manages to make it awkward. Winston later tells Julia, apparently as a compliment, "You're only a rebel from the waist downwards."

Of course, the police have been watching them. The two are arrested and imprisoned without being formally charged or tried before a jury of their peers.

As it happens, Orwell and Churchill held precisely the same view of the singular importance of not holding people without charging them. In fact, Churchill stated in an official memorandum in November 1942:

> The power of the Executive to cast a man into prison without formulating any charge known to the law, and particularly to deny him judgment by his peers for an indefinite period, is in the highest degree odious, and it is the foundation of all totalitarian Governments, whether Nazi or Communist. . . . Nothing can be more abhorrent to democracy than to imprison a person or keep him in prison because he is unpopular. This is really the test of a civilization.

Churchill made that succinct statement in instructing his subordinates to release the British fascist leader Oswald Mosley, who had been held since 1940, when there was a danger that if the Germans invaded, he would lead collaborators. Orwell had supported Churchill in both instances. "In 1940 it was a perfectly proper action to intern Mosley, and in my opinion it would have been quite proper to shoot him if the Germans had set foot in Britain. When it is a question of national existence, no government can stand on the letter of the law." But, he added, by 1943, Mosley was no longer a threat, merely "a ridiculous failed politician with varicose veins. To continue imprisoning him without trial was an infringement of every principle we are supposedly fighting for."

While in prison both Winston and Julia are broken by torture and forced to inform on each other. Winston's lead torturer is named O'Brien. The meaning of that name, if there is one, is not made clear. It is doubtful that Orwell knew it, but Hugh O'Donnell, the British Communist Party's representative to Spain—and someone known there by Orwell— was code-named "O'Brien" by the Soviet apparatus in the country. O'Brien tells Winston, a bit contemptuously, "You believe reality is something objective, eternal, existing in its own right. You also believe that the nature of reality is self-evident. . . . But I tell you, Winston, that reality is not external. . . . Whatever the Party holds to be truth *is* truth. It is impossible to see reality except by looking through the eyes of the Party."

The story ends with the two broken lovers meeting later, equally desolated. They confess to each other their betrayals, and then part. No hope is offered.

Published in June 1949, the book was successful in England, but had its greatest impact elsewhere. It was a "sensation" in Europe, recalled its publisher, Fredric Warburg. In the Europe of the day, Warburg said, "it was a political act of enormous importance. Because you must remember that after the war Russia, which had done so much to win it, was enormously powerful and in some ways admired, and this was—like *Animal Farm* but in a much different way—the most powerful anti-Soviet communism tract that you could find anywhere. And the Europeans treated it as such." It went on to sell millions, and has been celebrated as "probably the definitive novel of the 20th century."

As the book rose, Orwell declined. He was done for, and he knew it. "I have been very poorly, spitting up quantities of blood," he reported to his friend Richard Rees early in 1949. A few weeks later, he added, in another note to Rees, "I still can't do any work. Some days I take pen & paper and try to write a few lines, but it's impossible."

He was fading. Like Churchill in the final two volumes of his memoirs, Orwell's writing during and after *1984* begins to tire. His prose decreases in energy and his arguments become less trenchant. In mid-1948, he wrestled with the future of socialism in this fashion:

> Even if we squeeze the rich out of existence, the mass of people must either consume less or produce more. Or am I exaggerating the mess we are in? I may be, and I should be glad to find myself mistaken. But the point I wish to make is that this question, among people who are faithful to left ideology, cannot be genuinely discussed.

This is a passage that would not have been produced by a healthier Orwell, the man who just two years earlier had written "Politics and the English Language."

Orwell spent most of the last two years of his life hospitalized, sliding toward death. As he lay in his bed, he overheard the voices of unseen aristocratic visitors (he calls them "upper class"). He described them with devastating precision:

> And what voices! A sort of over-fedness, a fatuous self-confidence, a constant bah-bahing of laughter about nothing, above all a sort of heaviness & richness combined with a fundamental ill-will—people

who, one instinctively feels, without even being able to see them, are the enemies of anything intelligent or sensitive or beautiful.

But remember that this was also Eton-educated Orwell's own accent, and he was too honest a writer to ignore that, so he ended the diary note by including himself in the condemnation: "No wonder everyone hates us so."

His diaries end with that entry, made on April 17, 1949.

In September of that year, Malcolm Muggeridge, who himself had run afoul of the British left by honestly reporting on the famine in Ukraine in 1933, when the *New York Times* famously did not, went to visit Orwell in his London hospital. He wrote in his diary that night that Orwell "looks inconceivably wasted, and has, I should say, the appearance of someone who hasn't very long to live—a queer sort of clarity in his expression and elongation of his features."

The last article George Orwell would ever complete and publish was a review of the second volume of Churchill's war memoirs, *Their Finest Hour.* He was appreciative of the politician, despite the vast difference in their political views:

The political reminiscences which he has published from time to time have always been a great deal above average, in frankness as well as in literary quality. Churchill is among other things a journalist, with a real if not very discriminating feeling for literature, and he also has a restless, enquiring mind, interested in both concrete facts and in the analysis of motives, sometimes including his own motives. In general, Churchill's writings are more like those of a human being than of a public figure.

Coming from Orwell, this was high praise.

Orwell went on to review Churchill's performance in 1940. Churchill's achievement was to realize around the time of Dunkirk that just because France was beaten, it did not follow that Britain was as well. But Orwell faults Churchill for not grasping that the Soviets "hate Socialists more than they hate Conservatives," or that Mussolini's fascism "must of its nature be hostile to Britain."

Almost Orwell's last published words were these:

However much one may disagree with him [Churchill], however thankful one may be that he and his party did not win the 1945 election, one has to admire in him not only his courage but also a certain largeness and geniality which comes out even in formal memoirs of this type. . . .

After that review, and a handful of letters, he went silent.

On October 13, 1949, Orwell married Sonia Brownell, a vivacious member of the London literary scene who, like him, had been born in British India. She had turned him down the first time he proposed, but later accepted. "No one was under any illusion that she loved George," comments one of his biographers. A friend of Orwell's who knew both of his wives recalled that "Sonia was smart, hard-drinking, amusing, dangerous, quick-tempered—all the things Eileen was not." Another acquaintance remembered Sonia as "basically unbelievably unhappy."

There are no entries in Orwell's diary about Sonia, for he had stopped writing in it about six months earlier. Orwell sat up in bed for the ceremony, but was unable to stand. The best man at the macabre deathbed wedding was David Astor. For the ceremony, Orwell wore a mauve velvet smoking jacket over his pajamas.

Orwell spent much of the fall in bed reading Dante's *Divine Comedy*. On November 14, Muggeridge found that Orwell "has started losing weight again, and looked altogether pretty wretched." His fishing rods stood in the corner of the room, but he would never again use them.

ORWELL AND AMERICA

During one of Muggeridge's hospital visits, Orwell told him that he had five books in mind that he wanted to write. One possibility was a study of anti-British feeling in America. Orwell's views almost certainly would have been changed by traveling to the United States, but we cannot know just how. He already had begun reconsidering his distaste for twentieth-century America. "To be anti-American nowadays is to shout with the mob," he wrote about two years after the end of the war, in an essay that was not published at the time. But, he continued, if the members of the mob had to choose between Russia and America, "in spite of all the fashionable chatter of the moment, everyone knows in his heart that we should choose America."

Had Orwell been able to see the United States, he probably would have been repelled by much of it—the gargantuan size, and what he would have seen as the conspicuous consumption and swaggering and smugness. Most of all, he would have been alienated by America's determined, self-centered individualism. What he liked most about England was its strong sense of private community. In "The Lion and the Unicorn," he wrote of the English: "All the culture that is most truly native centres around things which even when they are communal are not official—the pub, the football match, the back garden, the fireside and the 'nice cup of tea.'"

The American self-image is far less collective than that. It is more about the lone individual. This begins as *The Deerslayer* and *The Virginian,* and becomes variants of gunslingers, such as *The Lone Ranger.* Every B-grade Western of the 1940s and 1950s seems to begin or end with a loner riding into or out of town. The image lives on as the motorcyclist roaring alone on an empty highway or the mountain climber soloing in the Rockies, the stuff of today's television commercials. Americans, far more than the English, identify with the rebel and the loner, such as Clint Eastwood's High Plains Drifter. A hit song recorded by the pop singer Dion in 1961 reduced this to its simplistic adolescent essence: "Yeah, I'm a wanderer, yeah, a wanderer / I roam around, around, around." In America, this was a role to emulate, not a fate to bemoan.

Had he visited America, Orwell also would have had a chance to see capitalism in a different, more robust and adaptive form.

But it clearly was not to be. Orwell was sinking. On December 21, Muggeridge wrote in his diary, "He looks quite shrunken now and somehow waxen. Said ruefully that he was having penicillin injections and they found difficulty in finding any meat into which to stick the needle."

On Christmas Day, Muggeridge saw him and recorded that "his face looks almost dead. . . . The stench of death was in the air, like autumn in a garden." In January 19, 1950, after another visit, he wrote in his diary that he doubted he would ever see Orwell alive again. He was right. Orwell died at about 2:30 in the morning of January 21, 1950. He was forty-six years old.

Orwell expired as the era he helped to name, "the Cold War," was getting under way. He had first used the term in a book review in December 1943, again in 1945—two months after the end of World War II—and then a third time in 1946. Muggeridge arranged the funeral. It was held on January 26, and was "a rather melancholy, chilly affair" in an unheated church, Muggeridge noted. Another Orwell friend, Anthony Powell, chose as the text for the funeral sermon the last book of Ecclesiastes. Suitably for the death of an author, at a ceremony organized by other authors, with many more in attendance, that chapter contains the phrase "of making many books there is no end."

Orwell's last desire was again a sign of his abiding pastoralism. He wished to be buried in an English churchyard. Learning of this, his friend

David Astor bought two cemetery plots. One was occupied by Orwell. When Astor's time came in 2001, he occupied the second. Buried nearby is Herbert Asquith, father of Churchill's close friend Violet (Asquith) Bonham Carter.

Churchill, reading *1984* for the second time, in February 1953, told his doctor, "It is a very remarkable book."

CHAPTER 15

CHURCHILL'S PREMATURE AFTERLIFE

1950–1965

In the year after Orwell's death, Churchill made one of the worst and saddest mistakes of his life: He took a second turn as prime minister. One can only conclude that he felt the need to avenge the stinging electoral loss of July 1945. That had been the first time he had stood for election as prime minister—in 1940, he had achieved office through appointment—and he had been rejected, loudly and publicly.

Historians tend to avert their eyes from his second time at the top, which began in October 1951. He was too old, he had been weakened by strokes and by a mild heart attack. Nor was he particularly interested in or adept at the two major tasks facing him—rebuilding the British economy at home and reducing its foreign policy to better fit the nation's diminished postwar status. If the 1930s were his wilderness years, the 1950s were his befuddled years.

As a peacetime prime minister, he also would miss the simplicity of his mission in World War II, to simply survive and then prevail over the Germans. Now there was no longer a Hitler to face. Churchill was, like his father, a natural oppositionist. "It is impossible to re-read the details of Churchill's life as Prime Minister of this second government without feeling that he was gloriously unfit for office," comments Roy Jenkins, generally quite understanding of Churchill's political moves. In April 1955, even Churchill, further weakened by a series of strokes, had to admit that it was time to step down.

And so, out of office, Churchill drifted away into his indulgences. Two years after he left the premiership, Evelyn Waugh spotted him in a Monte Carlo restaurant "gorging vast quantities of rich food." The novelist unkindly described the old man's face, in a letter to Ian Fleming's wife, as "elephant gray and quite expressionless." During the same Monte Carlo trip, Churchill, while waiting outside the casino for his car, was buttonholed by Frank Sinatra, the American singer, who rushed up to him and shook his hand, saying, "I've wanted to do that for twenty years." After the singer departed, a puzzled Churchill inquired of an assistant, "Who the hell was that?"

Churchill continued to live well: For a single flight across the Atlantic in 1961, his party required, over and above the usual first-class amenities, seven bottles of wine, two of cognac, and two pounds of Stilton cheese.

Yet even as the man and his mind waned, his reputation grew, supported in part by the worldwide popularity of his war memoirs, with the last one appearing in the United States in November 1953, which was the same year he was awarded the Nobel Prize in Literature.

He followed up that series by finishing and publishing *A History of the English-Speaking Peoples,* which he had started in the 1930s, and then put aside when he became prime minister. That history, sometimes romantic, often ragged, is the literary equivalent of his second term as prime minister. Ronald Lewin, a British historian sympathetic to Churchill, calls it "a fairy tale," adding, "No professional historian would turn to . . . [it] as a text-book." Another sympathetic critic found some of the work "incorrigibly amateurish." Even more than the World War II memoirs, these four volumes were a team effort, but it was a team overseen by a man who had outlived his powers.

In the late 1950s, as Churchill declined mentally and physically, several of his children also began to deteriorate. Two of them would predecease him: Marigold, the fourth child, had died in 1921 of a septic infection. Diana, the oldest, committed suicide in 1963 with an overdose of barbiturates. Randolph, the second child, having inherited all his father's vices and few of his virtues, ran six times for Parliament, losing every time he had an opponent. (He served from 1940 to 1945 after running unopposed under a wartime agreement between the parties.) After his second marriage failed, he characteristically dismissed that wife as "a paltry little middle-class bitch always anxious to please and failing owing to her dismal manners." When he went through a cancer scare and had a benign tumor removed, his sometime friend Evelyn Waugh remarked that it was typical of modern science to find the only part of him that was not malignant and remove it. Randolph was an alcoholic for most of his adult life, and would die just three years after Winston. (Waugh, by then drug addled, would precede him, dying in April 1966, just fifteen months after Churchill.)

The third child, Sarah, a frustrated actress, went through three ill-considered marriages and followed her brother into alcoholic decline. The fifth and last child, Mary, is the only one seen as having had a happy life. This record suggests that Churchill had severe shortcomings as a father. On the other hand, he had little example to go by in his own life.

In the public world, Churchill's reputation suffered a major blow in the late 1950s as the counter-battery fire of dissenting books about him began to appear, provoked in part by his own memoirs. Most notable was the publication in 1957 of the redacted memoirs of Field Marshal Alan Brooke. Next to surface were the die-hard imperialists who claimed that Churchill had sold out Britain. "Churchill's tragedy was his mixed blood," charged R. W. Thompson, a journalist and historian allied with the military theorist Basil Liddell Hart. "His English father and American mother were responsible for the ominous split in his loyalties," he wrote.

More recently, a small band of academics has surfaced with revisionist takes on Churchill carrying lurid titles such as *Churchill Unmasked.* But they appear to have little impact on the larger public, or even on more strategically minded scholars such as Eliot Cohen. Essentially these books consist of asking the reader to forget about the forest of Churchill's life and instead focus on a few trees that a given writer believes deserve more attention.

Today Churchill stands as a kind of folk figure, a fount of wisdom, the international equivalent of Yogi Berra, the New York Yankees baseball player almost as noted for the statements misattributed to him (such as: "Nobody goes there anymore. It's too crowded.") as for those he actually made. The false quotations have become so abundant that the Churchill Centre has on its Web site a section of quotes commonly attributed to the man that, in fact, he never uttered. For example, there is the famous story that Lady Astor said to him that if she were married to him, she would put poison in his coffee, and that he replied that if he were married to her, he would drink it. This exchange was determined actually to have its origin in a joke published in an American newspaper in 1900.

One quotation has been persistently misattributed to both Churchill and Orwell. This is the observation that "we sleep soundly in our beds because rough men stand ready in the night to visit violence on those who would do us harm." In fact, it came from neither of them. It first was written by a film critic in 1991 in the *Washington Times,* a conservative newspaper. The critic, Richard Grenier, made clear in the article that he was paraphrasing Orwell. Specifically, he seems to have been alluding to Orwell's comment in his essay on Kipling: "He sees clearly that men can only be highly civilised while other men, inevitably less civilised, are there to guard and feed them." Grenier had not used quotation marks, but a few years later, two other conservative American writers did so in repeating the comment—the *National Review*'s Kate O'Beirne and the columnist George Will. Then the conservative British historian Andrew Roberts picked it up. Finally, in 2006, the *National Review* completed the circle by misattributing the quote to Churchill.

But Churchill is invoked accurately in other places, some of them unexpected. In 1964, Fidel Castro disclosed that he was reading Churchill's World War II memoirs. "If Churchill hadn't done what he did to defeat the Nazis, you wouldn't be here, none of us would be here," he told a crowd that had gathered to see the new Cuban leader when he visited a Havana bookstore. "What is more, we have to take a special interest in him because he, too, led a little island against a great enemy."

Another surprising fan mention came from Keith Richards, the guitarist for the Rolling Stones, who defended his dissipated lifestyle by correctly citing Churchill's comment, "I've taken a lot more out of alcohol than it's ever taken out of me." Richards, who was born in 1943, during Churchill's first premiership, added, "I kind of feel the same way about the dope and stuff. I got something out of it." Sometimes genuine Churchill remarks have a paradoxical element that make them sound like they might have come from Yogi Berra, such as, "There are a terrible lot of lies going about the world, and the worst of it is that half of them are true."

But there has been a cost to the mythification of Churchill. Most notably, he made such an icon of "the special relationship" between Britain and the United States that some of his successors followed it without seeming to understand that it was devised to cast a warm glow over a hard-minded, and sometimes anguished, wartime alliance. As the historian Max Hastings put it, "British governments care to the point of obsession about the United States, and its administrations' view of us."

The low point of this pursuit of a special relationship came when it helped encourage the imprudent American-led invasion of Iraq in 2003. "I stood by America when it needed standing by," Tony Blair, prime minister from 1997 to 2007, states in his memoirs. It would be more accurate to say that when the United States needed the wise counsel of a true friend, Blair instead acted as a cheerleader. Trying to strike a Churchillian note, he said immediately after the 9/11 attacks, "We . . . here in Britain stand shoulder to shoulder with our American friends in this hour of tragedy, and we, like them, will not rest until this evil is driven from our world." He stepped up the nostalgic rhetoric when he visited New York City later that month, saying, inaccurately, that during the early days of World War II, "There was one country and one people which stood by us at that time." One must wonder what historically minded citizens of Canada, Australia, New Zealand, and South Africa—nations that aided Britain during the Blitz—thought of his assertion about who had helped Britain in 1939 and 1940, the time when the American ambassador in London was loudly predicting a German victory. As the Australian historian Robin Prior put it, "The defender of liberal democracy in 1940–41 was not Britain along with the United States; it was Britain and the Dominions. They fought freedom's battle while the largest democracy on earth occasionally threw them some crumbs."

In July 2002, Blair sent Bush a memorandum stating that, in the event of a confrontation with Iraq, "I will be with you, whatever." That memo was disclosed by an official British inquiry into the Blair government's decisions during the run-up to the Iraq War. Blair's blank-check statement made it "very difficult for the UK subsequently to withdraw its support" for the March 2003 invasion, the inquiry found.

If Blair had been as strategically adept as Churchill, he might well have opposed the American invasion of Iraq, which in fact would have made it very difficult for the United States government to go to war. To be sure, in the short run, open British disagreement over Iraq would have strained cross-Atlantic ties, but in the long run, declining to support the

Americans in Iraq would have been an act of genuine friendship—and also of strategic vision.

Instead, Blair went before the U.S. Congress in the summer of 2003, as questions grew about what America was doing in Iraq, and he urged Americans to press on. Don't worry about the lessons of history, he recklessly counseled. "There never has been a time when . . . except in the most general sense, a study of history provides so little instruction for our present day." By emphasizing the idea of the special relationship without seeming to grasp its complexity, and by sweeping aside history when he should have attended to it, Blair paradoxically did great damage to the Anglo-American relationship.

For himself, Churchill maintained his public allegiance to the United States to his death in January 1965, and even beyond it. At his funeral, which he designed, American flags were flown alongside the British ones. During the ceremony, "The Battle Hymn of the Republic" echoed into the gold and white arches and domes that dominate the interior of St. Paul's Cathedral. Yet the American president, Lyndon Johnson, perhaps remembering Churchill's slight of FDR's funeral twenty years earlier, declined to attend, or even to send his vice president.

CHAPTER 16

ORWELL'S EXTRAORDINARY ASCENSION

1950–2016

I t was a bright cold day in April, and the clocks were striking thirteen." So began a column written in April 2015 by Zahra Salahuddin for the Pakistani newspaper *Dawn.* Her complaint was about the new powers the state of Pakistan was giving itself to monitor the Internet. Big Brother, she concluded, was present, so she invoked the opening lines of *1984.*

Going by references, allusions, and tributes such as these, appearing daily in the media around the world, George Orwell is a contemporary figure in our culture. In recent years, he may even have passed Churchill, not in terms of historical significance but of current influence. It has been one of the most extraordinary posthumous performances in British literary history.

His current status would have shocked his contemporaries. He was for most of his life an obscure figure, even on the London literary scene. Not long after *Animal Farm* was published, Logan Pearsall Smith, himself a truly minor British-American writer, read it and then telephoned his old friend Cyril Connolly, an influential editor, to learn more about the book's author. Orwell, said Pearsall Smith, had seemed to come out of nowhere to "beat the lot of you."

Perhaps Pearsall Smith was in a prophetic frame of mind, as he died the day after making that call. His comment correctly captured the trajectory of Orwell's stature. He was close to unknown in the 1930s and of secondary standing at best until the mid-1940s. Since his death early in 1950 his stature has grown steadily, even inexorably. "His influence and example grow more radiant with each passing year," wrote a contributor to the *Financial Times* in 2014.

When he was alive, his book sales were measured in the hundreds and thousands. Since his death an estimated 50 million copies of his books have been sold.

Entire academic studies have been written solely about the details of Orwell's posthumous ascension, such as John Rodden's *George Orwell: The Politics of Literary Reputation*. It is not at all clear that Orwell would approve of these works, especially when they contain opaque sentences such as this: "Typically the primary watchword is the point of departure for the evolution of variants, but the variants may also serve as the basis for establishing the primary watchword. What distinguishes certain watchwords as 'primary' is not temporal priority but centrality and frequency of occurrence in a reception history." One must wonder how anyone who has read "Politics and the English Language" could write such a sentence. But the style is reflective of the larger fact that Orwell has not been well served by academia, often attracting the clumsy attentions of third-raters. The sociologist Neil McLaughlin argues that Orwell has been "relatively ignored" by university faculties precisely because he is so esteemed "in the popular culture"—and also perhaps because he has been so long embraced by conservatives. By contrast, over the last seven decades he has been promoted, and analyzed with care, by first-rate public intellectuals working mainly outside the walls of academe, such as Irving Howe, Norman Podhoretz, and Christopher Hitchens.

Only a few writers took much note of Orwell during his life, most notably Muggeridge and Arthur Koestler, who had gone to Spain as both a communist spy and a working journalist and had been imprisoned there by the Nationalists. As with Orwell, the experience of the Spanish Civil War left Koestler profoundly disappointed with both left and right. His public split with the Communist Party came after he returned to England to give speeches about Spain, but declined in them to denounce POUM, which he recalled was "at the time treated by the Communists as enemy number one." Instead, he said what he believed, which was that POUM's leaders had operated in good faith and that it was stupid and ugly to call them traitors.

Koestler and Muggeridge were exceptions, however, men who noticed Orwell because they were traveling the same difficult road as Orwell. All three were going into opposition against Stalinist-dominated communism.

Orwell's name did not appear in the British edition of *Who's Who* while he was alive. He has only one entry in the 1955 edition of *Bartlett's Quotations,* the first to be issued after his death. In 1956, Victor Gollancz, who published Orwell's early work but dropped him for criticizing Stalinism, told his daughter in a letter, "I think Orwell is enormously overrated."

As late as 1963, the poet and public intellectual Stephen Spender could dismiss Orwell as a fine prose stylist but even so, a decidedly minor figure of little or no lasting impact. Interestingly, he did this in a book dedicated to Orwell's widow, Sonia. When asked in an interview about Orwell, Spender delivered the most backhanded of compliments: "If you read his works carefully you often think he's arriving at the right conclusions for quite inadequate reasons." In his atrocious autobiography, Spender omits any mention of Orwell. However, he does rhapsodize like a minor-league Hemingway about his own time in Spain during the war: "There was always . . . the sense of living so dramatically within the moment that everything else was forgotten and therefore one was transfixed within a feeling of something uniquely Spanish." He also stated, illogically, "My poems from Spain are the poems of a pacifist who nevertheless supports military action." It comes as no surprise that Koestler, once while arguing politics with Spender in London's Café Royal (as noted previously, an Orwell hangout), contemptuously said, "Don't say any more, don't say any more, because I can predict everything you are going to say in the next twenty minutes."

Few subsequent critics would hold Orwell as low as Spender did. In the 1960s, at about the same time that Spender was writing him off, Orwell's reputation began its steady, multidecade rise. For the first time, collections of Orwell's essays were issued.

Since then, Orwell's reputation has taken off. Orwell is now seen as a major figure of his time, sometimes depicted as one of the most important writers of the century. A number of retrospective intellectual histories of the twentieth century focus on him.

In Peter Watson's *The Modern Mind,* first published in 2000, Orwell is elevated to the position of central figure, a point of reference. The first part of the four-part book is titled "Freud to Wittgenstein," and the second is "From Spengler to *Animal Farm.*" Orwell is also singled out, though not quite so highly, in the historian Tony Judt's final work, *Thinking the Twentieth Century.* A history of postwar Britain published in 2015 was titled *Orwell's Faded Lion.* As previously mentioned, when the *National Review,* a conservative American magazine, compiled a list of the most significant nonfiction books of the twentieth century, Orwell had two entries in the top ten—the only writer so honored—*Homage to Catalonia* and *The Collected Essays.* Topping the list was Churchill's World War II memoirs. Robert McCrum, literary editor of the London *Observer,* called Orwell "one of the most influential English writers of the twentieth century." The critic Philip French in the *Guardian* topped that by calling Orwell "possibly the greatest writer of the twentieth century," leaving out the question of nationality. More recently, the same newspaper described *1984* as "arguably the most famous English novel of the 20th century." In opinions issued by current members of the U.S. Supreme Court, Orwell was the third most cited author, coming after Shakespeare and Lewis Carroll.

In his ascendancy, Orwell has been the subject of some particularly poor analysis and commentary, but even that may be fitting, for few great writers produced as many bad works as he did.

ORWELL IN THE SOVIET BLOC

One of the drivers of Orwell's rise was the effect he had on eastern European and Russian intellectuals seeking to understand and describe their new communist rulers. "Even those who know Orwell only by hearsay are amazed that a writer who never lived in Russia should have so keen a perception into its life," remarked the Polish poet and diplomat Czesław Miłosz in *The Captive Mind*, written in 1953. At times, that book reads like an explication of *1984*. "The Party fights any tendency to delve into the depths of a human being, especially in literature and art," Miłosz observed. "What is not expressed does not exist. Therefore if one forbids men to explore the depths of human nature, one destroys in them the urge to make such explorations; and the depths in themselves slowly become unreal." The result, he warned, was that "in the East there is no boundary between man and society."

In a conscious nod to Orwell, the Soviet dissident Andrei Amalrik titled his 1970 critique of Soviet power *Will the Soviet Union Survive Until 1984?* In it, he accurately predicted that "any state forced to devote so much of its energies to physically and psychologically controlling millions of its own subjects could not survive indefinitely."

Orwell's star rose so high in the 1980s that intellectual skirmishing broke out over which ideological camp might claim him had he survived into old age. "I believe he would have been a neoconservative if he were alive today," Norman Podhoretz, the godfather of that movement, asserted in 1983.

Podhoretz based that argument on his own strongly held view that Orwell's core subject was the failings of the left-wing intelligentsia. But one of the pitfalls of literary criticism is attributing one's own views to one's subject. Criticizing the left from a newfound rightist perspective may have been Podhoretz's guiding light, but it was not Orwell's. Rather, the theme that runs powerfully through all of Orwell's writings, from his early work on *Burmese Days* through the late 1930s and then through the great essays, and into *Animal Farm* and *1984,* is the abuse of power in the modern world by both the left and the right. Sometimes this takes the form of examining the dealings of a master and a servant in colonial Burma, at other times between waiters and dishwashers in Depression-era Paris, but most often, in his essays and his works from 1937 on, it is the relationship between the state and the individual. It is for this reason, for example, that the Polish trade union movement embraced Orwell in the 1980s, issuing stamps with his image for its nonstate mail service. (Also, one must wonder how Podhoretz could disregard Orwell's opposition to the creation of Israel. Tosco Fyvel, a friend of Orwell's and a Zionist himself, recalled that to Orwell "the Zionists were white settlers like the British in India or Burma, and the Arabs were like the native Burmese. . . . He was against Jewish nationalism—against all nationalism." Fyvel in turn does not address the apparent contradiction that Orwell in his writings was a strong advocate of rural English life, amounting to a form of regionalism, if not nationalism.)

The most lasting aspect of the conservative embrace of Orwell is that the modern left has never been completely comfortable with the postwar Orwell. This is regrettable. Those who believe in free speech but also are skeptical of unrestrained capitalism should keep a place for him in their hearts and minds, and not allow him to be claimed solely by conservatives. Just because a faction or wing of political writers quotes an author does not necessarily mean that the author would agree with them. Anyone wondering about Orwell's political views would do well to remember that in November 1945, he had written, "I belong to the Left and must work inside it, much as I hate Russian totalitarianism." He was not someone who, as he observed of another writer, would let himself be "driven into a sort of perverse Toryism by the follies of the progressive party of the moment."

That said, during the late 1960s, Orwell probably would have been appalled by some of the narcissism of hippies, and by many aspects of the New Left, if his own writings are any guide. "Hedonistic societies do not endure," he once wrote. But he likely would have criticized the 1960s not as a conservative, but from the perspective of his agrarian village socialism. So he may well have embraced some other aspects of the 1960s and 1970s, such as the back-to-the-earth movement and other reactions against corporate agriculture and in favor of organic food grown by small farmers. Indeed, in his own life he was something of a back-to-the-lander, trying to fish and grow food in Scotland despite his ill health. Given his love of nature and his suspicion of large corporations, he likely also would have been engaged by the phenomenon of global warming.

Orwell's second great boost came thirty-four years after his death, with the arrival of the actual year 1984. In that year, *1984* itself again became a bestseller, with fifty thousand copies sold every day early that year. Steve Jobs and Apple gave Orwell another boost with a high-profile commercial that ran during that year's Super Bowl. The spot, which introduced the Macintosh computer, invoked the images of *1984,* with a Big Brother–like figure on a huge gray screen that was smashed by a flying hammer thrown by a colorful young woman in running clothes. Although shown only once, it became one of the most famous commercials ever made.

Had Orwell managed on his battered respiratory system to wheeze into the year 1984, when he would have become eighty-one years old, he probably would have continued his journey into slightly self-righteous English nonconformism, in the form of the hermetic agricultural life he tried to establish in the Inner Hebrides as he began dying. Stephen Spender, getting Orwell right for once, observed, "What he valued was the old concept of England based on the English countryside, in which to be conservative is to be against changes taking place, especially changes in the direction of producing inequality. He was opposed to the whole hard-faced industrial middle class which arose in the nineteenth century."

And had Orwell somehow been able to see the world of today, he almost certainly would have endorsed the criticism of growing wealth inequality in the United States, Britain, Russia, and China. Given the arc of his *Animal Farm,* he likely would have been unsurprised by the odyssey of modern China from its revolution through its Cultural Revolution and into the current unholy alliance between the Communist Party and its new billionaire oligarchs. One can only wonder what Orwell might have written had he been able to spend a year or two in today's China.

The only serious blows to Orwell's burgeoning reputation were two rounds of revelations, in 1998 and in 2003, that late in his life he had prepared a list of suspected communists for the British government. This act of informing, done from his hospital bed in May 1949, becomes more understandable when viewed in the context of his times. Orwell had seen friends imprisoned and executed without justice by the Soviets in Spain, and had some reason to fear for his own safety after the release of *Animal Farm*—which, as noted, itself had run into some prepublication obstacles placed by Peter Smollett, a British official secretly working for the Soviets. Smollett had been recruited by Kim Philby, who at that point was undetected, active in British life, and respected, along with other Soviet agents such as Guy Burgess and Sir Anthony Blunt. In September 1949, as Orwell lay dying, Philby was given the crucial post of chief of British intelligence at the British embassy in Washington, D.C.

Nonetheless, the fact remains that a key point of agreement between modern thinkers both of the right and the left is that Orwell's work has become central to our understanding of the previous century, and of our own as well. The neoconservative right bear-hugs him with phrases such as "called by some the most important writer of the twentieth century." The leftist Hitchens went even further, asserting, "He owns the twentieth century, as a writer about fascism and communism and imperialism, in a way that no other writer in English can claim." A writer in the *New Republic* in 2013 likened Orwell to both Montaigne and Shakespeare and dubbed him "Sage of the Century."

ORWELL'S POST-9/11 RESURRECTION

This point leads to the third, and perhaps least expected, of Orwell's posthumous booms. Some critics had speculated that Orwell would fade after the passing of 1984, or at least after the end of the Soviet Union. Harold Bloom predicted in 1987 that *1984* would come to be seen as "a period piece, such as *Uncle Tom's Cabin*." Even the literary critic Irving Howe, a longtime supporter of Orwell, had thought it possible that after the Cold War ended, "*1984* may have little more than 'historic interest.'"

Yet a new post–Cold War generation has found his words to have resonance. Instead of fading away, Orwell has enjoyed a new surge of popularity. The passing of the historical context of *1984* seems to have liberated the novel and allowed its message to be recognized as speaking to a universal problem of modern humankind.

The evidence for this is that in recent years, readers and writers around the world have responded to Orwell's depictions of a nearly omniscient state. "We live in a new age of surveillance, one where George Orwell's concept of living in a society whereby every citizen is under constant watch is becoming alarmingly prevalent," one blogger wrote matter-of-factly in July 2015. An Iraqi writer, Hassan Abdulrazzak, said in 2015, "I'm sure George Orwell didn't think: 'I must write an instructive tale for a boy from Iraq,' when he wrote *1984*. But that book explained Iraq under Saddam for me better than anything else before or since." In 2015, *1984* was listed as one of the ten bestselling books of the year in Russia.

In 2014, *1984* became so popular as a symbol among antigovernment protestors in Thailand that Philippine Airlines took to warning its passengers, in a list of helpful hints, that carrying a copy could cause trouble with customs officials and other authorities. "Emma Larkin," the pen name of an American journalist working in Southeast Asia, wrote, "In Burma there is a joke that Orwell wrote not just one novel about the country, but three: a trilogy comprised of *Burmese Days, Animal Farm* and *1984*."

Orwell seems to have resonated especially in modern China. Since the year 1984, some thirteen Chinese translations of *1984* have been published. Both it and *Animal Farm* also have been translated into Tibetan. Explaining the relevance of Orwell to China, one of his translators, Dong Leshan, wrote, "The twentieth century will soon be over, but political terror still survives and this is why *Nineteen Eighty-four* remains valid today."

Orwell's earlier meditations on the abuses of political power also found new audiences. An Islamic radical, reading *Animal Farm* while imprisoned in Egypt, realized that Orwell spoke to his private doubts. "I began to join the dots and think, 'My God, if these guys that I'm here with ever came to power, they would be the Islamist equivalent of *Animal Farm*,'" said Maajid Nawaz. In Zimbabwe, an opposition newspaper ran a serialized version of *Animal Farm* that underscored the point about a betrayed revolution by running illustrations in which Napoleon the pig is depicted wearing the big-rimmed eyeglasses favored by Zimbabwe's president-for-life, Robert Mugabe. In response, someone destroyed the newspaper's press with an antitank mine. A Cuban artist was jailed without trial for plans to stage a version of *Animal Farm* in 2014. To make sure the authorities got the point, he painted the names "Fidel" and "Raoul" on two pigs.

In the post-9/11 era, *1984* particularly has found a new relevance, and a new generation of Western readers, because of three interlocking aspects.

For present-day Americans, *1984*'s background of permanent warfare carries a chilling warning. In the book, as in American life today, the conflict is offstage, heard only as occasional rocket impacts in the distance. "Winston could not definitely remember a time when his country has not been at war," Orwell stated in *1984*. (The same is true of all Americans now in their early twenties or younger. In the novel, some even suspect the government is faking the war, claiming one is under way in order to maintain its hold on power.)

In an era when American wars are waged with drones firing precision-guided missiles, and with small numbers of Navy SEALs and other Special Operations forces on the ground in remote parts of the Middle East, with occasional enemy bombings in cities such as London, Paris, Madrid, and New York, this passage from the novel is eerily prescient:

It is a warfare of limited aims between combatants who are unable to destroy one another, [and] have no material cause for fighting. . . . [It] involves very small numbers of people, mostly highly trained specialists, and causes comparatively few casualties. The fighting, when there is any, takes place on the vague frontiers whose whereabouts the average man can only guess at. In the centres of civilization war means no

more than . . . the occasional crash of a rocket bomb which may cause
a few scores of deaths.

The second driver of the current Orwell boom is the post-9/11 rise of
the intelligence state. We live in a time of an intrusive, overweening state
in both the East and the West. In the early 2000s, the United States government routinely killed people in nations with which it was not officially at war, such as Pakistan and Yemen, using remote-controlled
aircraft. Many of those killed were not even identified, except by behavior patterns that the U.S. government considered threatening. Killing
such people became known as "signature strikes"—that is, a male of military age showing a pattern of behavior associated with terrorists, such as
talking to known terrorists on a telephone or attending a meeting with
them. Several hundred of these strikes have been carried out in Pakistan,
Yemen, and Somalia. (The Americans legalistically also noted that the
targeted men were armed, but that is a form of quibbling, as the men are
in areas such as the Afghan-Pakistan border, a kind of modern Dodge
City where adult males routinely carry weapons.) "Metadata"—the mani-
pulation of billions of bits of information in order to recognize previously
unseen patterns—allows governments to quietly compile dossiers on the
behavior of millions of individuals.

Of course, the American government acted in those lethal and intrusive ways in response to the 9/11 attacks. Orwell likely would have
roundly denounced both those attacks and also the panicky response of
the U.S. government. His guiding light was freedom of conscience—
both from government control and from extremists, whether religious or
ideological. Recall his observation quoted at the end of this book's intro-
ductory chapter: "If liberty means anything at all, it means the right to
tell people what they do not want to hear." In that vein, it is significant
that the greatest threat to freedom that Orwell's Winston sees in *1984* is
not from overseas, but from his own government.

Third, and perhaps most shocking, is the way the use of torture in *1984* foreshadows how today's state uses it in conducting an endless "war on terror." After 9/11, for the first time in American history, torture became official policy. (Before then it had been used occasionally but always in disregard of the law, and sometimes was prosecuted.) CIA officials have admitted that they used torture, almost daring a prosecutor to indict them—which has not happened.

There have been arguments on occasion among pundits about which predictive mid-twentieth-century author got the future more right—Aldous Huxley, with his vision in *Brave New World* in which people were controlled by the state through pleasure, or Orwell, with his darker view of a state built on the use of pain. (Huxley, in fact, briefly had been one of Orwell's French teachers at Eton.) Actually, it is a false distinction—both men are right. The great majority of people are content to be amused and not to challenge the state. But a dissident minority often emerges, and suppressing it generally seems to require harsher methods. As Orwell put it near the conclusion of *1984,* "The choice for mankind lay between freedom and happiness, and . . . for the great bulk of mankind, happiness was better." What's more, most Americans seem more or less comfortable with having their private communications monitored by the state's security apparatus. In both this and the use of torture, the American people tacitly consented to radical departures from their national traditions.

Other states also are following the American example in exploring the intrusive possibilities of high-tech electronic eavesdropping. During the 2014 upheaval in Ukraine, the pro-Russian government, beleaguered by protestors, sent them the most Orwellian of messages. It monitored the locations of cell phones near the protests and sent them all a mass text message. "Dear subscriber," it warned, "you are registered as a participant in a mass disturbance." That initial "dear" is particularly evocative of the mind-set of Big Brother.

Orwell was hardly all seeing. He feared the brute strength of totalitarianism, but as we've seen he never visited America, and so perhaps as a result did not grasp the resiliency of capitalism. Just as he misjudged the adaptivity of American soldiers during World War II, so too did he underestimate the robust, adaptive nature of their society. He wrote, in another context, in 1943, that "an economy ruled by the profit motive is simply not equal to re-arming on a modern scale." That assertion might have been true of the Britain of the 1930s, which had a declining economy that had failed to adequately fund innovation. But over the last eight decades, the United States has proved that assertion to be incorrect three times—first during World War II, then again during the Eisenhower-era buildup, and finally in the post-Vietnam rebuilding of the American military, when Reaganite spending combined with Silicon Valley to create a powerful, computer-based U.S. military machine.

As a consequence, Orwell also underestimated how intrusive Western states and companies could become. He predicted, incorrectly, in *Wigan Pier* that "the rate of mechanical progress will be much more rapid once Socialism is established." His vision may have been restricted by his location. His views on the limitations of capitalism were formed by what he observed in Britain—that is, stagnating late industrial age capitalism. Its highest goal was efficiency, which meant that the system depended on managers squeezing a little more money out of existing systems and workers. "The processes involved in making, say, an aeroplane are so complex as to be only possible in a planned, centralised society, with all the repressive apparatus that that implies," he wrote in 1945. "Unless there is some unpredictable change in human nature, liberty and efficiency must pull in opposite directions."

He could not see that with the dawn of the information age several decades later, efficiency would become far less economically significant than innovation and adaptiveness. Apple, Microsoft, Google, and myriad other late-twentieth-century companies did not make better typewriters, they created entirely new products, such as handheld computers and applications for them. They were not efficient in doing so, because innovation is necessarily a wasteful process, producing many more failures than successes. Indeed, these new companies could compete only by lavishing money and other benefits on workers capable of developing innovative products. Orwell could not also see that these companies, paradoxically inspired by a Californian ideology of personal liberation, soon would produce products that would intrude far deeper into private life than had the titans of the industrial age, with companies endlessly monitoring individuals in order to sell more goods to them. Today, data is not only powerful, it also has become hugely profitable. There is a saying in Silicon Valley that there is no such thing as a free app—if the app is free, then the individual using it *is* the product. In other words, today's Silicon Valley corporation views people as resources to be mined and exploited, not unlike, say, coal in the nineteenth century.

Orwell's new relevancy appears to have made him in recent years, for the first time, a kind of celebrity, frequently appearing in popular culture. A "Google alert" on "Orwell" maintained during the course of writing this book produced a steady flow, every day, of twenty to thirty citations of him in newspapers, magazines, Web sites, and other media around the world. Invariably, at least one entry began with the thought, "If Orwell were alive today, he would . . ."—usually, denounce whatever the entry writer objects to that day. In political commentary, he is simplified into a convenient club to swing at one's opponents. Here is a typical usage, from the *Wall Street Journal*'s right-wing editorial page: "To adapt George Orwell's motto for Oceania: Under Mr. Obama, friends are enemies, denial is wisdom, capitulation is victory." Here is another, written a few weeks later by a liberal college student: "America is not yet an Orwellian dystopia. . . . But while their policies are close enough to deserve that 'yet,' a vote for a Republican candidate is a vote that moves America toward *1984*." It is easy to mock these invocations of Orwell, but that would miss the point, because there is an important and beneficial aspect to them: It is clear that his works have instructed many people in how to be wary of the numbing rhetoric of government pronouncements, of pervasive official surveillance, and most of all, of state intrusion into the realm of the private individual.

There also is a more interesting flow of references to him in the world of arts and entertainment. Cumulatively, these make him, for all practical purposes, a current figure in our culture. In 2013, when the singer David Bowie compiled a list of his one hundred favorite books, he included three by Orwell. The coach of the Birmingham City soccer team listed *1984* as his favorite book. A happily loud young rock band from Chicago calling itself The Orwells won international fame on the strength of songs such as "Who Needs You?" and "Dirty Sheets," two titles George Orwell, were he musically inclined, might have composed. A Canadian indie duo named Town Heroes issued an album inspired by Orwell's advice to try to see what is in front of your nose.

Perhaps the most accomplished modern tribute to Orwell was *The Circle,* a lively novel by Dave Eggers, who recast *1984* in today's Silicon Valley. It is set at a company called The Circle, which appears to have absorbed Apple, Google, and Facebook, and perhaps several other information-based corporations. It follows the descent of a young woman named Mae into a world of voluntary total surveillance. It probably is not coincidental that the new headquarters building that Apple has been planning and constructing for several years is a perfect circle, sheathed in curved glass. There is in Apple's design an unintended echo of Jeremy Bentham's ideal prison, the circular Panopticon. But, as Eggers would appreciate, the Apple edifice is built not for the inward observation of prisoners, but to look outward into all of our lives.

The novel is fueled by the combination of Eggers's realistic portrayal of the worldview of Silicon Valley combined with his own view that the

Valley's corporate efforts ultimately will damage personal freedoms. "Everyone should have a right to know everything," says one of the three heads of the company. What's more, he says, if everyone were surveilled, "It would lead to a more moral way of life. . . . Mae, we would finally be compelled to be our best selves." Eggers slyly wraps that horrible thought in California-speak: *"We would finally realize our potential."*

Mae's overseers discover she has failed to share all her data about her experiences. They publicly interrogate her in a session that is seen by those around her as a form of spiritual growth. She summarizes for her approving peers what she has been forced to learn:

SECRETS ARE LIES
SHARING IS CARING
PRIVACY IS THEFT

Perhaps not surprisingly, the industry publication *Digital Trends* found parts of the book "almost offensive."

Meanwhile, in academia, scholars bushwhacked through the trivia of Orwell's career, such as the fact that Orwell, while working on *Down and Out in Paris and London,* had been jailed for a night in 1931, giving his name to the police as "Edward Burton." A journalist investigating Orwell's time as a village shopkeeper in Hertfordshire found, to no one's surprise, that he was considered by at least one neighbor to be "pretty useless" in that endeavor.

Today, of course, Orwell could make a comfortable income simply by sitting in that shop and signing his books. His literary executor in 2014 told a British publication that the income of Orwell's estate had grown 10 percent a year for the last three years—far outpacing the stagnant economy. The BBC commissioned a statue of its former employee, Orwell, with plans to have it in place in 2016. All told, in terms of contemporary influence, Orwell arguably has surpassed Churchill.

Do all these tributes overvalue Orwell today? Perhaps so, especially in casual references that portray him as an unparalleled seer about totalitarianism. Even so, the evidence is mainly in Orwell's favor. One reason he did not appear in accounts by contemporaries is that he understood their era better than they did. That was unprovable at the time, but has been borne out by the events of the six decades that have passed since he stopped writing.

Yet Orwell's most lasting contribution to Western culture may be the least noted. It is often observed that he is one of the few writers to have contributed words and phrases to our language—"doublethink," "Big Brother," "memory hole," "All animals are equal, but some are more equal than others."

Less noticed is that the distinctive style he used, especially in examining politics and culture, has become the accepted manner of modern discussion of such issues. In publications such as the *Times Literary Supplement,* the *New York Review of Books,* and op-ed pages in hundreds of newspapers, the prevailing approach tends to be, or at least tries to be, like his—plain, declarative, and offering observed but overlooked concrete facts as its justification. This is one reason his essays and reviews feel so contemporary. As an example, consider these two sentences from the twenty-first-century American political writer Ta-Nehisi Coates: "But all our phrasing—*race relations, racial chasm, racial justice, racial profiling, white privilege,* even *white supremacy*—serves to obscure that racism is a visceral experience, that it dislodges brains, blocks airways, rips muscle, extracts organs, cracks bones, breaks teeth. You must never look away from this." The wording, the rhythm, and, most of all, the fundamental instruction to look at how power is actually expressed are quintessentially Orwell.

It is a stretch, but perhaps not too much, to say that Churchill and

Orwell—along with many others—may have helped contribute to the conditions that made possible the economic boom of the late twentieth century. Churchill through his actions as a war leader made possible the postwar world. The Cold War was the consequence of World War II, and the conclusion of that conflict was ordained by the events of 1940, which had Churchill at their center. Russia and the United States, not then in the war, ultimately would win the war, but in 1940, Churchill was significant as "the one who did not lose it," observed the Hungarian-born historian John Lukacs, who himself was a prisoner of the Nazis during World War II. The British writer Paul Johnson probably put it best when he wrote, "Everyone who values freedom under law, and government by, for and from the people, can find comfort and reassurance in his life story."

Economic growth created space for the individual, and the opportunity it provides for creative self-expression. It is very unlikely that either fascism or communism would have been able to foster the late-twentieth-century economic boom. Despite its intrusive nature, the Internet remains more beneficial than not in its encouragement of individual expression. For most of the last two centuries, it usually took some wealth to become a publisher. That is no longer true. Now anyone with access to a computer can broadcast opinions, facts, and images to the world. The drawback is that governments and corporations can harness all that data and make the Internet resemble the two-way telescreen in *1984*, but even more all encompassing, a giant mechanism that combines state surveillance and capitalist commerce.

Orwell saw that people might become slaves of the state, but he did not foresee that they might also become something else that would horrify him—products of corporations, data resources to be endlessly mined and peddled elsewhere. He would no doubt have been a powerful critic of such things.

THE PATH OF CHURCHILL AND ORWELL

When they were confronted by a crucial moment in history, Churchill and Orwell responded first by seeking the facts of the matter. Then they acted on their beliefs. They faced a genuinely apocalyptic situation, in which their way of life was threatened with extinction. Many people around them expected evil to triumph and sought to make their peace with it. These two did not. They responded with courage and clear-sightedness. If there is anything we can take away from them, it is the wisdom of employing this two-step process, especially in times of mind-bending crisis: Work diligently to discern the facts of the matter, and then use your principles to respond.

They also often were wrong in their judgments, but they were determined to keep trying to get to the root of the matter, which is equally important. Orwell especially never stopped trying to see clearly through all the lies, obfuscations, and distractions. Instead of shaping facts to fit his opinions, he was willing to let facts change his opinions.

As we deal with terrorism, global warming, domestic inequality, and racism, and also with panicky politicians and demagogic leaders, we would do well to remember how these two men reacted to the over-whelming events of their own time. They were especially good at recognizing the delusions of their own social sets—always a useful tool, if not a good way to make and keep friends.

We should remember that most of us, most of the time, do not welcome the voices of people like Orwell and Churchill appearing in our midst. Most of us, when confronted with a crisis, do not dive into the matter. Rather, we practice avoidance. That is really what appeasement was in the 1930s—a way of not dealing with the matter, of sidestepping some hard, inevitable facts.

The term "psychological avoidance" is what Taylor Branch uses repeatedly in the first volume of his biography of Martin Luther King Jr. to describe the initial mainstream reaction in white America to the civil rights movement. The biggest problem civil rights activists faced in the America of the 1950s and 1960s was not prejudice per se, not even always in the South. Rather, it was a reluctance even among well-meaning people to address a festering wrong that could wait no longer.

In April 1963, Dr. King sat in a jail cell in Birmingham, Alabama, charged with breaking the law by conducting marches and sit-ins as part of a campaign for civil rights. His lawyer brought him the April 13 edition of the *Birmingham News*. On page 2, King read a headline: WHITE CLERGYMEN URGE LOCAL NEGROES TO WITHDRAW FROM DEMONSTRATIONS. In it, seven local religious figures who were white and had spoken in favor of integration were quoted as rejecting King's campaign, calling it "unwise and untimely." The proper thing to do, the moderate clergymen admonished, was for extremists on both sides to simmer down and give people time.

King began writing his response in the margins of the newspaper, having no other paper available. He finished writing four days later. In that "Letter from Birmingham City Jail," King, like Orwell and Churchill, simply asked people to see what was in front of their noses. He begins by stating what he is doing in his campaign and how he is doing it. Step one, he instructs the clergymen, is "Collection of the facts to determine whether injustices are alive." The other three steps, he continued, were "(2) negotiation; (3) self-purification; and (4) direct action."

Orwell would argue that the first step, collecting the facts, is the most revolutionary of acts, as it was for Winston in *1984*. King was arguing that in a world based on facts, in which the individual has the right to perceive and decide those facts on his or her own, the state must earn the allegiance of its citizens. When it fails to live up to its rhetoric, it begins to forfeit that loyalty. This is a thought at once profoundly revolutionary and very American.

King then set forth the facts of the matter before him:

> Birmingham is probably the most thoroughly segregated city in the United States. Its ugly record of police brutality is known in every section of this country. Its unjust treatment of Negroes in courts is a notorious reality. There have been more unsolved bombings of Negro homes and churches than in any city in this nation. These are the hard, brutal and unbelievable facts.

Is it not a contradiction that he is advocating breaking the law as a way to make the state treat its citizens decently? Not at all, he responds, invoking the enduring right of the individual to arrive at his or her own judgments. "Any law that uplifts human personality is just," he asserted. "Any law that degrades human personality is unjust."

Orwell likely would embrace that distinction. He also would have agreed with King's following thought: "If I lived in a communist country today where certain principles dear to the Christian faith are suppressed, I believe I would openly advocate disobeying these anti-religious laws."

A few pages later, King, expressing confidence in the ultimate victory of the civil rights movement, asserts that "right defeated is stronger than evil triumphant." There is an echo of Churchill's stance in the spring of 1940 in those words. Not surprisingly, King soon became a victim of state surveillance.

The avoidance that Churchill and Orwell faced about the rise of Hitler and the flaws of communism demonstrates how debilitating such behavior can be in shaping human responses to oppression. Even when faced with imminent military threat, the ruling class in Britain was unable to muster much will to defend its liberal democratic way of life. Confronting the Soviet threat after World War II was a more complex challenge, but it required at the very least that we see Stalinist communism for what it was—a deadly totalitarian ideology that extinguished people's freedom not merely to speak but to think, a notion that amounted to pure torture for such forceful and idiosyncratic thinkers as Orwell and Churchill.

As time passes, we come to recognize the real heroes of the recent past. We know now that the true leaders of the 1960s in the United States were Martin Luther King Jr., Bayard Rustin, Malcolm X, and others who declined to be patient. Overseas, we can recognize that among the people who helped lift the dead hand of communism from eastern Europe and Russia were Václav Havel, Czesław Miłosz, Lech Wałęsa, Pope John Paul II, Alexander Solzhenitsyn, Andrei Sakharov, and other dissidents.

Most of their peers went another way. The majority in such situations is almost always wrong, at least at the outset. The Czech-born writer Milan Kundera reminds us in *The Book of Laughter and Forgetting* that in the spring of 1948, when the Soviets imposed Stalinist communism on Czechoslovakia, they were greeted most eagerly by "the more dynamic, the more intelligent, the better. Yes, say what you will, the Communists were more intelligent. They had an imposing program. A plan for an entirely new world where everyone would find a place. The opponents had no great dream, only some tiresome and threadbare moral principles, with which they tried to patch the torn trousers of the established order."

After taking power, the communists of Czechoslovakia set out on a program that would not have surprised Orwell, that of systematically erasing the past. One of Kundera's characters, a historian about to be sent to prison for many years, puts it this way: "You begin to liquidate a people . . . by taking away its memory. You destroy its books, its culture, its history." Kundera himself went into exile.

To refuse to run with the herd is generally harder than it looks. To break with the most powerful among that herd requires unusual depth of character and clarity of mind. But it is a path we should all strive for if we are to preserve the right to think, speak, and act independently, heeding the dictates not of the state or of fashionable thought but of our own consciences. In most places and most of the time, liberty is not a product of military action. Rather, it is something alive that grows or diminishes every day, in how we think and communicate, how we treat each other in our public discourse, in what we value and reward as a society, and how we do that. Churchill and Orwell showed us the way. King, on the same path, found the means to redeem America, just as Lincoln had done at Gettysburg one hundred years earlier.

We can all endeavor to do the same, pursuing the facts of the matter, especially about the past of our own country. Facts are impressively dual in their effects. "Truth and reconciliation" meetings in Argentina, South Africa, and in parts of Spain's Basque country have demonstrated that facts are marvelously effective tools—they can rip down falsehoods but can also lay the foundations for going forward. For democracies to thrive, the majority must respect the rights of minorities to dissent, loudly. The accurate view almost always will, at first, be a minority position. Those in power often will want to divert people from the hard facts of a given matter, whether in Russia, Syria, or indeed at home. Why did it take so long for white Americans to realize that our police often treat black Americans as an enemy to be intimidated, even today? Why do we allow political leaders who have none of Churchill's fealty to traditional institutions to call themselves "conservatives"?

The struggle to see things as they are is perhaps the fundamental driver of Western civilization. There is a long but direct line from Aristotle and Archimedes to Locke, Hume, Mill, and Darwin, and from there through Orwell and Churchill to the "Letter from Birmingham City Jail." It is the agreement that objective reality exists, that people of goodwill can perceive it, and that other people will change their views when presented with the facts of the matter.

ACKNOWLEDGMENTS

I am grateful for the many forms of help provided to me at New America by Peter Bergen, Bailey Cahall, Anne-Marie Slaughter, and Rachel White. Research aid was ably provided there by Emily Schneider and Justin Lynch. The last round of research was done by David Sterman, who also did yeoman work in assembling the photographs.

I appreciate the support given to me by Arizona State University under the auspices of New America.

I also am pleased to note the support of the Bogliasco Foundation, which provided me with a wonderful place to write for a month, and a group of fine fellows to talk to at night.

I appreciate the research help provided to me earlier by Katherine Kidder and Stuart Montgomery, who were then at the Center for a New American Security, to which I also am obliged.

Several people read all or parts of the first draft and made helpful suggestions. Vernon Loeb once again generously volunteered to step in, and did so in imaginative ways that greatly helped me revise the manuscript. Lee Pollock's comments and referrals helped me sharpen and deepen several passages about Churchill. Richard Danzig's thoughts made me reconsider how to compare and contrast Churchill and Orwell. Karin Chenoweth's thoughts on the political context of the 1930s were both helpful and inspiring. Tim Noah also helped me quite a lot with thinking through the afterword. Cullen Murphy gave me a helpful overview of what needed to be done to make the book more accessible. Richard Wiebe brought a gimlet eye to the first draft, especially the gaps between what a chapter promised and what it delivered. Others who read the book and made valuable contributions were Michael Abramowitz, Ellen Heffelfinger, Richard Kohn, Anne-Marie Torres, James White, and Charles and Tunky Summerall. Seamus Osborne performed admirably as a volunteer watchdog on the manuscript. None of them are in any way responsible for anything said in this book. I have found in the course of writing five books that errors are inevitable, and that they are always all mine.

Thanks also to the helpful Web sites http://georgeorwellnovels.com and www.winstonchurchill.org. Also, to Parliamentary transcripts carried on the Web site at http://Hansard.millbanksystems.com.

I am happy to acknowledge my debt to the hundreds of scholars of Churchill, Orwell, and World War II whose works I read as I wrote this book. Among the works I relied on especially were those of Martin Gilbert, whose many studies of Churchill have been a guide to me for the last several years. But I wish to add that my favorite biography of Churchill is the multivolume work by William Manchester, perhaps because of his American perspective. Gilbert offers the authoritative record, but Manchester brings that record to life. I also was influenced by Roy Jenkins's biography of Churchill, which amounts to an informed gloss on all the others. Still, the most memorable books about Churchill are those by the man himself.

On the Orwell side of the ledger, I want to thank Andy Moursund for giving me, back in about 1982, the four-volume set of Orwell's collected essays.

And for his help on this book, as with my previous five, I want to thank

Scott Moyers, a great editor, and his team there—Christopher Richards, Kiara Barrow, and a crackerjack publicity operation led, for this book, by Gail Brussel. Without Scott, this would have been a very different and less interesting book. If copyediting were an Olympic event, Jane Cavolina would be wearing a gold medal. I also continue to depend on the counsel of Andrew Wylie, my literary agent. And I wish to thank the Dow Road Choir for its weekly encouragement.

As always, thanks to my wife for sticking with me on life's great journey.

NOTES

CHAPTER 1. THE TWO WINSTONS

1 **stepped out of a taxi:** Martin Gilbert, *Churchill and America* (New York: Free Press, 2005), 132.

2 **A Nationalist sharpshooter:** "Bullet in the Neck," in Audrey Coppard and Bernard Crick, *Orwell Remembered* (New York: Facts on File Publications, 1984), 158.

2 **Their paths never crossed:** Communications with Steven Wright, University College London, Special Collections, Orwell Archive, 14 July 2015, and with Louise Watling, archivist, Churchill Archives Centre, Churchill College, Cambridge University, Cambridge, 15 July 2015.

2 **he read it twice:** Sir Charles Wilson, later Lord Moran, *Churchill: Taken from the Diaries of Lord Moran* (Boston: Houghton Mifflin, 1966), 426.

3 **"arguing with a brass band":** Violet Bonham Carter, *Winston Churchill: An Intimate Portrait* (New York: Harcourt, Brace & World, 1965), 416.

3 **Isaiah Berlin observed:** Isaiah Berlin, "Winston Churchill in 1940," in *Personal Impressions,* 2nd ed. (Princeton, N.J.: Princeton University Press, 2001), 5.

3 **"I like bright colours":** Winston Churchill, *Painting as a Pastime* (Greensboro, N.C.: Unicorn Press, 2013), 64.

3 **"It is a war":** Winston Churchill, Parliamentary debate, 3 September 1939, accessed online at *Hansard, Parliamentary Debates.* Hereafter, *Hansard.*

3 **"We live in an age":** George Orwell, "Literature and Totalitarianism," *The Listener,* 19 June 1941, in *The Collected Essays, Journalism and Letters of George Orwell, Volume 2: My Country Right or Left, 1940–1943,* ed. Sonia Orwell and Ian Angus (New York: Harcourt Brace Jovanovich, 1968), 134. Hereafter, Orwell, *CEJL,* vol. 2.

4 **architects of their time:** Discussed as such in John Rodden and John Rossi, *The Cambridge Introduction to George Orwell* (Cambridge, U.K.: Cambridge University Press, 2012), 105.

4 **"the most unlikely of allies":** Simon Schama, "The Two Winstons" in the BBC television series *A History of Britain,* Series 3, presented by Simon Schama (2002; A&E Home Video), DVD.

4 **"Yes, and now bugger off":** Roy Jenkins, *Churchill* (New York: Farrar, Straus and Giroux, 2001), 849.

4 **Churchill had played a similar dual role:** See Simon Read, *Winston Churchill Reporting: Adventures of a Young War Correspondent* (Boston: Da Capo, 2015).

5 **"If liberty means anything":** Rodden and Rossi, *Cambridge Introduction to George Orwell,* 107.

CHAPTER 2. CHURCHILL THE ADVENTURER

6 **"a troublesome boy":** Winston Churchill, *My Early Life: 1874–1904* (New York: Touchstone, 1996), 8.

6 **"I have no doubt":** Peregrine Churchill and Julian Mitchell, *Jennie: Lady Randolph Churchill, a Portrait with Letters* (New York: Ballantine, 1976), 128–29.

7 **"three or four long intimate conversations":** Churchill, *My Early Life,* 31.

7 **"You never came to see me":** Randolph S. Churchill, *Winston S. Churchill: Youth, 1874–1900* (Boston: Houghton Mifflin, 1966), 79. See also Martin Gilbert, *Churchill: A Life* (New York: Henry Holt, 1991), 9.

7 **"You have never been":** R. Churchill, *Winston S. Churchill: Youth,* 119.

7 **taking perhaps nineteen lovers:** William Manchester, *The Last Lion: Visions of Glory, 1874–1932* (New York: Bantam, 1984), 137.

7 **"The number is suspiciously round":** Roy Jenkins, *Churchill* (New York: Farrar, Straus and Giroux, 2001), 8.

7 **"an active social life, to put it mildly":** Con Coughlin talk at the New America Foundation, Washington, D.C., 5 February 2014.

7 **a serpent inked on her left wrist:** Michael Shelden, *Young Titan: The Making of Winston Churchill* (New York: Simon & Schuster, 2013), 34.

7 **"I shall never get used to":** Paul Johnson, *Churchill* (New York: Penguin, 2010), 7.

8 **"Winston is going back to school":** R. Churchill, *Winston S. Churchill: Youth,* 99.

8 **"How I hated this school":** Churchill, *My Early Life,* 12.

8 **"French, History, lots of Poetry":** Ibid., 13.

8 **ranked last in conduct:** R. Churchill, *Winston S. Churchill: Youth,* 63.

8 **"his forgetfulness, carelessness":** Ibid., 109.

8 **"I got into my bones":** Churchill, *My Early Life,* 17.

8 **some fifteen million words:** David Freeman, "Putting Canards to Rest," *Finest Hour: The Journal of Winston Churchill* (Downers Grove, Il.: The Churchill Centre, Spring 2010): 38.

8 **"considerably discouraged":** Churchill, *My Early Life,* 39.

8 it took three tries: Ibid., 25.

9 "Those who were at the bottom": Ibid., 35.

9 "the uniforms of the cavalry": Ibid.

9 "With all the advantages you had": R. Churchill, *Winston S. Churchill: Youth,* 188–89.

9 "He was in the grip": Ibid., 191.

10 "I can never do anything right": Ibid., 202.

10 "I gained a lot by not overworking": Sir Charles Wilson, later Lord Moran, *Churchill: Taken from the Diaries of Lord Moran* (Boston: Houghton Mifflin, 1966), 281.

10 "it is a mistake to read too many": Winston S. Churchill, *Painting as a Pastime* (Greensboro, N.C.: Unicorn Press, 2013), 20.

10 "the desire for learning": Churchill, *My Early Life,* 109.

10 he chewed through Aristotle: Jonathan Rose, *The Literary Churchill* (New Haven, Conn.: Yale University Press, 2015), 24.

10 "I devoured Gibbon": Churchill, *My Early Life,* 111.

11 "When their long lances": Edward Gibbon, *The Decline and Fall of the Roman Empire,* vol. III, ed. J. B. Bury (New York: Heritage Press, 1946), 2042.

11 "As the successors of the Saracens": Churchill, *My Early Life,* 186.

11 twenty-five pages of Gibbon: Con Coughlin, *Churchill's First War: Young Winston at War with the Afghans* (New York: St. Martin's, 2014), 112.

11 "Good prose is like": George Orwell, "Why I Write," reprinted in *Orwell and Politics,* ed. Peter Davison (Harmondsworth, U.K.: Penguin Books Limited, 2001), 463.

11 "He likes to use four or five words": Moran, *Churchill,* 9.

11 "Churchill's language is": Isaiah Berlin, "Winston Churchill in 1940," in *The Proper Study of Mankind: An Anthology of Essays* (London: Pimlico, 1998), 6.

11 "a master of sham-Augustan prose": John Howard Wilson, "'Not a Man for Whom I Ever Had Esteem': Evelyn Waugh on Winston Churchill," in *Waugh Without End: New Trends in Evelyn Waugh Studies,* ed. Carlos Villar Flor and Robert Murray Davis (Bern, Switzerland: Peter Lang, 2005), 251.

11 He met Henry James: Ethel Barrymore, *Memories* (New York: Harper, 1955), 126.

12 "he had never heard of Henry James": Violet Bonham Carter, *Champion Redoubtable* (London: Weidenfeld & Nicolson, 1999), 21.

12 Keats's "Ode to a Nightingale": Violet Bonham Carter, *Winston Churchill: An Intimate Portrait.* (New York: Harcourt, Brace & World, 1965), 4.

12 not to have read *Hamlet*: Moran, *Churchill,* 559; and Rose, *The Literary Churchill,* 132.

12 "was astonishingly superficial": R. W. Thompson, *Churchill and Morton* (London: Hodder & Stoughton, 1976), 71.

12 painting, a hobby he picked up: Bonham Carter, *Winston Churchill,* 383.

12 he would keep himself talking: Moran, *Churchill,* 324–35.

12 "Writing a book": Churchill, *My Early Life,* 212.

12 "must fit on to one another": Ibid.

13 "Nothing in life is so exhilarating": Winston Churchill, *The Story of the Malakand Field Force* (Mineola, N.Y.: Dover, 2010), 131.

13 Lieutenant Donald McVean: Coughlin, *Churchill's First War*, 204.

13 His mother approached a literary agent: R. Churchill, *Winston S. Churchill: Youth*, 342, 353–54.

14 "I will 'boom' it judiciously": Ralph Martin, *Jennie: The Life of Lady Randolph Churchill*, vol. 2 (Englewood Cliffs, N.J.: Prentice-Hall, 1971), 125–26, 130.

14 "Luckily the religion of peace": Churchill, *The Story of the Malakand Field Force*, 29.

14 "About half a dozen shots": Ibid., 128.

14 "my style is good": R. Churchill, *Winston S. Churchill: Youth*, 365.

14 "Never before had Churchill been praised": Simon Read, *Winston Churchill Reporting* (Boston: Da Capo, 2015), 90.

15 he was off to South Africa: Churchill, *Winston S. Churchill: Youth*, 439.

15 "Eager for trouble": Churchill, *My Early Life*, 244.

16 "Hours crawl like paralytic centipedes": Ibid., 259.

16 "Then I hurled myself": Ibid., 274.

17 "The papers had . . . been filled": Ibid., 298.

17 Captain George Cornwallis-West: R. Churchill, *Winston Churchill: Youth*, 514.

17 "In Tory and social circles": Bonham Carter, *Winston Churchill*, 6.

18 "is almost more of a cad": John Ramsden, *Man of the Century: Winston Churchill and His Legend Since 1945* (New York: Columbia University Press, 2002), 39.

18 "Whether he will ultimately": Violet Bonham Carter, *Lantern Slides: The Diaries and Letters of Violet Bonham Carter*, ed. Mark Bonham Carter and Mark Pottle (London: Phoenix, 1997), 162.

19 "Range perfect—visibility perfect": Bonham Carter, *Winston Churchill*, 210.

19 her natural father was Bertram Mitford: Jenkins, *Churchill*, 133.

19 "Clementine was not entirely sure": Boris Johnson, *The Churchill Factor: How One Man Made History* (New York: Riverhead, 2014), 118.

19 "I am ordinary & love you": Mary Soames, ed., *Winston and Clementine: The Personal Letters of the Churchills* (Boston: Houghton Mifflin, 2001), 198.

19 at the ceremony, "Bertie" Mitford: Sonia Purnell, *Clementine: The Life of Mrs. Winston Churchill* (New York: Viking, 2015), 40, also 11, 18, 26.

19 "Like a sea-beast": Churchill, *Painting as a Pastime*, 36.

20 "It is a wild scene": Soames, *Winston and Clementine*, 116.

20 living shoulder to shoulder: This point was made to me in a conversation on March 9, 2016, by Peter Apps, author of *Churchill in the Trenches*, Amazon, 2015.

20 "large slabs of corned beef" . . . "heart & mind": Soames, *Winston and Clementine*, 164, 177.

21 "My Darling these grave public anxieties": Ibid., 195. Peter Apps drew this passage to my attention.

21 "When it came to sex": Christopher Ogden, *Life of the Party: The Biography of Pamela Digby Churchill Hayward Harriman* (New York: Little, Brown, 1994), 121.

21 "I drink champagne": Martin Gilbert, *Winston S. Churchill: The Prophet of Truth, Volume V: 1922–1939* (London: Minerva, 1990), 41.

21 **"Anyone can rat"**: Mary Lovell, *The Churchills in Love and War* (New York: W. W. Norton, 2011), 344.

22 **"he was hated"**: Lord Beaverbrook, *Politicians and the War, 1914–1916* (London: Collins, 1960), 25.

CHAPTER 3. ORWELL THE POLICEMAN

23 **the opium trade accounted for:** Sarah Deming, "The Economic Importance of Indian Opium and Trade with China on Britain's Economy, 1843–1890," Whitman College, Economics Working Papers 25, Spring 2011, 4.

24 **In his first winter:** "Mrs. Ida Blair's Diary for 1905," in Audrey Coppard and Bernard Crick, *Orwell Remembered* (New York: Facts on File Publications, 1984), 19.

24 **The first word spoken:** Gordon Bowker, *George Orwell* (London: Abacus, 2004), 15.

24 **"a little fat boy":** "The Brother-in-Law Strikes Back," in Coppard and Crick, *Orwell Remembered,* 128.

24 **"I barely saw my father":** George Orwell, "Why I Write," in, *Orwell and Politics,* ed. Peter Davison (Harmondsworth, U.K.: Penguin, 2001), 457.

24 **"appeared to me simply":** George Orwell, "Such, Such Were the Joys," in *The Collected Essays, Journalism and Letters of George Orwell, Volume 4: In Front of Your Nose, 1945–1950,* ed. Sonia Orwell and Ian Angus (New York: Harcourt Brace Jovanovich, 1968), 360. Hereafter, Orwell, *CEJL,* vol. 4.

24 **"At eight years old":** Ibid., 359.

25 **"the great, abiding lesson":** Ibid., 333–34.

25 **"It was the poor":** Ibid., 339.

25 **"break the rules":** Ibid., 362.

26 **a poor early impression:** Bowker, *George Orwell,* 91–92.

26 **his early essay "A Hanging":** George Orwell, *The Collected Essays, Journalism and Letters of George Orwell, Volume 1: An Age Like This, 1920–1940,* ed. Sonia Orwell and Ian Angus (New York: Harcourt Brace Jovanovich, 1968), 45. Hereafter, Orwell, *CEJL,* vol. 1.

26 **"Much of it is simply reporting":** Orwell, *CEJL,* vol. 4, 114.

26 **"the dirty work of Empire":** George Orwell, "Shooting an Elephant," in *Orwell and Politics,* 18.

27 **"His face was very haggard":** George Orwell, *Burmese Days* (New York: Harcourt Brace Jovanovich, 1974), 16–17.

27 **the "hideous" birthmark:** Ibid., 17.

28 **the European Club:** Ibid.

28 **"Little pot-bellied niggers":** Ibid., 22–23.

28 **"In some ways they are getting":** Ibid., 29.

28 **"It's our job to kick":** Ibid., 208.

28 **"the lie that we're here":** Ibid., 39.

28 **The empire, he asserts:** Ibid., 43.

28 **"The British Empire is simply a device":** Ibid., 40.

29 "I wanted to write": Orwell, "Why I Write," in *Orwell and Politics,* 459.

29 "No European cares anything": Orwell, *Burmese Days,* 12.

29 "had forgotten that most people": Ibid., 118.

29 "Master wouldn't hurt you": Ibid., 280.

30 "Learn from me": Orwell, *CEJL,* vol. 1, 142.

30 "When the white man turns tyrant": Orwell, "Shooting an Elephant," in *Orwell and Politics,* 22.

30 "He was looking for dirt": "The Brother-in-Law Strikes Back," in Coppard and Crick, *Orwell Remembered,* 127.

30 his old police trainer: "An Old Burma Hand," in Coppard and Crick, *Orwell Remembered,* 64. Also, Emma Larkin, *Finding George Orwell in Burma* (New York: Penguin, 2005), 249.

31 "the oppressed are always right": George Orwell, *The Road to Wigan Pier* (New York: Harvest, 1958), 148.

31 "She was beautiful": Quoted in Michael Shelden, *Orwell: The Authorized Biography* (New York: HarperCollins, 1991), 126.

32 "I am a happy, honest": Harold Nicolson, *The War Years: 1939–1945* (New York: Atheneum, 1967), 234.

32 an aristocratic ring of Soviet spies: Stephen Dorril, *Black Shirt: Sir Oswald Mosley and British Fascism* (Harmondsworth, U.K.: Penguin, 2007), 522. See also passim, Michael Bloch, *Closet Queens: Some 20th Century British Politicians* (New York: Little, Brown, 2015).

32 "We are humane, charitable": Nicolson, *The War Years,* 57.

32 "the masses do not care": Ibid., 325.

32 "Wouldn't it be awful": Ibid., 433, 435.

32 "What do the majority": Orwell, *Down and Out in Paris and London (*New York: Mariner Books, 1972), 120.

33 "I pulled her off the bed": Ibid., 14.

33 "I came to understand that": "A Philosopher in Paris," in Coppard and Crick, *Orwell Remembered,* 211. Oddly, many years later, in 1987, Ayer was at a party in New York when he looked into a bedroom and saw the boxer Mike Tyson forcing himself on the model Naomi Campbell. He intervened, provoking Tyson to say, "Do you know who the fuck I am? I'm the heavyweight champion of the world." Ayer responded, "And I am the former Wykeham Professor of Logic [at Oxford]. We are both pre-eminent in our field; I suggest we talk about this like rational men." Ben Rogers, *A. J. Ayer: A Life* (New York: Grove, 2000), 344. Ayer was the stepfather of the television chef Nigella Lawson. He also had been a wartime colleague of Orwell's friend Malcolm Muggeridge. Muggeridge, *Like It Was: The Diaries of Malcolm Muggeridge,* ed, John Bright-Holmes (London: Collins, 1981), 364.

34 "There is nothing for it": Orwell, *Down and Out,* 18.

34 Orwell limns the status structure: Ibid., 70–71.

34 "There is a sharp social line": Ibid., 168.

34 "gagger," "moocher," and "clodhopper": Ibid., 174.

34 he "stood jammed": Ibid., 89.
35 his milk became undrinkable: George Orwell, *Diaries,* ed. Peter Davison (New York: W. W. Norton, 2012), 141.
35 "sheets [that] stank": Orwell, *Down and Out,* 130.
35 "In a corner by himself a Jew": Ibid., 132.
35 "A horrible old Jew": Ibid., 36.
35 "Trust a snake": Ibid., 73.
35 write extensively against anti-Semitism: George Orwell, "Antisemitism in Britain," in *The Collected Essays, Journalism and Letters of George Orwell, Volume 3: As I Please, 1943–1945,* ed. Sonia Orwell and Ian Angus (New York: Harcourt Brace Jovanovich, 1968), 332–41. Hereafter, Orwell, *CEJL,* vol. 3.
35 little to say about the Holocaust: John Newsinger, "Orwell, Anti-Semitism and the Holocaust," in *The Cambridge Companion to George Orwell,* ed. John Rodden (Cambridge, U.K.: Cambridge University Press, 2007), 124.
36 "he was at heart strongly anti-Semitic": Muggeridge, *Like It Was,* 376.
36 "He led me down": Orwell, *Down and Out,* 55–56.
36 "was disgusting filth": Ibid., 68.
37 "the shape of rich men": Ibid., 120, 121.
37 "small dark room": George Orwell, *Keep the Aspidistra Flying,* in George Orwell omnibus (London: Secker & Warburg, 1976), 578.
37 "not a natural novelist": Mary McCarthy, "The Writing on the Wall," *New York Review of Books,* 30 January 1969, accessed online.
38 "As the alarm clock": Orwell omnibus (London: Secker & Warburg, 1976), 255.
38 wrote two early novels: Bernard Crick, "Orwell: A Photographic Essay," in *Reflections on America, 1984: An Orwell Symposium,* ed. Robert Mulvihill (Athens, Ga., and London: University of Georgia Press, 1986), 76.
38 Orwell's friend Jack Common: "Jack Common's Recollections," in Coppard and Crick, *Orwell Remembered,* 142.
38 "Apart from projections": "A Memoir by Anthony Powell," in Coppard and Crick, *Orwell Remembered,* 244.
38 "There are two or three books": Orwell, *CEJL,* vol. 4, 205.
39 "Unfortunately you do not solve": Orwell, *Down and Out,* 154.
39 "Smell as in common lodging houses": Orwell, *Diaries,* 29.
39–40 "Bitter wind. They had to send a steamer": Ibid., 37.
40 "To see what is in front": Orwell, "In Front of Your Nose," in *CEJL,* vol. 4, 125.
40 Orwell became a shopkeeper: Shelden, *Orwell,* 236.
40 he sold bacon, sugar: Orwell, *Diaries,* 80.
40 "They had a proper bacon slicer": Stephen Wadhams, ed., *Remembering Orwell* (Harmondsworth, U.K.: Penguin, 1984), 115.
40 "white bread and margarine": Orwell, *Wigan Pier,* 95–96.
41 "kneeling in the cindery mud": Orwell, *Wigan Pier,* 104.
41 "Most of the things": Ibid., 21.
41 "blackened to the eyes": Ibid., 35.

41 "a curiously uneven achievement": Peter Stansky and William Abrahams, *Orwell: The Transformation* (Palo Alto, Calif.: Stanford University Press, 1994), 186.

41 "the mere words 'Socialism' and 'Communism'": Orwell, *Wigan Pier,* 174.

42 "all that dreary tribe": Ibid., 182.

42 "*The lower classes smell*": Orwell's italics, ibid., 127.

42 "You can have an affection": Ibid., 128.

42 "a terrible book," said Kay Ekevall: "Hampstead Friendship," in Coppard and Crick, *Orwell Remembered,* 102.

42–43 "'half-gramophones, half-gangsters'": Victor Gollancz, foreword to Orwell, *Wigan Pier,* xix.

43 "The Left Book Club has": Ibid., x.

43 frame of mind that: This last sentence borrows from the language of a note the writer Timothy Noah sent to me about this paragraph.

43 married in June 1936: Bernard Crick, *George Orwell: A Life* (New York: Penguin, 1980), 295.

43 challenged his "sweeping statement": Ibid., 204.

44 a local ten-year-old boy: Shelden, *Orwell,* 246.

44 war began in Spain: Crick, *George Orwell,* 312.

CHAPTER 4. CHURCHILL: DOWN AND OUT IN THE 1930S

45 "the end of Western civilization": Stephen Spender, *The Thirties and After* (New York: Random House, 1978), 4.

45 The end of the Western way of life: This paragraph relies heavily on the research presented by Richard Overy in his fine book, *The Twilight Years: The Paradox of Britain Between the Wars* (New York: Penguin, 2009), 273. The Toynbee comments are on 38 and 43; the quotation from Rowse is on 273; the Fischer remark is on 316; the Woolf comment appears on 345.

46 "the garrison state": Harold Lasswell, *Essays on the Garrison State* (New Brunswick, N.J.: Transaction, 1997), 43.

46 found him "very changed": Harold Nicolson, *Diaries and Letters, 1930–1939,* ed. Nigel Nicolson (London: Collins, 1966), 41.

46 George Bernard Shaw and Nancy Astor: Stanley Weintraub, *Shaw's People: Victoria to Churchill* (University Park, Pa., and London: Penn State University Press, 1996), 229.

47 causing him in 1931 to break: Martin Gilbert, *Winston Churchill: The Wilderness Years* (Boston: Houghton Mifflin, 1984), 33.

47 "the boneless wonder": See Winston Churchill, *Blood, Toil, Tears and Sweat: The Great Speeches,* ed. David Cannadine (Harmondsworth, U.K.: Penguin, 1990), xxxiv.

47 "a guy who's not well": William Manchester, *The Caged Lion: Winston Spencer Churchill, 1932–1940* (London: Abacus, 1994), 88.

47 Churchill faced serious financial problems: David Reynolds, *In Command of History:*

Churchill Fighting and Writing the Second World War (New York: Random House, 2005), xx.

47 **"in the political wilderness"**: Winston S. Churchill, *The Second World War, Volume I: The Gathering Storm* (Boston: Houghton Mifflin, 1948), 667.

47 **extent of his political exile**: See, for example, Stuart Ball, "Churchill and the Conservative Party," in *Winston Churchill in the Twenty-First Century,* ed. David Cannadine and Roland Quinault (Cambridge, U.K.: Cambridge University Press, 2004), 78.

47 **"in no circumstances fight"**: Jonathan Rose, "England His Englands," in *The Cambridge Companion to George Orwell,* ed. John Rodden (Cambridge U.K.: Cambridge University Press, 2007), 37.

48 **"whether the British ruling class"**: George Orwell, "Looking Back at the Spanish War," in *Orwell in Spain,* ed. Peter Davison (Harmondsworth, U.K.: Penguin, 2001), 358.

48 **"The Ribbentrops are intimate"**: Robert Rhodes James, ed., *Chips: The Diaries of Sir Henry Channon,* ed. Robert Rhodes James (London: Weidenfeld & Nicolson, 1967), 62.

48 **pronounced the German leader "very agreeable"**: Ian Kershaw, *Making Friends with Hitler: Lord Londonderry, the Nazis and the Road to World War II* (New York: Penguin, 2004), 141, 177, 222.

48 **a bitter conversation over dinner**: Ibid., xvii, 175, 258, 319.

49 **"very much in love"**: Randolph S. Churchill, *Twenty-One Years* (Boston: Houghton Mifflin, 1965), 27.

49 **"I don't mind people"**: Charlotte Mosley, ed., *The Mitfords: Letters Between Six Sisters* (New York: HarperCollins, 2007), 28.

49 **"awfully good" imitation of Churchill**: Ibid., 87, 89. See also David Cannadine, *Aspects of Aristocracy: Grandeur and Decline in Modern Britain* (New Haven, Conn.: Yale University Press, 1994), 142.

49 **"I think Hitler must be"**: Mosley, *The Mitfords,* 103.

49 **"He talked a lot about Jews"**: Ibid., 68.

50 **Neville Chamberlain's sister-in-law**: David Faber, *Munich, 1938* (New York: Simon & Schuster, 2010), 88–89.

50 **expressed some admiration**: John Ramsden, *Man of the Century: Winston Churchill and His Legend Since 1945* (New York: Columbia University Press, 2002), 44.

50 **"He is convinced of"**: Thomas Jones, *A Diary with Letters, 1931–1950* (Oxford: Oxford University Press, 1954), 181. See also William McNeill, *Arnold J. Toynbee: A Life* (Oxford: Oxford University Press, 1989), 172.

50 **Americans' distaste for the Nazis**: Jones, *A Diary with Letters,* 390.

50 **"they would prefer to see Hitler"** . . . **"we cannot possibly fight"**: Nicolson, *Diaries and Letters, 1930–1939),* 342–43.

50 **the "Right Club"**: Jonathan Freedland, "Enemies Within," *The Spectator,* 11 February 2012.

50 **"Special weight was held"**: Lord Halifax foreword to John Wrench, *Geoffrey Dawson and Our Times* (London: Hutchinson, 1955), 12.

51 "Herr Hitler, whatever one may think": No author, *The History of The Times, Volume IV, The 150th Anniversary and Beyond, Part II: 1921–1948* (London: Office of the Times, 1952), 887.

51 "I do my utmost": Wrench, *Geoffrey Dawson and Our Times*, 361.

51 the newspaper, "like the Government": *History of The Times*, vol. IV, part II, 946, 1009.)

51 "a piece of my mind": Quoted in Anthony Cave Brown, *C: The Secret Life of Sir Stewart Menzies, Spymaster to Winston Churchill* (New York: Macmillan, 1987), 183.

52 "as a realist, I must do": Keith Feiling, *The Life of Neville Chamberlain* (London: Macmillan, 1946), 323.

52 "a man who could be relied": Kershaw, *Making Friends with Hitler*, 243.

52 "a remarkable man": Jones, *A Diary with Letters*, 247.

52 "The rise of Germany": Quoted in Gilbert, *Churchill: The Wilderness Years*, 60.

52 "the great dominant fact": Winston Churchill, Parliamentary debate, 7 November 1933, accessed online at *Hansard, Parliamentary Debates*. Hereafter, *Hansard*.

52 "What is the great new fact": *Hansard*, 28 November 1934.

53 refrain from an arms race: Faber, *Munich, 1938*, 16.

53 pressure the French government: Gilbert, *Churchill: The Wilderness Years*, 78.

53 "we do not think": *Hansard*, 11 March 1935.

53 Chamberlain sought to reconcile: Gilbert, *Churchill: The Wilderness Years*, 215.

53–54 "no policy of immediate adventure": Martin Gilbert, *Winston S. Churchill: The Prophet of Truth, Volume V: 1922–1939* (London, Minerva, 1990), 889.

54 "a policy of negotiation": *Hansard*, 24 March 1938.

54 "rightly or wrongly": Thomas Jones letter to Abraham Flexner, in Jones, *A Diary with Letters*, 125.

54 "We have abundant evidence": Ibid., 175.

54 "Hitler believes in you": Ibid., 208.

54 make "strongly the case": Ibid., 219.

54 an "overtalented outsider": Tony Judt with Timothy Snyder, *Thinking the Twentieth Century* (New York: Penguin Press, 2012), 68.

54 "We all know that": *Hansard*, 13 March 1930.

54 "a Malay running amok": Gilbert, *Churchill: The Wilderness Years*, 113.

54 called "derisive laughter": Ibid., 106.

55 "there is scarcely a single Tory": W. P. Crozier, *Off the Record: Political Interviews 1933–1943*, ed. A. J. P. Taylor (London: Hutchinson, 1973), 32.

55 "Although one hates to criticise": *Hansard*, 2 May 1935.

55 thought him "very unbalanced": Gilbert, *Churchill: The Wilderness Years*, 146.

55 his political career was "finished": Ibid., 171.

55 "it was almost the universal view": Churchill, *The Second World War, Vol. I: The Gathering Storm*, 219.

55 "Whatever dangers there may be": *Hansard*, 18 December 1934.

55 **Baron Ponsonby of Shulbrede:** Information on Ponsonby's forebears is from Overy, *The Twilight Years,* 237.

55 **"the greatest possible admiration":** *Hansard,* 4 October 1938.

55 **"shot or hanged":** Brian Gardner, *Churchill in Power: As Seen by His Contemporaries* (Boston: Houghton Mifflin, 1970), 11.

56 **"You won't be satisfied":** Gilbert, *Churchill: Prophet of Truth,* 822.

56 **"Mrs. Simpson's pinched our king":** Iona Opie and Peter Opie, *The Lore and Language of Schoolchildren* (Oxford: Oxford University Press, 1959), 6.

56 **"The upper classes mind her":** Nicolson, *Diaries and Letters,* 280.

57 **"England may be very clever":** Churchill, *The Second World War, Vol. I: The Gathering Storm,* 222–24.

57 **"We seem to be moving":** *Hansard,* 14 April 1937.

57 **"I watched the daylight":** Churchill, *The Second World War, Vol. I: The Gathering Storm,* 258.

57 **"For five years I have talked":** *Hansard,* 24 March 1938.

57 **players gave the Nazi salute:** Faber, *Munich, 1938,* 177.

58 **"It was a disagreeable business":** Gilbert, *Churchill: Prophet of Truth,* 925.

58 **"established a certain confidence":** Quoted in A. L. Rowse, *Appeasement: A Study in Political Decline, 1933–1939* (New York: W. W. Norton, 1963), 83.

58 **"a fatal delusion":** Gilbert, *Churchill: Prophet of Truth,* 978–79.

59 **Most members of the House:** All quotations are from *Hansard,* 3 October 1938.

59–60 **"I will begin by saying"** . . . **"What is Czechoslovakia?":** *Hansard,* 5 October 1938.

60 **"Anybody who had been through":** *Hansard,* 6 October 1938.

60 **"The hard fact":** Roy Jenkins, *Churchill* (New York: Farrar, Straus and Giroux, 2001), 530, 534.

61 **enjoyed a burst of popularity:** Harold Nicolson, *The War Years: 1939–1945* (New York: Atheneum, 1967), 355.

61 **"Our foreign policy":** Faber, *Munich, 1938,* 432.

61 **"the democracies would be crushed":** Jones, *A Diary with Letters,* 411.

61 **he attacked Churchill:** Gilbert, *Churchill: Prophet of Truth,* 1016.

62 **"I shall have to say something":** Faber, *Munich, 1938,* 432.

62 **the issue of Jewish refugees:** Robert Self, *Neville Chamberlain: A Biography* (London and Burlington, Vt.: Ashgate, 2006), 344–45.

62 **never "expressed a word of sympathy":** Crozier, *Off the Record,* 120.

62 **His Christmas card that year:** Simon Schama, *A History of Britain, Volume 3: The Fate of Empire: 1776–2000* (London: BBC, 2003), 384.

62 **"at the next general election":** Jenkins, *Churchill,* 535.

62 **looked "extremely dangerous":** Gilbert, *Churchill: Prophet of Truth,* 1039.

62 **"Now it will take some time":** Ibid., 1041.

63 **"a far away country":** L. S. Amery, *My Political Life, Volume 3: The Unforgiving Years, 1929–1940* (London: Hutchinson, 1955), 279.

63 **Some revisionists contend that:** Williamson Murray, "Innovation: Past and Future," *Military Innovation in the Interwar Period,* ed. Williamson Murray and Allan Millett (Cambridge, U.K.: Cambridge University Press, 2006), 307.

63 **unfold his plans for war:** *"Bericht ueber Besprechung am 23.5.1939"* [Minutes of a Conference on 23 May 39], Evidence Code Document 79, Nuremberg Documents. Accessed online at Harvard Law School Nuremberg Trials Project.

63 **he envisioned fighting the United States:** Gerhard Weinberg, *A World at Arms: A Global History of World War II,* 2nd ed. (Cambridge, U.K.: Cambridge University Press, 2006), 239 and passim.

63–64 **"The right honorable Gentleman":** *Hansard,* 8 June 1939.

64 **"had no intention":** Wrench, *Geoffrey Dawson and Our Times,* 394.

64 **"all along has prophesied":** *Hansard,* 24 August 1939.

CHAPTER 5. ORWELL BECOMES "ORWELL": SPAIN 1937

65–66 **"there was a belief":** George Orwell, *Homage to Catalonia* (New York: Harvest, 1980), 6.

66 **"A new world":** David Boyd Haycock, *I Am Spain: The Spanish Civil War and the Men and Women Who Went to Fight Fascism* (London: Old Street, 2012), 67.

66 **Popeye the Sailor Man:** Ibid., 69.

66 **"variants of Jack the Giant-Killer":** George Orwell, *The Collected Essays, Journalism and Letters of George Orwell, Volume 1: An Age Like This, 1920–1940,* ed. Sonia Orwell and Ian Angus (New York: Harcourt Brace Jovanovich, 1968), 459. Hereafter, Orwell, *CEJL,* vol. 1.

66 **"as if we had been landed":** Ibid., 37.

66 **he would be tortured . . . communist-run jail:** Ibid., 256.

66 **"He won me over":** "Jennie Lee to Margaret M. Goalby," in George Orwell, *Orwell in Spain,* ed. Peter Davison (Harmondsworth, U.K.: Penguin, 2001), 5.

66 **he recorded his occupation:** Adam Hochschild, *Spain in Our Hearts: Americans in the Spanish Civil War, 1936–1939* (Boston: Houghton Mifflin Harcourt, 2016), 65.

66 **"He came striding towards me":** "With the ILP in Spain," in Audrey Coppard and Bernard Crick, *Orwell Remembered* (New York: Facts on File Publications, 1984), 146–47.

67 **"We were near the front line":** Orwell, *Homage to Catalonia,* 16.

67 **"We had just dumped our kits":** Ibid., 20.

67 **The POUM newspaper had:** Bernard Crick, *George Orwell: A Life* (New York: Penguin, 1992), 322.

68 **"the Trotskyist organization POUM":** Christopher Andrew and Vasili Mitrokhin, *The Sword and the Shield: The Mitrokhin Archive and the Secret History of the KGB* (New York: Basic Books, 1999), 76.

68 **dog with the letters POUM:** Orwell, *Homage to Catalonia,* 18.

68 **black poodle he named Marx:** Gordon Bowker, *George Orwell* (London: Abacus, 2004), 230.

68 "nothing happened, nothing ever happened": Orwell, *Homage to Catalonia*, 72.

68 "he was very practical": "In the Spanish Trenches" in Audrey Coppard and Bernard Crick, *Orwell Remembered* (New York: Facts on File Publications, 1984), 149.

68 ventured into the no-man's-land: Ibid.

68 "Everything was quiet": Stephen Wadhams, ed., *Remembering Orwell* (Harmondsworth, U.K.: Penguin, 1984), 79.

69 executing members who displayed "Trotskyite tendencies": Ibid., 85.

69 "I was allowed to stay": Michael Shelden, *Orwell: The Authorized Biography* (New York: HarperCollins, 1991), 258.

69 "Then what a rest we will have": Orwell, *CEJL*, vol. 1, 266.

69 "the revolutionary atmosphere": Orwell, *Homage to Catalonia*, 109.

69 "We, at the front": Ibid., 110.

69 An official propaganda campaign: Andrew and Mitrokhin, *The Sword and the Shield*, 74.

70 A sense of looming danger: Orwell, *Homage to Catalonia*, 117.

70 The storm broke on May 3: Ibid., 121.

70 Hotel Colón, where Churchill had stayed: Geert Mak, *In Europe: Travels Through the Twentieth Century* (New York: Vintage, 2008), 321. See also Winston S. Churchill, *The Second World War, Volume I: The Gathering Storm* (Boston: Houghton Mifflin, 1948), 185. Churchill does not identify the hotel in his memoir, but letters and telegrams in the Churchill Archives sent to him in mid-December 1935 were addressed to the Colón. See Churchill Papers, Churchill College, Cambridge, Document CHAR 2/238/131.\.

70 "In a window near the last O": Orwell, *Homage to Catalonia*, 131.

70 "Trotskyists, Fascists, traitors": Ibid., 64.

71 "You had all the while": Ibid., 147.

71 "The Communist Party, with Soviet Russia": Ibid., 51.

71–72 "One of the dreariest effects": Ibid., 65.

72 This set him on his life's work: This and several earlier paragraphs reflect conversations with the writer Karin Chenoweth.

72 "Franco's Fifth Column": Ibid., 160.

72 Posters appeared on Barcelona walls: Wadhams, *Remembering Orwell*, 88–89.

72 "Roughly speaking it was" . . . "Gosh! Are you hit?": Orwell, *Homage to Catalonia*, 185.

72 "I thought he wouldn't make it": Shelden, *Orwell*, 267.

73 "I took it for granted": Orwell, *Homage to Catalonia*, 186.

73 his voice was a croak: "Bullet in the Neck," in Coppard and Crick, *Orwell Remembered*, 159.

74 On June 15, Andreu Nin: Andrew and Mitrokhin, *The Sword and the Shield*, 73.

74 Orwell returned to Barcelona: Shelden, *Orwell*, 270.

74 *Get out!* . . . Get out": Orwell, *Homage to Catalonia*, 204.

74 "The POUM's been suppressed": Ibid., 205, 198.

74 "the 'Stalinists' were in the saddle": Ibid., 198.

74 "as though we had been": Ibid., 208.

74 "One must remember that the police": Ibid., 224.

75 the Orwells' passports: Haycock, *I Am Spain*, 256.

75 "He had learned": Ernest Hemingway, *For Whom the Bell Tolls* (New York: Scribner, 1993), 229.

75 "It was a heresy": Ibid., 247.

75 "boozy, preoccupied with the image": Malcolm Muggeridge, *Chronicles of Wasted Time* (Vancouver, B.C., Canada: Regent College, 2006), 488.

76 "Their correspondence reveals": "Escape from Spain," in *Orwell in Spain*, 26. For a slightly different translation, see Bowker, *George Orwell*, 227.

76 many of his British socialist friends: The end of this paragraph is drawn from a series of e-mail exchanges with Karin Chenoweth.

76 "It was still the England": Orwell, *Homage to Catalonia*, 231–32.

77 "If someone drops a bomb": George Orwell, "Review of *The Tree of Gernika* by G. L. Steer; *Spanish Testament* by Arthur Koestler," *Time and Tide*, 5 February 1938, in Orwell, *CEJL*, vol. 1, 296.

77 Before Spain, he had been: George Orwell, *Orwell and Politics*, ed. Peter Davison (Harmondsworth, U.K.: Penguin, 2001), 26.

77 "a leftist at odds": Hugh Kenner, "The Politics of the Plain Style," in *Reflections on America, 1984: An Orwell Symposium*, ed. Robert Mulvihill (Athens, Ga., and London: University of Georgia Press, 1986), 63.

77 "It is unfortunate": George Orwell, "Spilling the Spanish Beans," in *CEJL*, vol. 1, 270.

77 "The Spanish war and other": George Orwell, "Why I Write," in *Orwell and Politics*, ed. Peter Davison (Harmondsworth, U.K.: Penguin, 2001), 461.

78 "a communist and a fascist": George Orwell, "Unsigned editorial," *Polemic*, 3 May 1946, ibid., 455.

78 "In Spain, for the first time": George Orwell, *The Collected Essays, Journalism and Letters of George Orwell, Volume 2: My Country Right or Left, 1940–1943*, ed. Sonia Orwell and Ian Angus (New York: Harcourt Brace Jovanovich, 1968), 257. Hereafter, Orwell, *CEJL*, vol. 2.

78 "doesn't approve at all": Shelden, *Orwell*, 281.

79 "one of the most important documents": Lionel Trilling, introduction to Orwell, *Homage to Catalonia*, v.

79 *National Review* named it: "The 100 Best Non-Fiction Books of the Century," *National Review*, May 3, 1999.

79 fewer than 1,500 copies: Bowker, *George Orwell*, 237.

79 In 1941, the printing plates: Orwell, *Orwell and Politics*, 104.

80 "Whatever faults the post-war government": Orwell, *Homage to Catalonia*, 181.

80 "an anachronism," a feudalist: Ibid.

80 "Franco was not strictly comparable": Orwell, *Orwell in Spain*, 171.

81 "It would seem today": Quoted in Dorothy Boyd Rush, "Winston Churchill and the Spanish Civil War," *Social Science* (Spring 1979): 90. This paragraph draws on the conclusions of that article.

81 "The night before the Russo-German pact": Orwell, *CEJL*, vol. 1, 539.

82 a final moment of clarity: This end of this paragraph is drawn from another series of e-mail exchanges with Karin Chenoweth.

82 literary critic and editor Raymond Mortimer: Orwell, *Orwell in Spain*, 269–73.

82 *The Long Week-End:* Robert Graves and Alan Hodge, *The Long Week-End: A Social History of Great Britain, 1918–1939* (London: Faber & Faber, 1940; reprinted New York: W. W. Norton, 1963). See Sir Charles Wilson, later Lord Moran, *Churchill: Taken from the Diaries of Lord Moran* (Boston: Houghton Mifflin, 1966), 319.

83 "then you can't eat them": Shelden, *Orwell*, 359.

83 "war is almost certain": George Orwell, *Diaries*, ed. Peter Davison (New York: W. W. Norton, 2012), 224–25.

83 "very pessimistic views": Ibid., 230.

83 "Invasion of Poland began": Ibid., 232.

CHAPTER 6. CHURCHILL BECOMES "CHURCHILL": SPRING 1940

84 "This is the last picture": Martin Gilbert, *Winston S. Churchill: The Prophet of Truth, Volume V: 1922–1939* (London: Minerva, 1990), 1013.

84 "Before the harvest is gathered": Walter Thompson, *Beside the Bulldog: The Intimate Memoirs of Churchill's Bodyguard* (London: Apollo, 2003), 76.

85 "This is a sad day": Neville Chamberlain, Parliamentary debate, 3 September 1939, accessed online at *Hansard, Parliamentary Debates.* Hereafter, *Hansard.*

85 "I felt a serenity": Winston S. Churchill, *The Second World War, Volume I: The Gathering Storm* (Boston: Houghton Mifflin, 1948), 409.

85 "We are fighting": *Hansard*, 3 September 1939.

85 "Intellectual liberty . . . without a doubt": George Orwell, "Orwell's Proposed Preface to *Animal Farm*," in *Orwell and Politics,* ed. Peter Davison (Harmondsworth, U.K.: Penguin, 2001), 311.

85 "if this war": George Orwell, *The Collected Essays, Journalism and Letters of George Orwell, Volume 3: As I Please, 1943–1945,* ed. Sonia Orwell and Ian Angus (New York: Harcourt Brace Jovanovich, 1968), 199. Hereafter, Orwell, *CEJL,* vol. 3.

86 Unity Mitford walked into a park: Charlotte Mosley, ed., *The Mitfords: Letters Between Six Sisters* (New York: HarperCollins, 2007), 143.

86 "I shall at all times welcome it": Warren F. Kimball, ed., *Churchill & Roosevelt: The Complete Correspondence, Volume 1: Alliance Emerging, October 1933–November 1942* (Princeton, N.J.: Princeton University Press, 1987), 24.

86 Churchill responded with alacrity: Churchill, *The Second World War, Vol. I: The Gathering Storm,* 440. See also the discussion of Kennedy in Norman Gelb, *Dunkirk: The Complete Story of the First Step in the Defeat of Hitler* (New York: William Morrow, 1989), 46–47.

86 the first of about 800: Winston S. Churchill, *The Second World War, Volume II: Their Finest Hour* (Boston: Houghton Mifflin, 1949), 23.

86 "The President thinks: David Nasaw, *The Patriarch: The Remarkable Life and*

Turbulent Times of Joseph P. Kennedy (New York: Penguin Press, 2012), 315. See also 497.

86 **"possibly under other names"**: Ibid., 373.

86 **"disloyal to his country"**: Ibid., 331.

87 **"we have snubbed"**: David Dilks, ed., *The Diaries of Sir Alexander Cadogan, 1938–1945,* (New York: G. P. Putnam's Sons, 1972), 37.

87 **"The lack of all sense"**: Churchill, *The Second World War, Vol. I: The Gathering Storm,* 255.

87 **"Somehow the light faded"**: Ibid., 433. Additional details from Martin Gilbert, *Winston S. Churchill: Finest Hour, Volume VI: 1939–1941* (London: Heinemann, 1983), 32.

87 **his first major speech**: Paul Johnson, *Churchill* (New York: Penguin, 2010), 104.

88 **"very frank talk"**: Robert Self, *Neville Chamberlain: A Biography* (London and Burlington, Vt.: Ashgate Publishing, 2006), 388.

88 **Churchill sent thirteen analytical letters**: Roy Jenkins, *Churchill* (Farrar, Straus and Giroux, 2001), 553.

88 **"Winston's ceaseless industry"**: John Colville, *The Fringes of Power: 10 Downing Street Diaries, 1939–1955* (New York: W. W. Norton, 1985), 143.

88 **"has not appeared"**: Quoted in Harold Nicolson, *The War Years: 1939–1945* (New York: Atheneum, 1967), 186.

88 **"rather shocked by"**: Ibid., 251.

88 **Churchill drank champagne**: Sir Ian Jacob, in John Wheeler-Bennett, ed., *Action This Day: Working with Churchill (*New York: St. Martin's, 1969),183.

89 **May 10, 1940**: The following two pages rely heavily on Gilbert, *Churchill: Finest Hour.* 306–17. Just behind that source stands Churchill's own account at the end of *The Gathering Storm,* the first volume of his World War II memoirs. Several other sources were used for particular aspects of this key transition. On King George's preference for Halifax, see Joseph Lash, *Roosevelt and Churchill, 1939–1941: The Partnership That Saved the West* (New York: W. W. Norton 1976), 110–11, and also Brian Gardner, *Churchill in Power: As Seen by His Contemporaries* (Boston: Houghton Mifflin, 1969), 39. On the question of how Halifax would have dealt with Germany had he become premier, see Dennis Showalter, "Phony and Hot War, 1939–1940," in Dennis Showalter and Harold Deutsch, ed., *If the Allies Had Fallen: Sixty Alternate Scenarios of World War II* (London/New York: Frontline/Skyhorse, 2010). After the war, Clementine Churchill found herself seated at a French embassy dinner next to Halifax, who complained that her husband was becoming a burden on the Conservative Party. Clementine hotly responded, "If the country had depended on you, we might have lost the war." Sir Charles Wilson, later Lord Moran, *Churchill: Taken from the Diaries of Lord Moran* (Boston: Houghton Mifflin, 1966), 472. She almost certainly was correct. As the historian Sebastian Haffner puts it, "But for Churchill in 1940 and 1941, it is quite conceivable that Hitler might have won the war and would have founded a Greater Germanic SS state extending from the

Atlantic to the Urals or beyond." Sebastian Haffner, *Churchill* (London: Haus, 2003), 104.

89 **"Mr. Chamberlain was inclined"**: Churchill, *The Second World War, Vol. I: The Gathering Storm,* 662.

90 **"Haggard and worn"**: Ibid.

90 **"I hope that it is"**: Thompson, *Beside the Bulldog,* 84.

90 **"the greatest adventurer"**: Colville, *The Fringes of Power,* 122.

91 with **"total horror"**: Joshua Levine, *Forgotten Voices of the Blitz and the Battle for Britain* (London: Ebury, 2007), 37.

91 **"bring the United States into the war"**: Anthony Cave Brown, *C: The Secret Life of Sir Stewart Menzies, Spymaster to Winston Churchill* (New York: Macmillan, 1987), 263.

91 **"a profound sense of relief"**: Churchill, *The Second World War, Vol. I: The Gathering Storm,* 667.

91 **"The Tories don't trust Winston"**: Gilbert, *Churchill: Finest Hour,* 327.

91 **"Winston won't last"**: Andrew Roberts, *Eminent Churchillians* (London: Phoenix, 1995), 159.

92 **"Very ungrateful of them"**: Ibid., 168.

92 **"In the early weeks"**: Robert Rhodes James, ed., *Chips: The Diaries of Sir Henry Channon,* (London: Weidenfeld & Nicolson, 1967), 252. See also Richard Toye, *The Roar of the Lion: The Untold Story of Churchill's World War II Speeches* (Oxford: Oxford University Press, 2013), 42. Churchill quotation is from Churchill, *The Second World War, Vol. II: Their Finest Hour,* 10.

92 the welcoming speeches: Nicolson, *The War Years,* 85.

92 **"I have nothing to offer"** . . . **"towards its goal"**: *Hansard,* 13 May 1940.

92 **"The Age of Bronze"**: Michael Shelden, *Young Titan: The Making of Winston Churchill* (New York: Simon & Schuster, 2013), 7.

93 **"For the first time in decades"**: George Orwell, "Letter to the Editor of *Time and Tide,*" in *The Collected Essays, Journalism and Letters of George Orwell, Volume 2: My Country Right or Left, 1940–1943,* ed. Sonia Orwell and Ian Angus (New York: Harcourt Brace Jovanovich, 1968), 28. Hereafter, Orwell, *CEJL,* vol. 2.

93 **"drag the United States in"**: Gilbert, *Churchill: Finest Hour,* 358.

93 **"The first thing is"**: Stephen Roskill, *Churchill and the Admirals* (New York: William Morrow, 1978), 126.

93 **"The situation is terrible"**: Nasaw, *The Patriarch,* 447.

93 **"nothing but slaughter ahead"**: Ibid., 350.

94 **"British navy would be against us"**: Orville Bullitt, ed., *For the President: Personal and Secret: Correspondence Between Franklin D. Roosevelt and William C. Bullitt* (Boston: Houghton Mifflin, 1972), 428.

94 **"he dissolved into tears"**: Hastings Ismay, *The Memoirs of Lord Ismay* (London: Heinemann, 1960), 116.

94 **Several hundred thousand**: Gelb, *Dunkirk,* 316.

94 **"The German mobile columns"**: Alistair Horne, *To Lose a Battle: France 1940* (Harmondsworth, U.K.: Penguin, 2007), 610.

94 **"We could not understand"**: Hans von Luck, *Panzer Commander: The Memoirs of Colonel Hans von Luck* (New York: Dell, 1989), 42.

95 **"avoid inflicting a humiliating defeat"**: Stephen Bungay, *The Most Dangerous Enemy: A History of the Battle of Britain* (London: Aurum Press, 2001), 31. See also Levine, *Forgotten Voices of the Blitz*, 19–20.

95 **Hitler's order stopping his ground forces**: John Lukacs, *Five Days in London: May 1940.* (New Haven, Conn.: Yale University Press, 2001), 42, 192. See also Churchill, *The Second World War, Vol. II: Their Finest Hour*, 76.

95 **"Churchill was quite unable"**: Carlo D'Este, *Warlord: A Life of Winston Churchill at War, 1874–1945* (New York: HarperCollins, 2008), 425.

95 **"My tanks were kept halted"**: Earl Ziemke, "Rundstedt," in Correlli Barnett, ed., *Hitler's Generals* (London: Weidenfield & Nicolson, 1989), 191.

95 **"his aim was to make peace"**: B. H. Liddell Hart, *The German Generals Talk* (New York: Berkley, 1958), 113, 115.

95 **"a face-saving rationalization"**: Ian Kershaw, *Fateful Choices: Ten Decisions That Changed the World, 1940–1941* (New York: Penguin, 2007), 27; Gerhard Weinberg, *A World at Arms: A Global History of World War II*, 2nd ed. (Cambridge, U.K.: Cambridge University Press, 2006), 131.

96 **"left to the Luftwaffe"**: Horne, *To Lose a Battle*, 610.

96 **Orwell's wife's brother**: Michael Shelden, *Orwell: The Authorized Biography* (New York: HarperCollins, 1991), 330,

96 **"Her hair was unbrushed"**: Ibid., 331.

96 **"He did not talk"**: Ibid.

96 **"Winston talked the most frightful rot"**: Kershaw, *Fateful Choices*, 41.

96 **England's negotiating position**: Colville, *Fringes of Power*, 141.

97 **"fighting for his political life"**: Boris Johnson, *The Churchill Factor: How One Man Made History* (New York: Riverhead, 2014), 22.

97 **"his government would be untenable"**: Jenkins, *Churchill*, 602.

97 **Halifax grumbled to**: Dilks, *Diaries of Sir Alexander Cadogan*, 291.

97 **"apologies and affection"**: Jenkins, *Churchill*, 604.

97 **there would be no surrender**: Lukacs, *Five Days in London*, 149, 155, 182–83.

97 **"If this long island story"**: Hugh Dalton, *The Fateful Years* (London: Frederick Muller, 1957), 336.

97 **"England will never quit"**: Churchill, *The Second World War, Vol. II: Their Finest Hour*, 90.

98 **"Hitler's peace terms"**: John Charmley, *Churchill: The End of Glory* (New York: Harcourt Brace, 1993), 400.

98 **"the first great battle"**: Simon Schama, *A History of Britain, Volume 3: The Fate of Empire: 1776–2000* (London: BBC, 2003), 398.

98 **"Churchill and his gang"**: W. P. Crozier, *Off the Record: Political Interviews, 1933–1943*, ed. A. J. P. Taylor (London: Hutchinson, 1973), 221.

98 "A compromise government": Richard Overy, *The Battle of Britain: The Myth and the Reality* (New York: W. W. Norton, 2001), 17.

98 "Halifax may succeed Churchill": Bungay, *The Most Dangerous Enemy,* 13.

98 possibility of Churchill being replaced: Ibid., 112. See also Roberts, *Eminent Churchillians,* 137–38.

99 "When a week ago" . . . "liberation of the old": *Hansard,* 4 June 1940.

99 He stood perhaps five foot seven: Anthony Storr, *Churchill's Black Dog, Kafka's Mice, and Other Phenomena of the Human Mind* (New York: Ballantine, 1990), 9.

100 the locations of fighting: Bungay, *The Most Dangerous Enemy,* 22.

100 "This afternoon Winston made the finest speech": Nicolson, *The War Years,* 93.

100 "I remember being very frightened": Levine, *Forgotten Voices of the Blitz,* 43–44.

100 Churchill's voice became "our hope": C. P. Snow, "Winston Churchill," in *Variety of Men* (London: Macmillan, 1967), 111.

100 "It will be necessary to withdraw": Gelb, *Dunkirk,* 213.

101 "Britain was not just expelled": Cathal Nolan, *The Allure of Battle: A History of How Wars Have Been Won and Lost* (New York: Oxford University Press, 2017), 445.

101 Left behind in the sand dunes: Harold Macmillan, *The Blast of War, 1939–1945* (New York: Harper & Row, 1968), 81. See also Gelb, *Dunkirk,* 311.

101 200 first-rate tanks: Churchill, *The Second World War, Vol. II: Their Finest Hour,* 256.

101 the 1st London: Len Deighton, *Battle of Britain* (New York: Coward, McCann & Geoghegan, 1980), 84.

101 Anthony Eden, then overseeing: Statement made to and quoted by Crozier in *Off the Record,* 184.

101 civilians were shot: Daniel Todman, *Britain's War: Into Battle, 1937–1941* (Oxford: Oxford University Press, 2016), 379.

101 Britain braced for invasion: Levine, *Forgotten Voices of the Blitz,* 57–58.

101 lost 250 modern fighter planes: Gelb, *Dunkirk,* 301.

102 wheelbarrows of archived documents: Ismay, *Memoirs of Lord Ismay,* 127.

102 "crowned like a volcano": Gardner, *Churchill in Power,* 47.

102 "I was dumbfounded": Churchill, *The Second World War, Vol. II: Their Finest Hour,* 47.

102 "In all battles": Winston S. Churchill, *Painting as a Pastime* (Greensboro, N.C.: Unicorn Press, 2013), 48.

102 "We will starve Germany": Gardner, *Churchill in Power,* 47.

102 "mental and moral prostration": Churchill, *The Second World War, Vol. II: Their Finest Hour,* 243.

102 "The news from France": Ibid., 217.

102 "Great Britain was left": Walter Millis, *Arms and Men: A Study in American Military History* (New Brunswick, N.J.: Rutgers University Press, 1981), 275.

102 "The whole fury and might": *Hansard,* 18 June 1940.

102 the significance of this speech: Jenkins, *Churchill,* 611. Along these lines, there is a Web site devoted to comparing Churchill and Lincoln, www.lincolnandchurchill.com.

103 "nearly everyone who was anti-Nazi": George Orwell, "London Letter," *Partisan Review,* July–August 1942, in *Orwell and Politics,* 162.

104 "Never give in": Winston Churchill, "Never Give In" (speech, Harrow School, 29 October 1941), accessed online at the Web site of the Churchill Society.

104 "It is impossible": George Orwell, *Diaries,* ed. Peter Davison (New York: W. W. Norton, 2012), 286.

104 "if the worst comes": Ibid., 292.

104 had to explain to Parliament: Gilbert, *Churchill: Finest Hour,* 642.

105 "Chamberlain [had] presided": Sir Ian Jacob, in Wheeler-Bennett, *Action This Day,* 159.

105 yet unemployment increased: Todman, *Britain's War,* 225.

105 "sedate, sincere, but routine:" Churchill, *The Second World War, Vol. I: The Gathering Storm,* 650.

105 demanding "Action This Day": Lukacs, *Five Days in London,* 190.

105 "the beam of a searchlight": Lord Normanbrook, in Wheeler-Bennett, *Action This Day,* 22.

105 "All round Whitehall": Sir Ian Jacob, ibid., 168.

106 "mental field was well lit": Churchill, *The Second World War, Vol. I: The Gathering Storm,* 158.

106 "'Attack, attack, attack'": R. W. Thompson, *Churchill and Morton* (London: Hodder & Stoughton, 1976), 95.

106 aggressive moves by British forces: Churchill, *The Second World War, Vol. II: Their Finest Hour.* 243.

106 "overcome the difficulties": Winston S. Churchill, *The Second World War, Volume IV: The Hinge of Fate* (Boston: Houghton Mifflin, 1950), 934.

106 "any error towards the enemy": Churchill, *The Second World War, Vol. II: Their Finest Hour,* 681.

107 "You need not argue": David Jablonsky, *Churchill: The Making of a Grand Strategist* (Carlisle, Pa.: Strategic Studies Institute, U.S. Army War College, 1990), 72.

107 "Much is being thrown upon": Churchill, *The Second World War, Vol. I: The Gathering Storm,* 459.

107 "The tendency of every Station Commander": Ibid., 662.

108 "This decision was undoubtedly correct": Bungay, *The Most Dangerous Enemy,* 101.

CHAPTER 7. FIGHTING THE GERMANS,
REACHING OUT TO THE AMERICANS: 1940–1941

109 "wipe the British Air Force from the sky": Ronald Lewin, *Ultra Goes to War* (London: Hutchinson, 1978), 86.

109 Luftwaffe's commanders estimated: Stephen Bungay, *The Most Dangerous Enemy: A History of the Battle of Britain* (London: Aurum Press, 2001), 111. See also 152.

109 "would be inevitable": Martin Gilbert, *Churchill and America* (New York: Free Press, 2005), 200–201.

110 **wheeled and dueled in the skies:** Richard Overy, *The Battle of Britain: The Myth and the Reality* (New York: W. W. Norton, 2001), 45.

110 **"Who would have believed":** George Orwell, *Diaries,* ed. Peter Davison (New York: W. W. Norton, 2012), 282.

110 **"The coming of Winston":** Thomas Jones, *A Diary with Letters, 1931–1950 (*Oxford: Oxford University Press, 1954), 460.

110 **"Winston is now":** Ibid., 466.

110 **"I shall always be":** No author, *The History of The Times, Volume IV, The 150th Anniversary and Beyond, Part II: 1921–1948* (London: Office of the Times, 1952), 1022.

110 **Orwell argued with a young pacifist:** *The Collected Essays, Journalism and Letters of George Orwell, Volume 3: As I Please, 1943–1945,* ed. Sonia Orwell and Ian Angus (New York: Harcourt Brace Jovanovich, 1968), 132. Hereafter, Orwell, *CEJL,* vol. 3. The Café Royal was, for one example, where Frank Harris met with Oscar Wilde in 1895 to urge him to drop his libel suit against the Marquess of Queensberry, saying, "You don't know what is going to happen to you." Wilde angrily refused, and went on to ruin his own life. Stanley Weintraub, *Shaw's People: Victoria to Churchill.* (University Park, Pa., and London: State University Press, 1996), 46. Harris, a well-connected Victorian gentleman with more than a few skeletons in his own closet, years later would help Winston Churchill negotiate a lucrative publishing contract. Peter Clarke, *Mr. Churchill's Profession: The Statesman as Author and the Book That Defined the "Special Relationship"* (London: Bloomsbury Press, 2012), 27. Harris is remembered now primarily as the author of *My Life and Loves,* a four-volume account of his sexual adventures.

111 **"Never in the field"** . . . **"springboards of invasion":** *Hansard,* 20 August 1940.

111 **"I don't think we were":** Joshua Levine, *Forgotten Voices of the Blitz and the Battle for Britain* (London: Ebury, 2007), 302.

111 **central London was bombed:** Overy, *Battle of Britain,* 91.

112 **"Should they fall into an area":** Winston S. Churchill, *The Second World War, Volume II: Their Finest Hour* (Boston: Houghton Mifflin, 1949), 657.

112 **the signal CROMWELL:** Harold Nicolson, *The War Years: 1939–1945* (New York: Atheneum, 1967), 111.

112 **his life expectancy:** Levine, *Forgotten Voices of the Blitz,* 91.

112 **348 German bombers:** Peter Stansky, *The First Day of the Blitz* (New Haven, Conn.: Yale University Press, 2007), 1.

113 **"I'll bet you five to one":** David Nasaw, *The Patriarch: The Remarkable Life and Turbulent Times of Joseph P. Kennedy* (New York: Penguin Press, 2012), 474.

113 **British to accept defeat:** Ibid., 477.

113 **"imminent sense of apocalypse":** Peter Ackroyd, introduction to Levine, *Forgotten Voices of the Blitz,* 2.

113 **"the heat blistered":** Neil Wallington, *Firemen at War: The Work of London's Fire Fighters in the Second World War* (Huddersfield, U.K.: Jeremy Mills Publishing, 2007), 91.

113 "You see, he really cares": Martin Gilbert, *Winston S. Churchill: Finest Hour, Volume VI: 1939–1941* (London: Heinemann, 1983), 775.

114 Churchill's visit, September 15: This account of Churchill's visit to the Fighter Group headquarters on 15 September 1940 is based primarily on Churchill, *The Second World War, Vol. II: Their Finest Hour*, 332–36. It also relies on several other sources: Sir Charles Wilson, later Lord Moran, *Churchill: Taken from the Diaries of Lord Moran* (Boston: Houghton Mifflin, 1966), 320–21; Levine, *Forgotten Voices of the Blitz*, 289; and the entry for 15 September 1940 in the Royal Air Force's "Fighter Command Operational Diaries" Web site.

114 "the culminating date": Churchill, *The Second World War, Vol. II: Their Finest Hour*, 332.

115 "the odds were great": Ibid., 336.

115 For fifty minutes: Bungay, *The Most Dangerous Enemy*, 330.

115 "What a slender thread": Gilbert, *Churchill: Finest Hour*, 729.

115 thousands of German bombs: Len Deighton, *Battle of Britain* (New York: Coward, McCann & Geoghegan, 1980), 174.

115 RAF lost twenty-eight: Bungay, *The Most Dangerous Enemy*, 371.

116 "A bomb had struck": James Leutze, ed., *The London Journal of General Raymond E. Lee, 1940–1941* (Boston: Little, Brown, 1971), 62.

116 Churchill would tell friends: Moran, *Churchill*, 348.

116 "PM was very pleasant": Field Marshal Lord Alanbrooke, *The War Diaries: 1939–1945*, ed. Alex Danchev and Daniel Todman (Berkeley: University of California Press, 2002), 107.

116 "While he brooded": John Colville, *The Fringes of Power: 10 Downing Street Diaries, 1939–1955* (New York: W. W. Norton, 1985), 370, 364, 394, 403, 442, 509.

116 "he read a Horatio Hornblower": The Hornblower reference is in Winston S. Churchill, *The Second World War, Volume III: The Grand Alliance* (Boston: Houghton Mifflin, 1950), 429. The Austen reference is in Winston S. Churchill, *The Second World War, Volume V: Closing the Ring* (Boston: Houghton Mifflin, 1951), 425.

117 British early warning system: Bungay, *The Most Dangerous Enemy*, 376–84.

117 They gathered information, quickly: Robin Prior, *When Britain Saved the West: The Story of 1940* (New Haven, Conn.: Yale University Press, 2015), 181.

117 "The whole theory of fighter defence": Levine, *Forgotten Voices of the Blitz*, 137.

118 "astonishingly amateur," concluded Bungay: Bungay, *The Most Dangerous Enemy*, 125.

118 "flying over England": Ibid., 162.

118 a conservative army: John Lukacs, *The Duel: The Eighty-Day Struggle Between Churchill and Hitler* (Boston: Ticknor & Fields, 1991), 158.

118 "I experienced a Spitfire formation": Levine, *Forgotten Voices of the Blitz*, 137.

119 they had 1,438: Bungay, *The Most Dangerous Enemy*, 244.

119 British pilots could fly many missions: Levine, *Forgotten Voices of the Blitz*, 199, 239.

119 RAF lost more bomber crew members: Bungay, *The Most Dangerous Enemy*, 292, 371–74.

119 **a poll conducted:** Tom Harrisson, *Living Through the Blitz* (Harmondsworth, U.K.: Penguin, 1990), 105.

119 **if the German army had landed:** Bungay, *The Most Dangerous Enemy*, 115.

119 **"The margin of victory":** Ibid., 368.

120 **"The unspeakable depression":** Orwell, *Diaries,* 319.

120 **"this misleading Kennedy stuff":** Churchill, *The Second World War, Vol. II: Their Finest Hour,* 675.

120 **"Democracy is finished in England":** Nasaw, *The Patriarch,* 498.

120 **"I never want to see":** Michael Beschloss, *Kennedy and Roosevelt: The Uneasy Alliance* (New York: W. W. Norton, 1980), 229.

121 **"the British position is hopeless":** Charles Lindbergh, *The Wartime Journals of Charles A. Lindbergh* (Harcourt Brace Jovanovich, 1970), 420.

121 **"At this moment, when the New Year":** Churchill, *The Second World War, Vol. III: The Grand Alliance,* 22.

121 **he dispatched Harry Hopkins:** George McJimsey, *Harry Hopkins: Ally of the Poor and Defender of Democracy* (Cambridge, Mass.: Harvard University Press, 1987), 316.

121 **A former social worker:** The description of Hopkins as being the advisor closest to President Roosevelt is from Warren Kimball, *The Juggler: Franklin Roosevelt as Wartime Statesman* (Princeton, N.J.: Princeton University Press, 1991), 9.

122 **Churchill really was "unsteady":** "Unsteady" is from Roy Jenkins, *Churchill* (Farrar, Straus and Giroux, 2001), 573; "drunk half the time" is from David Reynolds, *The Creation of the Anglo-American Alliance 1937–41: A Study in Competitive Co-operation* (Chapel Hill, N.C.: University of North Carolina Press, 1982), 114.

122 **Pan American Clipper service:** Robert E. Sherwood, *Roosevelt and Hopkins: An Intimate History* (New York: Harper & Brothers, 1948), 232, 234, 302. Details of legs of the flight are from Thomas Parrish, *To Keep the British Isles Afloat: FDR's Men in Churchill's London, 1941* (London: Collins, 2009).

122 **greeted there by Brendan Bracken:** The significance of Bracken meeting Hopkins is underscored in Parrish, *To Keep the British Isles Afloat,* 133.

122 **"A rotund—smiling—red-faced"** . . . **"responsible for the impression":** Quotations in this and the subsequent paragraph from Sherwood, *Roosevelt and Hopkins,* 238.

123 **"We seek no treasure"** . . . **"Hitler gets licked":** Gilbert, *Churchill: Finest Hour,* 985–86.

123 **"It just doesn't make sense":,** Martin Gilbert, ed., *The Churchill War Papers: The Ever-Widening War, 1941* (New York: W. W. Norton, 1995), 59, 61, 76.

124 **"Seems simple and nice":** David Dilks, ed., *The Diaries of Sir Alexander Cadogan, 1938–1945,* (New York: G. P. Putnam's Sons, 1972), 348.

124 **Hopkins stood and said:** Moran, *Churchill,* 6. The whispered level of Hopkins's voice is remembered in Hastings Ismay, *The Memoirs of Lord Ismay* (London: Heinemann, 1960), 216. Some twenty-six years later, Bob Dylan, while on his controversial tour of the U.K. in which he played electric guitar and was called a "Judas," would stay at the same Glasgow hotel and while there record several songs. One of them was an obscure title that Hopkins might have appreciated: "What Kind

of Friend Is This?" Steve Hendry, "The King in Queen Street," Glasgow *Daily Record,* 4 October 2015, accessed online.

124 **"Europe First" strategy:** Churchill, *The Second World War, Vol. II: Their Finest Hour,* 690.

124 **"I don't think Hitler can lick these people":** Parrish, *To Keep the British Isles Afloat,* 188.

124 **Churchill assured the Americans:** Winston Churchill, *Blood, Toil, Tears and Sweat: The Great Speeches,* ed. David Cannadine (Harmondsworth, U.K.: Penguin, 1990), 213.

125 **"What bravado Churchill":** Leutze, *The London Journal of General Raymond E. Lee,* 258.

125 **Churchill almost certainly knew:** Richard Toye, *The Roar of the Lion: The Untold Story of Churchill's World War II Speeches* (Oxford: Oxford University Press, 2013), 91.

125 **"The active belligerency":** Christopher Thorne, *Allies of a Kind: The United States, Britain, and the War Against Japan, 1941–1945* (Oxford: Oxford University Press, 1979), 111.

CHAPTER 8. CHURCHILL, ORWELL, AND THE CLASS WAR IN BRITAIN: 1941

126 **"It does not seem probable":** George Orwell, "The Lion and the Unicorn," in *The Collected Essays, Journalism and Letters of George Orwell, Volume 2: My Country Right or Left, 1940–1943,* ed. Sonia Orwell and Ian Angus (New York: Harcourt Brace Jovanovich, 1968), 88. Hereafter, Orwell, *CEJL,* vol. 2.

126 **"They won't have me":** George Orwell, *The Collected Essays, Journalism and Letters of George Orwell, Volume 1: An Age Like This, 1920–1940,* ed. Sonia Orwell and Ian Angus (New York: Harcourt Brace Jovanovich, 1968), 410. Hereafter, Orwell, *CEJL,* vol. 1.

126 **In a 1938 medical examination:** Michael Shelden, *Orwell: The Authorized Biography* (New York: HarperCollins, 1991), 289.

126 **Air Ministry's public relations office:** Bernard Crick, *George Orwell: A Life* (New York: Penguin, 1980), 391–92.

127 **"It is a terrible thing":** George Orwell, "Letter to John Lehmann," in *CEJL,* vol. 2, 29.

127 **"At any normal time":** George Orwell, *Diaries,* ed. Peter Davison (New York: W. W. Norton, 2012), 325.

127 **one hundred pieces of journalism:** John Rodden and John Rossi, *The Cambridge Introduction to George Orwell* (Cambridge, U.K.: Cambridge University Press, 2012), 26.

127 **"Mr. Auden's brand of amoralism":** Orwell, *CEJL,* vol. 1, 516.

127 **"Outside my work":** Orwell, *CEJL,* vol. 2, 24.

128 **"our job, he said, was to die":** Orwell, *Diaries,* 308.

128 **"easier to throw downstairs than up":** Shelden, *Orwell,* 237.

128 **"almost certain that England":** George Orwell, "Letter to the Editor of *Time and Tide,*" in *CEJL,* vol. 2, 27.

128 "He felt enormously at home": Cyril Connolly, *The Evening Colonnade* (London: David Bruce & Watson, 1973), 383.

128 she would turn off the lights: Shelden, *Orwell,* 330.

128 no bomb crater deeper: Orwell, *Diaries,* 312.

129 "hardness of the seats": Ibid., 313.

129 dogs quickly learned: Ibid., 316.

129 "On nights when the raids are bad": Orwell, *CEJL,* vol. 2, 54.

129 "The Lion and the Unicorn," an essay: John Rossi, "'My Country, Right or Left': Orwell's Patriotism," in *The Cambridge Companion to George Orwell,* ed. John Rodden (Cambridge, U.K.: Cambridge University Press, 2007), 94.

129 "opponents professed to see": Orwell, "The Lion and the Unicorn," in *CEJL,* vol. 2, 67.

129 "This war, unless we are defeated": Ibid., 78.

130 writer H. G. Wells: George Orwell, "Wells, Hitler and the World State," ibid, 142.

130 "Read my early works": Gordon Bowker, *George Orwell* (London: Abacus, 2004), 293. See also Orwell, *Diaries,* 366.

130 "that Trotskyite with big feet": Stephen Wadhams, ed., *Remembering Orwell* (Harmondsworth, U.K.: Penguin, 1984), xii.

130 "Churchill's oratory is really good": Orwell, *Diaries,* 344.

130 that "with individual exceptions": Ibid., 295.

130 The stations of the London Underground: Daniel Todman, *Britain's War: Into Battle, 1937–1941* (Oxford: Oxford University Press, 2016), 478.

130 "I was assured": Joshua Levine, *Forgotten Voices of the Blitz and the Battle for Britain* (London: Ebury, 2007), 345–48, and Churchill, *The Second World War, Volume II: Their Finest Hour,* 351.

131 "Now the working class": Quoted in Robert Hewison, *Under Siege: Literary Life in London, 1939–45* (New York: Oxford University Press, 1977), 39.

131 "The lady in the Rolls-Royce": Orwell, "The Lion and the Unicorn," in Orwell, *CEJL,* vol. 2, 90.

131 "with the help of some other people": Levine, *Forgotten Voices of the Blitz and the Battle for Britain,* 377. See also obituary of "Squadron Leader 'Stapme' Stapleton," *Telegraph* (London), 22 April 2010, accessed online.

131 "There is a possibility": James Leutze, ed., *The London Journal of General Raymond E. Lee, 1940–1941* (Boston: Little, Brown, 1971), 339.

131 "there is no sign of weakness": Ibid., 463.

132 "the ruling-class orbit": Orwell, "The Lion and the Unicorn," in *CEJL,* vol. 2, 71.

132 "motor mechanics in uniforms": Len Deighton, *Battle of Britain* (New York: Coward, McCann & Geoghegan, 1980), 32.

132 "when the Air Force": Evelyn Waugh, *Officers and Gentlemen* (New York: Dell, 1961), 255.

132 "the coloured troops": Hugh Dundas, *Flying Start: A Fighter Pilot's War Years* (New York: St. Martin's Press, 1989), 6.

132 Class differences also reached: Levine, *Forgotten Voices of the Blitz,* 226.

132 "breach has been made in the class system": George Orwell, "London Letter, 8 May 1942," in *Orwell and Politics,* ed. Peter Davison (Harmondsworth, U.K.: Penguin, 2001), 167.

132 "the heirs of Nelson": Orwell, "The Lion and the Unicorn," in *CEJL,* vol. 2, 109.

133 "almost entire failure": John Colville, *The Fringes of Power: 10 Downing Street Diaries, 1939–1955* (New York: W. W. Norton, 1985), 282.

133 Of the three thousand pilots: Deighton, *Battle of Britain,* 93.

133 compared with World War I: Anthony Cave Brown, *C: The Secret Life of Sir Stewart Menzies, Spymaster to Winston Churchill* (New York: Macmillan, 1987), 113.

133 "They left it to the lower middle class": Colville, *The Fringes of Power,* 278.

133 "They have saved this country": Ibid., 278, 433.

133 a silver lapel pin: John Ramsden, *Man of the Century: Winston Churchill and His Legend Since 1945* (New York: Columbia University Press, 2002), 575.

133 "We failed you in 1938": Margaret Thatcher, *The Path to Power* (New York: HarperCollins, 1995), 27.

133–34 "careful that class prejudice" . . . "of class or fortune": Churchill, *The Second World War, Vol. I: The Gathering Storm,* 760–63.

134 "We lost him altogether": Martin Gilbert, *Winston S. Churchill: Finest Hour, Volume VI: 1939–1941* (London: Heinemann, 1983), 148.

135 "He has been behaving like a child": Field Marshal Lord Alanbrooke, *The War Diaries: 1939–1945,* ed. Alex Danchev and Daniel Todman (Berkeley: University of California Press, 2002), 347.

135 "the matter of distinctive patches": Eliot Cohen, *Supreme Command: Soldiers, Statesmen, and Leadership in Wartime* (New York: Anchor, 2003), 127.

135 "I should be glad": Winston S. Churchill, *The Second World War, Volume IV: The Hinge of Fate* (Boston: Houghton Mifflin, 1950), 916.

135 "the most class-ridden country": Orwell, "Lion and the Unicorn," in *CEJL,* vol. 2, 67.

135 "Until the Churchill government": Ibid., 85.

136 "It is significant": George Orwell, "The English People," in *The Collected Essays, Journalism and Letters of George Orwell, Volume 3: As I Please, 1943–1945,* ed. Sonia Orwell and Ian Angus (New York: Harcourt Brace Jovanovich, 1968), 21. Hereafter, Orwell, *CEJL,* vol. 3.

136 "a Tory anarchist": Bowker, *George Orwell,* 123.

136 among some Britishers: Some people maintain that "Britisher" is not a real word, but George Marshall used it in his correspondence with British officials. See, for example, his note of 25 October 1950 to Lord Louis Mountbatten in *The Papers of George Catlett Marshall, Volume 7: "The Man of the Age,"* ed. Mark Stoler and Daniel Holt (Baltimore, Md.: Johns Hopkins University Press, 2016), 26.

136 "Lord Haw-Haw": This is pointed out in the discussion of World War II in James Bowman, *Honor: A History* (New York: Encounter, 2006), 157.

136 bowl of boiled eels: Crick, *George Orwell,* 431.

136 "I never saw him wearing": Orwell's style of dress: George Woodcock, *The Crystal Spirit: A Study of George Orwell* (Boston: Little, Brown, 1966), 23. Also, Audrey

Coppard and Bernard Crick, *Orwell Remembered* (New York: Facts on File Publications, 1984), 203.

137 **"For a popular leader"**: George Orwell, "London Letter," *Partisan Review,* July–August 1943, in *Orwell and Politics,* ed. Peter Davison (Harmondsworth, U.K.: Penguin, 2001), 181.

137 **"half an alien"**: Martin Gilbert, *Churchill and America* (New York: Free Press, 2005), 157.

137 **it was the Labour members**: Max Hastings, *Winston's War: Churchill 1940–1945* (New York: Vintage, 2011), 40.

137 **"He was an aristocrat"**: C. P. Snow, *Variety of Men* (London: Macmillan, 1967), 112–13.

138 **"The proper course"**: Orwell, *Diaries,* 333.

138 **"People don't have scruples"**: Ibid., 345.

138 **"the rich swine"**: Ibid., 316.

138 **"how the wealthy are still behaving"**: Ibid., 317.

138 **"my political predictions"**: Ibid., 339.

138 **"The thing that most disturbs"**: Ibid., 342.

139 **"a long, dreary exhausting war"**: Ibid., 358.

139 **"having let the side down"**: Michael Simpson, *A Life of Admiral of the Fleet Andrew Cunningham* (Abingdon, U.K., and New York: Routledge, 2012), 62.

139 **"We have got away with it"**: Winston S. Churchill, *The Second World War, Volume III: The Grand Alliance* (Boston: Houghton Mifflin, 1950), 242. My italics.

140 **"You should obtain accurate information"**: Quoted in Ronald Lewin, *Churchill as Warlord* (London: Scarborough, 1973), 72.

140 **"the most awful outburst"**: Alanbrooke, *The War Diaries,* 207.

140 **"was a complete parrot house"**: Ibid., 226.

140 **"Have you not got a single general"**: Ibid.

140 **"Warships are meant"**: Winston S. Churchill, *The Second World War, Volume II: Their Finest Hour* (Boston: Houghton Mifflin, 1949), 443.

141 **"preferred to work by intuition"**: Alanbrooke, *The War Diaries,* 207, 273.

141 **"the level of events"**: A. L. Rowse, *The Churchills: The Story of a Family* (New York: Harper & Row, 1966), 471.

141 **"it is not possible"**: Churchill, *The Second World War, Vol. III: The Grand Alliance,* 28.

141 **"Painting a picture"**: Winston S. Churchill, *Painting as a Pastime* (Greensboro, N.C.: Unicorn Press, 2013), 45–46.

142 **"It is a crime"**: Churchill, *The Second World War, Volume II: Their Finest Hour,* 548.

142 **"People have visions of Stalin"**: Orwell, *Diaries,* 354.

142 **"We shall fight him by land"**: Winston S. Churchill, *The Second World War, Vol. III: The Grand Alliance,* 372.

143 **Churchill's speech as "very good"**: Orwell, *Diaries,* 353.

143 **erase the memory of Stalin's treaty**: George Orwell, "Notes on Nationalism," in Orwell, *CEJL,* vol. 3, 370.

143 **"as strong as Singapore"**: George Orwell, *The War Commentaries,* ed. W. J. West (New York: Schocken Books, 1986), 40.

143 **salute Churchill for delivering**: Ibid., 213–14.

144 **"heavy casualties on both sides"**: Ibid., 138.

144 **"although he wrote so well"**: "That Curiously Crucified Expression," in Coppard and Crick, *Orwell Remembered,* 171.

144 **"*Hamlet* is the tragedy"**: George Orwell, "*Macbeth,*" 17 October 1943, in *Orwell: The Lost Writings,* ed. W. J. West (New York: Arbor House, 1985), 160–61.

144 **"Good, sensitive, loyal work"**: Bowker, *George Orwell,* 294.

144 **"Its atmosphere is"**: Orwell, *Diaries,* 361.

144 **"The thing that strikes one"**: Ibid., 390–91.

145 **"A huge army of them"**: Ibid., 386.

145 **a vacation in Worcestershire**: Bowker, *George Orwell,* 294.

145 **"When I look back"**: George Orwell, *Coming Up for Air,* in George Orwell omnibus (London: Secker & Warburg, 1976), 476.

145 **he caught almost nothing**: Orwell, *Diaries,* 392.

145 **"All propaganda is lies"**: Ibid., 361–62.

146 **"And it is important to realise"**: George Orwell, "Literature and Totalitarianism," in *CEJL,* vol. 2, 135.

146 **"conceived without pleasure"**: Jeremy Lewis, *David Astor* (London: Jonathan Cape, 1980), chapter 2. No page number available from Kindle version.

146 **Astor was working at the *Observer***: Stephen Pritchard, "Astor and the *Observer,*" *Observer,* 8 December 2001.

146 **enliven the newspaper**: Roger Lewis, "How the *Observer*'s Celebrated Owner-Editor Coped with Being So Rich," *Guardian,* 18 February 2016.

146 **"As soon as I met him"**: "David Astor and the *Observer,*" in Coppard and Crick, *Orwell Remembered,* 184.

146 **"unfit for service overseas"**: Crick, *George Orwell,* 421.

CHAPTER 9. ENTER THE AMERICANS: 1941–1942

148 **"was the difference between"**: Field Marshal Lord Alanbrooke, *The War Diaries: 1939–1945,* ed. Alex Danchev and Daniel Todman (Berkeley: University of California Press, 2002), 209; Roy Jenkins, *Churchill* (Farrar, Straus and Giroux, 2001), 800.

148 **"England would live"**: Winston S. Churchill, *The Second World War, Volume III: The Grand Alliance* (Boston: Houghton Mifflin, 1950), 607.

149–50 **"if my father had been American"**: Winston Churchill, *Blood, Toil, Tears and Sweat: The Great Speeches,* ed. David Cannadine (Harmondsworth, U.K.: Penguin, 1990), 226.

150 **"in our darkest days"**: Ibid., 227.

150 **"The forces ranged against us"**: Ibid., 228–29.

150 **"drawn the sword for freedom"**: Ibid., 230.

151 **"What kind of people"**: Ibid., 232.

151 **won "the loudest response"**: Sir Charles Wilson, later Lord Moran, *Churchill: Taken*

from the Diaries of Lord Moran (Boston: Houghton Mifflin, 1966), 16. See also
Churchill, *The Second World War, Vol. III: The Grand Alliance,* 671.

151 **mild heart attack:** Moran, *Churchill,* 17.

151 **"We are no longer single, but married":** Churchill, *The Second World War, Vol. III:
The Grand Alliance,* 686.

151 **dined with Roosevelt and Harry Hopkins:** Robert E. Sherwood, *Roosevelt and
Hopkins: An Intimate History* (New York: Harper & Brothers, 1948), 444.

152 **"He thinks they are arrogant":** Martin Gilbert, *Winston S. Churchill: The Prophet of
Truth, Volume V: 1922–1939* (London: Minerva, 1990), 301.

152 **"your known hostility to America":** Mary Soames, ed., *Winston and Clementine: The
Personal Letters of the Churchills* (Houghton Mifflin, 2001), 331–32.

152 **"My own relations with him":** Winston S. Churchill, *The Second World War, Volume II:
Their Finest Hour* (Boston: Houghton Mifflin, 1949), 553.

152 **"We crawl too much":** Andrew Roberts, *Eminent Churchillians* (London: Phoenix,
1995), 49.

152 **"our new alliance":** George Orwell, *The Collected Essays, Journalism and Letters of
George Orwell, Volume 2: My Country Right or Left, 1940–1943,* ed. Sonia Orwell and
Ian Angus (New York: Harcourt Brace Jovanovich, 1968), 177. Hereafter, Orwell,
CEJL, vol. 2.

153 **"nineteenth century America":** George Orwell, "As I Please," 22 November 1946, in
*The Collected Essays, Journalism and Letters of George Orwell, Volume 4: In Front of
Your Nose, 1945–1950,* ed. Sonia Orwell and Ian Angus (New York: Harcourt Brace
Jovanovich, 1968), 247. Hereafter, Orwell, *CEJL,* vol. 4.

153 **"The State hardly existed":** George Orwell, "Mark Twain—The Licensed Jester," in
CEJL, vol. 2, 326.

153 **biography of Mark Twain:** Bernard Crick, *George Orwell: A Life* (New York: Penguin,
1980), 247.

153 **he was introduced:** Randolph S. Churchill, *Winston S. Churchill: Youth, 1874–1900*
(Boston: Houghton Mifflin, 1966), 369, 525.

153 **Orwell's favorite authors:** Gordon Bowker, *George Orwell* (London: Abacus, 2004),
62. See also "Quixote on a Bicycle," in Audrey Coppard and Bernard Crick, *Orwell
Remembered* (New York: Facts on File Publications, 1984), 256.

153 *Martin Chuzzlewit,* **a novel based:** Charles Dickens, *The Life and Adventures
of Martin Chuzzlewit* (New York: Penguin, 1986), 338, also 336–37, 346–47,
592, 607.

153 **"a curious blind spot":** Christopher Hitchens, *Why Orwell Matters* (New York: MJF
Books, 2002), 104.

154 **"More and more Americans":** Norman Longmate, *The G.I.'s: The Americans in
Britain, 1942–1945* (New York: Scribner, 1975), 228, 43, 36.

154 **"Back Every Fortnight":** John Charmley, *Churchill: The End of Glory* (New York:
Harcourt Brace, 1993), 449.

154 **"a great deal of bad news":** Parliamentary debates, 27, 28, 29 January 1942, *Hansard,
Parliamentary Debates.* Hereafter, *Hansard.*

156 "his heart and conscience": Ibid.

156 "to receive the stigmata": Harold Nicolson, *The War Years: 1939–1945* (New York: Atheneum, 1967), 209,

156 "the worst disaster": Winston S. Churchill, *The Second World War, Volume IV: The Hinge of Fate* (Boston: Houghton Mifflin, 1950), 92.

156 "Up to the fall of Singapore": Orwell, *CEJL*, vol. 2, 209.

156 "I now make entries": George Orwell, *Diaries*, ed. Peter Davison (New York: W. W. Norton, 2012), 396–97.

157 "Eileen's appearance was": Stephen Wadhams, ed., *Remembering Orwell* (Harmondsworth, U.K.: Penguin, 1984), 129–30.

157 "she used to say that": Ibid., 130.

157 "We were lifted out": Crick, *George Orwell*, 432.

158 "bringing them into touch": Churchill, *The Second World War, Vol. IV: The Hinge of Fate*, 209.

158 "it was 'China'": Ibid., 134.

158 "I know you will not mind": Ibid., 201.

159 "The Soviet machine": Winston S. Churchill, *The Second World War, Volume V: Closing the Ring* (Boston: Houghton Mifflin, 1951), 270.

159 "I am greatly concerned": Warren F. Kimball, ed., *Churchill & Roosevelt: The Complete Correspondence, Volume 1: Alliance Emerging, October 1933–November 1942* (Princeton, N.J.: Princeton University Press, 1987), 447–48.

159 "tactless utterances of Americans": Orwell, *Diaries*, 371.

159 "Tobruk has surrendered": *Hansard*, July 2, 1942.

160 "just plain bad leadership": Simon Berthon and Joanna Potts, *Warlords: An Extraordinary Re-creation of World War II Through the Eyes and Minds of Hitler, Churchill, Roosevelt, and Stalin* (Cambridge, Mass.: Da Capo, 2006), 150.

160 "What can we do to help?": Churchill, *The Second World War, Vol. IV: The Hinge of Fate*, 382–83. The account given here also relies on Hastings Ismay, *The Memoirs of Lord Ismay* (London: Heinemann, 1960), 254–55; on Sherwood, *Roosevelt and Hopkins*, 204; and on Department of State, *Foreign Relations of the United States, The Second Washington Conference* (Washington, D.C.: U.S. Government Printing Office, 1968), 437.

161 "Tobruk has fallen": Moran, *Churchill*, 41.

161 "sideswipes at the American way": Kim Philby, *My Silent War* (New York: Modern Library, 2002), 174. See also Andrew Marr, *A History of Modern Britain* (London: Pan Macmillan, 2009), 141.

161 "It is always best": John Charmley, "Churchill and the American Alliance," in *Winston Churchill in the Twenty-First Century*, ed. David Cannadine and Roland Quinault (Cambridge, U.K.: Cambridge University Press, 2004), 146.

161 "the heavy labour": Max Hastings, *Winston's War: Churchill 1940–1945* (New York: Vintage, 2011), 149.

161 "Most of them feel kindly": Harold Nicolson, *Diaries and Letters, 1930–1939*, ed. Nigel Nicolson (London: Collins, 1966), 205.

161 "something about the smarminess": Ibid., 189.

162 "We are far more advanced": Harold Nicolson, *The War Years: 1939–1945* (New York: Atheneum, 1967), 328.

162 "President was no friend" . . . "This anti-colonialism": Harold Macmillan, *The Blast of War, 1939–1945* (New York: Harper & Row, 1968), 121, 359.

162 "President's entourage very Jewish": Oliver Harvey, *War Diaries, 1941–1945,* ed. John Harvey (New York: HarperCollins, 1978), 37.

162 "a hundred years behind": Ibid., 85.

162 "It is rather a scandal": Ibid., 141.

163 "How is it that": James Boswell, *The Life of Samuel Johnson, Volume III* (Oxford: Talboys and Wheeler, 1826), 180.

163 "some section of the press": Andrew Roberts, *"The Holy Fox": A Biography of Lord Halifax* (London: Weidenfeld & Nicolson, 1991), 281–82.

163 "we were playing tennis": Anthony Eden, *The Reckoning: The Memoirs of Anthony Eden* (Boston: Houghton Mifflin, 1965), 158–59.

CHAPTER 10. GRIM VISIONS OF THE POSTWAR WORLD: 1943

164 "Where we mounted": Norman Longmate, *The G.I.'s: The Americans in Britain, 1942–1945* (New York: Scribner, 1975), 62.

164 "They wear on their faces": George Orwell, *The Collected Essays, Journalism and Letters of George Orwell, Volume 2: My Country Right or Left, 1940–1943,* ed. Sonia Orwell and Ian Angus (New York: Harcourt Brace Jovanovich, 1968), 236. Hereafter, Orwell, *CEJL,* vol. 2.

165 "Our staff preparation": *George C. Marshall: Interviews and Reminiscences for Forrest C. Pogue,* ed. Larry I. Bland (Lexington, Va.: George C. Marshall Foundation, 1996), 608, 613.

165 an entire shipload of well-educated: Martin Gilbert, *Winston S. Churchill: Road to Victory, Volume VII: 1941–1945* (London: Heinemann, 1989), 293.

165 "every time they brought up": Eric Larrabee, *Commander in Chief: Franklin Delano Roosevelt, His Lieutenants, and Their War* (New York: Harper & Row, 1987), 184.

165 7 million tons: Ronald Lewin, *Churchill as Warlord* (London: Scarborough, 1973), 184.

165 invasion of Sicily: Hastings Ismay, *The Memoirs of Lord Ismay* (London: Heinemann, 1960), 288.

165 "Marshall has got practically": Field Marshal Lord Alanbrooke, *The War Diaries: 1939–1945,* ed. Alex Danchev and Daniel Todman (Berkeley: University of California Press, 2002), 364.

166 FDR favored the Mediterranean plan: Gilbert, *Churchill: Road to Victory,* 296.

166 crossing the channel in 1943: "Joint Chiefs of Staff Minutes of a Meeting at the White House, January 7, 1943," *Foreign Relations of the United States: The Conferences at Washington, 1941–1942, and Casablanca, 1943* (Washington, D.C.: U.S. Government Printing Office, 1968), 510.

166 **"a long period of training"**: "Meeting of Roosevelt with the Joint Chiefs of Staff, January 15, 1943, 10 A.M., President's Villa," *Foreign Relations of the United States, Washington and Casablanca Conferences,* 559.

166 **reorganization of his planning staff:** Steven Rearden, *Council of War: A History of the Joint Chiefs of Staff, 1942–1991* (Washington, D.C.: NDU Press, 2012), 13–14.

166 **"We came, we listened":** Albert Wedemeyer, *Wedemeyer Reports!* (New York: Henry Holt, 1958), 191–92. Long after the war, Marshall would write to Churchill: "I don't know anyone with whom I had more arguments than with you, and I don't know anyone whom I admire more." *The Papers of George Catlett Marshall, Volume 7: "The Man of the Age,"* ed. Mark Stoler and Daniel Holt (Baltimore, Md.: Johns Hopkins University Press, 2016), 986.

167 **"Americans are still amateurish":** Oliver Harvey, *War Diaries, 1941–1945,* ed. John Harvey (New York: HarperCollins, 1978), 287.

167 **"some American officers":** Alanbrooke, *The War Diaries,* 419.

167 **Brooke "did not get on":** Sir Charles Wilson, later Lord Moran, *Churchill: Taken from the Diaries of Lord Moran* (Boston: Houghton Mifflin, 1966), 767.

167 **"I am afraid the American troops":** Alanbrooke, *The War Diaries,* 384.

167 **"the Americans run away":** Harold Nicolson, *The War Years: 1939–1945* (New York: Atheneum, 1967), 347.

167 **"The IId American Army Corps":** Winston S. Churchill, *The Second World War, Volume IV: The Hinge of Fate* (Boston: Houghton Mifflin, 1950), 733–34.

167 **France "until 1945 or 1946":** "Meeting of the Combined Chiefs of Staff, May 13, 1943, 10:30 A.M., Board of Governors Room, Federal Reserve Building," *Foreign Relations of the United States: The Conferences at Washington and Quebec, 1943* (Washington, D.C.: Government Printing Office, 1970), 45.

168 **"absolute madness," he wrote:** Alanbrooke, *The War Diaries,* 233.

168 **"nasty cut at the Russians":** David Dilks, ed., *The Diaries of Sir Alexander Cadogan, 1938–1945,* (New York: G. P. Putnam's Sons, 1972), 484.

168 **Breakfasting at the British embassy:** Field Marshal Lord Alanbrooke, *The War Diaries,* 370.

168 **underwear made of pale pink silk:** Violet Bonham Carter, *Winston Churchill: An Intimate Portrait* (New York: Harcourt, Brace & World, 1965), 172.

168 **variety of loathed foods:** William Manchester, *The Caged Lion: Winston Spencer Churchill, 1932–1940* (London: Abacus, 1994), 25.

168 **sixteen cigars a day:** G. S. Harvie-Watt, *Most of My Life* (London: Springwood, 1980), 53.

168 **"anyone could smoke so much":** Eleanor Roosevelt, "Churchill at the White House," *Atlantic Monthly,* March 1965, accessed online.

169 **"Surveying the whole military scene":** Winston S. Churchill, *The Second World War, Volume V: Closing the Ring* (Boston: Houghton Mifflin, 1951), 405.

169 **"A bloody lot":** Moran, *Churchill,* 145.

169 **as if he held the senior role:** Warren F. Kimball, ed., *Churchill & Roosevelt: The*

Complete Correspondence, Volume 2: Alliance Forged, November 1942–February 1944 (Princeton, N.J.: Princeton University Press, 1987), 596.

169 **President Roosevelt declined:** Robert E. Sherwood, *Roosevelt and Hopkins: An Intimate History* (New York: Harper & Brothers, 1948), 781. Color of pencil is from Richard Overy, *Why the Allies Won* (New York: W. W. Norton, 1996), 246.

169 **small dinner party:** Warren F. Kimball, ed., *Churchill & Roosevelt: The Complete Correspondence, Volume 1: Alliance Emerging, October 1933–November 1942* (Princeton, N.J.: Princeton University Press, 1987), 206, 642. Elliott Roosevelt, *As He Saw It* (New York: Duell, Sloan and Pearce, 1946), 190. Stalin is credited as host of the dinner in Jon Meacham, *Franklin and Winston: An Intimate Portrait of an Epic Friendship* (New York: Random House, 2004), 258. Also, a somewhat sanitized account of this dinner, which even in classified form did not mention Elliott Roosevelt's intervention, is offered in U.S. Department of State, *Foreign Relations of the United States: The Conferences at Cairo and Tehran* (Washington, D.C.: U.S. Government Printing Office, 1961), 552-55.

170 **he was "only playing":** Churchill, *The Second World War, Vol. 5: Closing the Ring*, 374.

170–71 **execution of twenty thousand Polish officers:** Benjamin Fischer, "The Katyn Controversy: Stalin's Killing Field," *Studies in Intelligence*, CIA (Winter 1999–2000), accessed online.

171 **beginning of *Unconditional Surrender*:** This synopsis, which has been excised from editions of the complete trilogy, is available online at www.abbotshill.freeserve.co .uk/USIntro.htm.

171 **"bored by this Conference":** Dilkes, *Diaries of Sir Alexander Cadogan*, 580.

171 **"He said he could still":** Alanbrooke, *The War Diaries*, 544.

172 **"the big Russian bear":** Violet Bonham Carter, *Champion Redoubtable* (London: Weidenfeld & Nicolson, 1999), 312–13.

172 **"a rather nice pig":** John Colville, *The Fringes of Power: 10 Downing Street Diaries, 1939–1955* (New York: W. W. Norton, 1985), 158.

172 **"the good little pig":** Diana Cooper, *Trumpets from the Steep* (London: Century, 1960), 154.

172 **"like a hippopotamus":** Moran, *Churchill*, 22.

172 **three totalitarian superstates:** See George Orwell, "Letter to Roger Senhouse," in *The Collected Essays, Journalism and Letters of George Orwell, Volume 4: In Front of Your Nose, 1945–1950*, ed. Sonia Orwell and Ian Angus (New York: Harcourt Brace Jovanovich, 1968), 132.

172 **Orwell left the BBC:** George Orwell, "Letter to L. F. Rushbrook-Williams," in *CEJL*, vol. 2, 316.

173 **"Even if you steer clear":** George Orwell, *The Collected Essays, Journalism and Letters of George Orwell, Volume 3: As I Please, 1943–1945*, ed. Sonia Orwell and Ian Angus (New York: Harcourt Brace Jovanovich, 1968), 54.

CHAPTER 11. *ANIMAL FARM:* 1943–1945

174 "What a pity": Malcolm Muggeridge, *Like It Was: The Diaries of Malcolm Muggeridge,* ed. John Bright-Holmes (London: Collins, 1981), 410.

174 "He had a great influence": Sir Charles Wilson, later Lord Moran, *Churchill: Taken from the Diaries of Lord Moran* (Boston: Houghton Mifflin, 1966), 199.

175 "It was still possible": George Orwell, "On Kipling's Death," in *The Collected Essays, Journalism and Letters of George Orwell, Volume 1: An Age Like This, 1920–1940,* ed. Sonia Orwell and Ian Angus (New York: Harcourt Brace Jovanovich, 1968), 159–60. Hereafter, Orwell, *CEJL,* vol. 1.

175 "'Now my dears'": Beatrix Potter, *The Tale of Peter Rabbit,* accessed online at Project Gutenberg.

175 Tiring of his cleaning tasks: Kenneth Grahame, *The Wind in the Willows* (New York: Grosset & Dunlap, 1913), 3.

175 "I like your clothes awfully": Ibid., 11–12.

176 "A toad has about": George Orwell, "Some Thoughts on the Common Toad," in *The Collected Essays, Journalism and Letters of George Orwell, Volume 4: In Front of Your Nose, 1945–1950,* ed. Sonia Orwell and Ian Angus (New York: Harcourt Brace Jovanovich, 1968), 142. Hereafter, Orwell, *CEJL,* vol. 4.

176 "a recently dead fish": George Orwell, *Diaries,* ed. Peter Davison (New York: W. W. Norton, 2012), 380.

177 drink at the Red Lion: This double appearance of the Red Lion is noted by Jeffrey Meyers in *Orwell: Life and Art* (Champaign, Ill.: University of Illinois Press, 2010), 112. However, "Red Lion" is the most common name for British pubs, with more than five hundred in existence, according to one recent count by Pubs Galore. Among those is a Red Lion in Willingdon.

177 "The pigs did not actually work": George Orwell, *Animal Farm* (New York: New American Library, 1974), 35.

177 "Four legs good": Ibid., 40–41.

177 "the turning point": Orwell, *Diaries,* 471.

177 "had the animals stood up": Quoted in Gordon Bowker, *George Orwell* (London: Abacus, 2004), 358–59.

177 "It was noticed": Orwell, *Animal Farm,* 58.

178 "four young porkers": Ibid., 59.

178 "And so the tale of confessions": Ibid., 83.

178 "two legs better!": Ibid., 122.

178 "All animals are equal": Ibid., 123.

178 "the totalitarian state is": George Orwell, "Literature and Totalitarianism," *The Listener,* 19 June 1941, in *The Collected Essays, Journalism and Letters of George Orwell, Volume 2: My Country Right or Left, 1940–1943,* ed. Sonia Orwell and Ian Angus (New York: Harcourt Brace Jovanovich, 1968), 134. Hereafter, Orwell, *CEJL,* vol. 2.

179 "Totalitarianism demands, in fact": George Orwell, *Orwell and Politics,* ed. Peter Davison (Harmondsworth, U.K.: Penguin, 2001), 384.

179 "The creatures outside": Orwell, *Animal Farm,* 128.

179 "satire on the Russian revolution": No. 3128, "To Dwight Macdonald," 5 December 1946, in Peter Davison, ed., *The Complete Works of George Orwell, Volume 18* (London: Secker & Warburg, 1998), 507.

179 he read aloud: Stephen Wadhams, ed., *Remembering Orwell* (Harmondsworth, U.K.: Penguin, 1984), 131.

179 influenced E. B. White: E. B. White, "A Letter from E. B. White," on the Web site of HarperCollins.

180 Trotsky himself had been assassinated: Christopher Andrew and Vasili Mitrokhin, *The Sword and the Shield: The Mitrokhin Archive and the Secret History of the KGB* (New York: Basic Books, 1999), 87.

180 Russian defector, Walter Krivitsky: Anthony Cave Brown, *Treason in the Blood: H. St. John Philby, Kim Philby, and the Spy Case of the Century* (Boston: Houghton Mifflin, 1994), 222.

180 Philby had operated: Andrew and Mitrokhin, *The Sword and the Shield*, 67. See also Brown, *Treason in the Blood*, 79.

180 campaign of kidnapping and murder: Andrew and Mitrokhin, *The Sword and the Shield*, 74–75.

181 "I could not possibly publish:" Bernard Crick, *George Orwell: A Life* (New York: Penguin, 1980), 454.

181 rejected the book: Ibid., 458. Also see Alison Flood, "'It Needs More Public-Spirited Pigs': T. S. Eliot's Rejection of Orwell's Animal Farm," *Guardian*, 26 May 2016. For the total number of rejections by publishers: John Rodden and John Rossi, *The Cambridge Introduction to George Orwell* (Cambridge, U.K.: Cambridge University Press, 2012); and Crick, *George Orwell*, 452–62.

181 warned off by Peter Smollett: Rodden and Rossi, *Cambridge Introduction to Orwell*, 77.

181 "I'm having hell and all": George Orwell, *The Collected Essays, Journalism and Letters of George Orwell, Volume 3: As I Please, 1943–1945*, ed. Sonia Orwell and Ian Angus (New York: Harcourt Brace Jovanovich, 1968), 141. Hereafter, Orwell, *CEJL*, vol. 3.

182 "Eileen was very happy": Wadhams, *Remembering Orwell*, 131.

182 "the kind of marginal area": Crick, *George Orwell*, 465.

182 "wanted to go into Germany": Audrey Coppard and Bernard Crick, *Orwell Remembered* (New York: Facts on File Publications, 1984), 186–87.

182 as "silly potboilers": Bowker, *George Orwell*, 472. Interestingly, this memorandum is not included in Orwell's *Collected Essays, Journalism and Letters*.

182 Her funeral was held: Bowker, *George Orwell*, 329.

182 "I don't think he felt": Coppard and Crick, *Orwell Remembered*, 187.

183 "Eileen is dead": Orwell, *CEJL*, vol. 3, 359.

183 "his first wife Eileen": George Woodcock, *The Crystal Spirit* (New York: Schocken Books, 1984), 31.

183 "printed as many copies": Coppard and Crick, *Orwell Remembered*, 197.

183 "It's a terribly long time": Orwell, *CEJL*, vol. 4, 104.

183 Orwell purchased a pistol: Bowker, *George Orwell*, 330–31.

183 **listed for execution:** Rodden and Rossi, *Cambridge Introduction to Orwell,* 59.

184 **One friend, Celia Kirwan:** Bowker, *George Orwell,* 484.

184 **Anne Popham, a neighbor:** Wadhams, *Remembering Orwell,* 166.

184 **He summarizes his points:** George Orwell, "Politics and the English Language," in *Orwell and Politics,* 409.

185 **"Political language . . . is designed":** Ibid., 410.

185 **"Defenceless villages are":** Ibid., 406.

186 **"man who cannot say":** Manchester, *The Caged Lion,* 26.

186 **"He waged continual war":** Sir John Martin, in John Wheeler-Bennett, ed., *Action This Day: Working with Churchill* (New York: St. Martin's, 1969), 146–47.

186 **Fowler's *Modern English Usage*:** John Colville, *Winston Churchill and His Inner Circle* (New York: Wyndham, 1981), 155.

186 **repeatedly misspelling "inadmissible":** Winston S. Churchill, *The Second World War, Volume VI: Triumph and Tragedy* (Boston: Houghton Mifflin, 1953), 749.

186 **called "Local Defense Volunteers":** Winston S. Churchill, *The Second World War, Volume I: The Gathering Storm* (Boston: Houghton Mifflin, 1948), 166.

186 **examples of offending verbosity:** Quoted in Harold Macmillan, *The Blast of War 1939–1945* (New York: Harper & Row, 1968), 84.

187 **"nearly always better":** Warren F. Kimball, ed., *Churchill & Roosevelt: The Complete Correspondence, Volume 2: Alliance Forged, November 1942–February 1944* (Princeton, N.J.: Princeton University Press, 1987), 712.

187 **apologizes to the reader:** Winston S. Churchill, *The Second World War, Volume II: Their Finest Hour* (Boston: Houghton Mifflin, 1949), 431.

CHAPTER 12. CHURCHILL (AND BRITAIN) IN
DECLINE AND TRIUMPH: 1944–1945

188 **Irving Berlin was visiting:** John Colville, *The Fringes of Power: 10 Downing Street Diaries, 1939–1955* (New York: W. W. Norton, 1985), 471–72.

188 **After the composer left:** Laurence Bergreen, *As Thousands Cheer: The Life of Irving Berlin* (New York: Viking, 1990), 431.

188–89 **Churchill's weakened state:** George Orwell, "London Letter," *Partisan Review,* 17 April 1944," in *The Collected Essays, Journalism and Letters of George Orwell, Volume 3: As I Please, 1943–1945,* ed. Sonia Orwell and Ian Angus (New York: Harcourt Brace Jovanovich, 1968), 123. Hereafter, Orwell, *CEJL,* vol. 3.

189 **"obstinate old cripple":** Artemis Cooper, ed., *A Durable Fire: The Letters of Duff and Diana Cooper, 1913–1950* (London: HarperCollins, 1983), 305.

189 **"the King's First Minister":** Winston Churchill (speech, Lord Mayor's Luncheon, 10 November 1942), accessed online at the Web site of the Churchill Society.

190 **"My God how tired I am":** Field Marshal Lord Alanbrooke, *The War Diaries: 1939–1945,* ed. Alex Danchev and Daniel Todman (Berkeley: University of California Press, 2002), 515.

190 **"I often doubt":** Ibid., 521.

190 "He has lost all balance": Ibid., 528.

190 "I feel like": Ibid., 534.

190 "We had a long": Ibid., 561.

190 "a complete amateur": Ibid., 568.

190 "admired and despised": Ibid., 590.

190 "He was very tired": Ibid., 566.

190 faults as a war leader: For more on this, see Carlo D'Este, *Warlord: A Life of Winston Churchill at War, 1874–1945* (New York: HarperCollins, 2008), 395.

191 see aircraft carriers as: See, for example, his memorandum of 12 September 1939, reprinted in Winston S. Churchill, *The Second World War, Volume I: The Gathering Storm* (Boston: Houghton Mifflin, 1948), 434–35.

191 impact that German submarines: David Reynolds, *In Command of History: Churchill Fighting and Writing the Second World War* (New York: Random House, 2005), 114.

191 "misconceptions, if not delusions": Maurice Ashley, *Churchill as Historian* (New York: Scribner, 1969), 189.

191 "only one sure path": Colville, *The Fringes of Power*, 186–87. See also Winston S. Churchill, *The Second World War, Volume III: The Grand Alliance* (Boston: Houghton Mifflin, 1950), 806–7.

191 "Winston adored funny operations": R. W. Thompson, *Churchill and Morton* (London: Hodder & Stoughton, 1976), 48.

191 the landing at Anzio: See, for example, Sir Charles Wilson, later Lord Moran, *Churchill: Taken from the Diaries of Lord Moran* (Boston: Houghton Mifflin, 1966), 169.

191 experience of World War I: Sir Ian Jacob, in John Wheeler-Bennett, ed., *Action This Day: Working with Churchill* (New York: St. Martin's, 1969), 201.

192 "always right to probe": Churchill, *The Second World War, Vol. I: The Gathering Storm*, 462.

192 "a continuous audit" . . . "He saw war policy": Eliot Cohen, *Supreme Command: Soldiers, Statesmen, and Leadership in Wartime* (New York: Anchor, 2003), 118.

192 "with complete conviction": Moran, *Churchill*, 759.

193 that Brooke hated him: David Fraser, "Alanbrooke," in *Churchill's Generals*, ed. John Keegan (New York: Grove Weidenfeld, 1991), 90. The same anecdote is worded slightly differently in Fraser's earlier *Alanbrooke* (London: Arrow Books, 1983), 295.

193 "our terrible enemy, America": Simon Heffer, *Like the Roman: The Life of Enoch Powell* (London: Weidenfeld & Nicolson, 1998), 75.

193 trained in field security: Ibid., 62.

193 "growth of animosity against America": George Orwell, "Letter from England," *Partisan Review*, 3 January 1943, in *The Collected Essays, Journalism and Letters of George Orwell, Volume 2: My Country Right or Left, 1940–1943*, ed. Sonia Orwell and Ian Angus (New York: Harcourt Brace Jovanovich, 1968), 278–79. Hereafter, Orwell, *CEJL*, vol. 2.

194 a "policy of appeasement": Max Hastings, *Winston's War: Churchill, 1940–1945* (New York: Vintage, 2011), 437.

194 "become very unpopular": Colville, *The Fringes of Power*, 574.

194 "The cynics felt": Ralph Ingersoll, *Top Secret* (New York: Harcourt, Brace, 1946), 67.

194 the commander be American: Winston S. Churchill, *The Second World War, Volume V: Closing the Ring* (Boston: Houghton Mifflin, 1951), 85.

194 "We shall be able": Ibid., 129.

195 "maybe you British can't": J. Lawton Collins, *Lightning Joe* (Baton Rouge: Louisiana State University Press, 1979), 292.

195 "ruled by narrow-minded" . . . "faintly disreputable": First quote is from George Orwell, "Wells, Hitler and the World State," in *CEJL*, vol. 2, 143–44. Second quote is from George Orwell, "Such, Such Were the Joys," in *The Collected Essays, Journalism and Letters of George Orwell, Volume 4: In Front of Your Nose, 1945–1950*, ed. Sonia Orwell and Ian Angus (New York: Harcourt Brace Jovanovich, 1968), 336. Hereafter, Orwell, *CEJL*, vol. 4.

195 "It is discouraging": Winston S. Churchill, *The Second World War, Volume VI: Triumph and Tragedy* (Boston: Houghton Mifflin, 1953), 713.

196 "The Industrial Revolution": Ronald Lewin, *Churchill as Warlord* (London: Scarborough, 1973), 19.

196 "creating the mass vulgarity": George Trevelyan, *English Social History: A Survey of Six Centuries from Chaucer to Queen Victoria* (New York: Longman, 1978), 457.

196 victims of "over-hasty, botched": Correlli Barnett, *The Audit of War: The Illusion & Reality of Britain as a Great Nation* (London: Macmillan, 1986), 161, 164, 180–81.

197 the historian David Edgerton: David Edgerton, "The Prophet Militant and Industrial: The Peculiarities of Correlli Barnett," in *Twentieth Century British History* 2, no. 3 (1991), accessed online.

197 two dominant impressions: Bernard Lewis, "Second Acts," *Atlantic Monthly*, November 2007, 25.

197 noted Raymond Lee: James Leutze, ed., *The London Journal of General Raymond E. Lee, 1940–1941* (Boston: Little, Brown, 1971), 319, 341.

197 three times the size: For the comparison of British and American fielded forces in the spring of 1945, see Lord Normanbrook, in Wheeler-Bennett, ed., *Action This Day*, 32.

198 "I was grossly wrong": George Orwell, "London Letter," to *Partisan Review*, December 1944, in *CEJL*, vol. 3, 293, 297.

198 "Up to July 1944": Moran, *Churchill*, 614.

199 "the first important divergence": Churchill, *The Second World War, Vol. VI: Triumph and Tragedy*, 57.

199 "a suitable place": "First Plenary Meeting, November 28, 1943," U.S. Department of State, *Foreign Relations of the United States: The Tehran Conference* (Washington, D.C.: U.S. Government Printing Office, 1961), 490.

199 "advance up the Rhone Valley": Warren F. Kimball, ed., *Churchill & Roosevelt: The Complete Correspondence, Volume 3: Alliance Declining, February 1944–April 1945* (Princeton, N.J.: Princeton University Press, 1987), 228, 263.

199 "Ike said no": Captain Harry C. Butcher, *Three Years with Eisenhower* (New York: Simon & Schuster, 1946), 634, 644. See also D.K.R. Crosswell, *Beetle: The Life of General Walter Bedell Smith* (Lexington: University Press of Kentucky, 2010), 677.

200 "had the opposite effects": Churchill, *The Second World War, Vol. VI: Triumph and Tragedy*, 120.

200 "they would be too late": Ibid., 59.

200 "The Americans were right": Williamson Murray and Allan R. Millett, *A War to Be Won: Fighting the Second World War* (Cambridge, Mass.: Harvard University Press, 2000), 433.

200 One quarter of all Allied supplies: Steven Zaloga, *Operation Dragoon 1944: France's Other D-Day* (Oxford: Osprey, 2013), 6.

200 the Allies were moving 501,000: Roland Ruppenthal, *The European Theater of Operations: Logistical Support of the Armies, Volume II: September 1944–May 1945* (Washington, D.C.: U.S. Army Center of Military History, 1959), 124.

201 the "Black Dog": See Moran, *Churchill*, 179–80, 195.

201 "a terrible world": Violet Bonham Carter, *Champion Redoubtable* (London: Weidenfeld & Nicolson, 1999), 314.

201 "brave new world": Moran, *Churchill*, 197.

201 "deaf to certain passages": Colville, *The Fringes of Power*, 513.

201 "two main factors": Alanbrooke, *The War Diaries*, 630.

201 "out of Eisenhower's hands": Ibid.

201 "how well Monty can handle him": Ibid.

202 "raw, immature and uneducated": Sir Henry Pownall, *Chief of Staff: The Diaries of Lieutenant General Sir Henry Pownall, Volume II: 1940–1944* (Hamden, Conn.: Archon, 1974), 190.

202 "looking very old": Alanbrooke, *The War Diaries*, 647.

202 "a slender contact with life": Churchill, *The Second World War, Vol. VI: Triumph and Tragedy*, 397.

202 "President Truman should come": Martin Gilbert, *Winston S. Churchill: Road to Victory, Volume VII: 1941–1945* (London: Heinemann, 1989), 1294.

202 danced a Viennese waltz: Ibid., 1296.

202 "remarkably unmoved" by FDR's death: Christopher Thorne, *Allies of a Kind: The United States, Britain, and the War Against Japan, 1941–1945* (Oxford: Oxford University Press, 1979), 120.

203 "cast of Roosevelt's mind": Moran, *Churchill*, 322.

203 "any ideas at all": Ibid., 350.

203 "link between Churchill and Roosevelt": Roy Jenkins, *Churchill* (Farrar, Straus and Giroux, 2001), 785.

203 "Churchill was one of the few": Robert E. Sherwood, *Roosevelt and Hopkins: An Intimate History* (New York: Harper & Brothers, 1948), 442.

203 "blinded him to Roosevelt's aim": Thompson, *Churchill and Morton*, 30.

204 "British firms were unable": Alfred D. Chandler Jr., *Scale and Scope: The Dynamics of Industrial Capitalism* (Cambridge, Mass.: Harvard University Press, 1994), 334.

204 "Britain's postwar descent": Barnett, *The Audit of War,* 304.

204 "there are snipers": Alanbrooke, *The War Diaries,* 677.

204 an "eternal childhood": Violet Bonham Carter, *Lantern Slides: The Diaries and Letters of Violet Bonham Carter,* ed. Mark Bonham Carter and Mark Pottle (London: Phoenix, 1997), 318.

205 "With a restraint and poise": Winston Churchill, *Blood, Toil, Tears and Sweat: The Great Speeches,* ed. David Cannadine (Harmondsworth, U.K.: Penguin, 1990), 259–60.

206 "On the continent of Europe": Ibid., 266.

206 "the policeman's knock": Ibid., 286, 288.

206 "No Socialist Government": Ibid., 274.

206 "discarded the role": Malcolm Muggeridge, "Twilight of Greatness," in *Tread Softly for You Tread on My Jokes* (London: Collins, 1966), 238.

206 "I have predicted": George Orwell, *CEJL,* vol. 3, 381.

207 "such demonstrations of emotion": Simon Schama, "Rescuing Churchill," *New York Review of Books,* 28 February 2002, accessed online.

207 "when two large tears": Harold Nicolson, *The War Years: 1939–1945* (New York: Atheneum, 1967), 344–45.

207 "occasionally a tear": Richard Toye, *The Roar of the Lion: The Untold Story of Churchill's World War II Speeches* (Oxford: Oxford University Press, 2013), 112.

208 "Tears streamed down": Alanbrooke, *The War Diaries,* 324.

208 67,000 British civilians: Jasper Copping, "Records of WW2 Dead Published Online," *Daily Telegraph,* 17 November 2013.

208 "orator is the embodiment": Winston Churchill, "The Scaffolding of Rhetoric," accessed online at the Web site of the Churchill Society.

208 "never had any idea": Thompson, *Churchill and Morton,* 53, 65. See also Churchill, *The Second World War, Vol. I: The Gathering Storm,* 80.

208 "none other gods": Robert Boothby, *I Fight to Live* (London: Victor Gollancz, 1947), 46.

209 more "American exaggerations": Alanbrooke, *The War Diaries,* 709.

209 Churchill traveled into Berlin: David Dilks, ed., *The Diaries of Sir Alexander Cadogan, 1938–1945* (New York: G. P. Putnam's Sons, 1972), 763.

209 "I saw it": Moran, *Churchill,* 306.

209 "Churchill stood for": John Charmley, *Churchill: The End of Glory* (New York: Harcourt Brace, 1993), 649.

210 "Through Churchill's stewardship": Williamson Murray, "British Grand Strategy, 1933–1942," in Williamson Murray, Richard Hart Sinnreich, James Lacey, eds., *The Shaping of Grand Strategy: Policy, Diplomacy and War* (Cambridge, U.K.: Cambridge University Press, 2011), 180.

CHAPTER 13. CHURCHILL'S REVENGE: THE WAR MEMOIRS

211 his account of the war: David Reynolds, *In Command of History: Churchill Fighting and Writing the Second World War* (New York: Random House, 2005), 537.

211 **only account of World War II**: John Keegan, introduction to Winston Churchill, *The Second World War* (Boston: Houghton Mifflin, 1985), xi.

211 **"I was now well content"**: Winston S. Churchill, *The Second World War, Volume II: Their Finest Hour* (Boston: Houghton Mifflin, 1949), 447.

212 **"I am much disquieted"**: Winston S. Churchill, *The Second World War, Volume III: The Grand Alliance* (Boston: Houghton Mifflin, 1950), 834.

212 **"quick-winged from"**: Winston S. Churchill, *The Second World War, Volume IV: The Hinge of Fate* (Boston: Houghton Mifflin, 1950), 797.

212 **"I had been struck"**: Winston S. Churchill, *The Second World War, Volume I: The Gathering Storm* (Boston: Houghton Mifflin, 1948), 440.

212 **had "always disliked him"**: Michael Beschloss, *Kennedy and Roosevelt: The Uneasy Alliance* (New York: W. W. Norton, 1980), 200.

212 **"the scaly wings"**: Churchill, *The Second World War, Vol. I: The Gathering Storm,* 26.

213 **"The Rhine, the broad, deep"**: Ibid., 7.

213 **"frothing pious platitudes"**: Ibid., 85.

213 **"a picture of British fatuity"**: Ibid., 89.

213 **"the truculent and transient"**: Ibid., 62.

213 **"led by a handful"**: Ibid., 209.

213 **"The German munition plants"**: Ibid., 211.

213 **"was alert, business-like"**: Ibid., 222.

213 **"the demon-genius sprung"**: Ibid., 249.

214 **"It was nearly a thousand years"**: Churchill, *The Second World War, Vol. II: Their Finest Hour,* 257.

214 **"They were gaunt"**: Ibid., 362

214 **"the last time"**: Churchill, *The Second World War, Vol. I: The Gathering Storm,* 272.

214 **a "hyena" act**: Ibid., 347.

215 **"Nothing surpasses 1940"**: Churchill, *The Second World War, Vol. II: Their Finest Hour,* 628.

215 **"The Battle of France was lost"**: Ibid., 630.

215 **"the U-boat peril"**: Ibid., 598.

215 **one convoy from Canada**: Ibid., 600.

215 **large, well-funded research group**: Reynolds, *In Command of History,* 501.

216 **"South of the British sector"**: Churchill, *The Second World War, Vol. IV: The Hinge of Fate,* 773.

216 **U.S. Navy and Air Force**: Ibid., 254.

216 **May 19, 1943**: Ibid., 798, 800.

216 **"Very little of 'American Naval Victories'"**: Reynolds, *In Command of History,* 300.

217 **Morison himself stumbled across**: Ibid., 353–54. Reynolds is actually mistaken in calling this unique. There is another such mysterious footnote on p. 202 of Volume VI of the memoirs, referring the reader, without explanation, to "H. St. G. Saunders, *The Green Beret.*"

217 **"The Battle of Coral Sea"**: Samuel Eliot Morison, *History of United States Naval*

Operations in World War II, Volume IV: Coral Sea, Midway and Submarine Actions, May 1942–August 1942 (Boston: Little, Brown, 1975), 63.

217 **Churchill's account stated:** Churchill, *The Second World War, Vol. IV: The Hinge of Fate,* 247.

217 **"The whole audience clapped":** Ibid., 828.

218 **"a general harmony":** Winston S. Churchill, *The Second World War, Volume V: Closing the Ring* (Boston: Houghton Mifflin, 1951), 426.

218 **"This vast operation":** Winston Churchill, Parliamentary debate, 6 June 1944, accessed online at *Hansard, Parliamentary Debates.*

219 **"What has happened":** Malcolm Muggeridge, *Like It Was: The Diaries of Malcolm Muggeridge,* ed, John Bright-Holmes (London: Collins, 1981), 410. For the serialization issue, see Muggeridge, *Chronicles of Wasted Time* (Vancouver, B.C., Canada: Regent College, 2006), 167.

219 **"still Churchill's book":** Reynolds, *In Command of History,* 436.

219 **"He could no longer tell":** John Colville, *Winston Churchill and His Inner Circle* (New York: Wyndham, 1981), 135.

220 **the official missives are separated:** Winston S. Churchill, *The Second World War, Volume VI: Triumph and Tragedy* (Boston: Houghton Mifflin, 1953), 214, 216.

220 **"a most unhappy time":** Ibid., 456.

220 **"in danger of degenerating":** Simon Schama, *A History of Britain, Volume 3: The Fate of Empire: 1776–2000* (London: BBC, 2003), 408.

CHAPTER 14. ORWELL IN TRIUMPH AND DECLINE: 1945–1950

221 **"Spring is here":** George Orwell, "Some Thoughts on the Common Toad," in *The Collected Essays, Journalism and Letters of George Orwell, Volume 4: In Front of Your Nose, 1945–1950,* ed. Sonia Orwell and Ian Angus (New York: Harcourt Brace Jovanovich, 1968), 142, 144–45. Hereafter, Orwell, *CEJL,* vol. 4.

222 **"battered, grey and tired-looking":** "Orwell at Tribune," in Audrey Coppard and Bernard Crick, *Orwell Remembered* (New York: Facts on File Publications, 1984), 212.

222 **Bread rationing had been:** Jonathan Rose, "England His Englands," in *The Cambridge Companion to George Orwell,* ed. John Rodden (Cambridge, U.K.: Cambridge University Press, 2007), 41.

222 **"For anyone outside":** Orwell, *CEJL,* vol. 4, 185.

222 **Iron Curtain speech:** Winston Churchill, "The Sinews of Peace ('Iron Curtain Speech')," accessed online at the Web site of the Churchill Society.

223 **"age of the totalitarian state":** George Orwell, "Literature and Totalitarianism," *The Listener,* 19 June 1941, in *The Collected Essays, Journalism and Letters of George Orwell, Volume 2: My Country Right or Left, 1940–1943,* ed. Sonia Orwell and Ian Angus (New York: Harcourt Brace Jovanovich, 1968), 134. Hereafter, Orwell, *CEJL,* vol. 2.

223 **"the most remote place"**: "David Astor and the *Observer,*" in Coppard and Crick, *Orwell Remembered,* 188. Timing of writing is from John Rodden and John Rossi, *The Cambridge Introduction to George Orwell* (Cambridge, U.K.: Cambridge University Press, 2012); and Crick, *George Orwell,* 29, 81.

223 **"for a person in delicate health"**: Stephen Wadhams, ed., *Remembering Orwell* (Harmondsworth, U.K.: Penguin, 1984), 170.

223 **cold, storm-raked island**: "His Jura Laird," in Coppard and Crick, *Orwell Remembered,* 226.

223 **"a fire in every room"**: George Orwell, *Diaries,* ed. Peter Davison (New York: W. W. Norton, 2012), 427.

223 **"so violent that"**: Ibid., 469.

223 **"in a self-destructive mood"**: Wadhams, *Remembering Orwell,* 180.

223 **"nearly always short of bread"**: Orwell, *CEJL,* vol. 4, 200.

224 **"winter may be pretty bleak"**: Ibid., 376.

224 **"We were flung this way"**: Wadhams, *Remembering Orwell,* 190–92.

224 **fishing in two nearby lochs**: Orwell, *Diaries,* 516.

224 **finish writing the book**: "His Jura Laird," in Coppard and Crick, *Orwell Remembered,* 227.

224 **"made a fairly good start"**: Orwell, *CEJL,* vol. 4, 329.

224 **September 5, 1947**: Orwell, *Diaries,* 520. Parentheses are Orwell's.

224 **October 13, 1947**: Ibid., 529.

224 **September 16, 1948**: Ibid., 551.

225 **October 13, 1948**: Ibid., 555.

225 **December 19, 1948**: Ibid., 561.

225 **sanatorium for TB victims**: John J. Ross, "Tuberculosis, Bronchiectasis, and Infertility: What Ailed George Orwell?" *Clinical Infectious Diseases* (December 1, 2005): 1602.

225 **two-story recording studio**: Like Orwell's hero, one of the leaders of that band, John Lennon, who was born on October 9, 1940, near the end of the Battle of Britain, was named in part for Churchill—his middle name was Winston, though as an adult he added to it Ono, for his second wife, Yoko Ono. (Philip Norman, *John Lennon: The Life* [New York: Ecco, 2009], 598. See also Ken Lawrence, *John Lennon: In His Own Words* [Kansas City, Mo.: Andrews McMeel, 2001], 5.) Lennon, who read Churchill's memoirs as a boy, would join his partial namesake on a list of the greatest Britons compiled by the BBC in 2002. Mark Lewisohn, *The Beatles: All These Years, Volume 1: Tune In* (New York: Crown, 2013), 16, 33. Churchill was ranked first, while Lennon was eighth. (See "100 Greatest Britons" BBC Poll, 2002, accessed online.) Ironically, it was Churchill, the warrior-politician, who would die in bed at a very advanced age, while the songwriter-musician was murdered with hollow-point bullets when he was forty years old. Lennon also was a fan of Orwell, displaying his works in his house. Philip Norman, *John Lennon* (New York: Ecco, 2009), 383.

225 "clocks were striking thirteen": George Orwell, *1984* (New York: Signet, 1981), 5.

226 There is universal surveillance: George Orwell, *1984,* in George Orwell omnibus (London: Secker & Warburg, 1976), 789.

226 the three slogans: Orwell, *1984* (Signet), 6–7.

226 "the really frightening one": Ibid., 8.

226 the character of Winston: Ibid., 27.

226 "a sourish, composite smell": Orwell, *1984* (Secker & Warburg), 777.

227 "DOWN WITH BIG BROTHER": Orwell, *1984* (Signet), 19.

227 "Freedom is the freedom": Orwell, *1984* (Secker & Warburg), 790.

227 "the nature and limits": John Stuart Mill, *On Liberty,* in Great Books of the Western World, Volume 43 (Edinburgh, Scotland: Encyclopædia Britannica, 1971), 267.

227 "the inward domain": Ibid., 272.

227 "empirical habit of thought": Orwell, *1984* (Secker & Warburg), 855.

228 "the human heritage": Orwell, *1984* (Signet), 26.

228 "If the Party could": Ibid., 32.

228 "people who had been vaporized": Orwell, *1984* (Secker & Warburg), 767.

228 "If there is hope": Ibid., 783, 791.

229 "visions of a totalitarian future": Orwell, *CEJL,* vol. 2, 261.

229 "Heavy physical work": Orwell, *1984* (Secker & Warburg), 785.

229 "to one another": Ibid., 841.

229 "know any proles": Thomas Pynchon, foreword to George Orwell, *Nineteen Eighty-Four* (New York: Penguin, 2003), xviii.

229–30 "He had pulled her down": Orwell, *1984* (Secker & Warburg), 814.

230 "It was a political act": Ibid., 818.

230 "You're only a rebel": Ibid., 836.

230 "the power of the Executive": Winston Churchill, "Prime Minister to Home Secretary, 21 November 43," reprinted in Winston S. Churchill, *The Second World War, Volume V: Closing the Ring* (Boston: Houghton Mifflin, 1951), 679.

231 "a perfectly proper action": George Orwell, *The Collected Essays, Journalism and Letters of George Orwell, Volume 3: As I Please, 1943–1945,* ed. Sonia Orwell and Ian Angus (New York: Harcourt Brace Jovanovich, 1968), 266–67. Hereafter, Orwell, *CEJL,* vol. 3.

231 code-named "O'Brien": This weird fact is mentioned in Adam Hochschild, "Orwell: Homage to the 'Homage'," *New York Review of Books,* 19 December 2013.

231 "Whatever the Party holds": Orwell, *1984* (Secker & Warburg), 886.

231 "it was a political act of enormous": "His Second, Lasting Publisher," in Coppard and Crick, *Orwell Remembered,* 198.

231 "the definitive novel": Robert McCrum, *Observer,* 10 May 2009, accessed online.

232 "I have been very poorly": Orwell, *CEJL,* vol. 4, 487.

232 "can't do any work": Ibid., 498.

232 "Even if we squeeze the rich": George Orwell, "Writers and Leviathan," in *Orwell and Politics,* ed. Peter Davison (Harmondsworth, U.K.: Penguin, 2001), 486.

232–33 "And what voices!" . . . "No wonder everyone hates us so": Orwell, *Diaries,* 564–65.

233 "looks inconceivably wasted": Malcolm Muggeridge, *Like It Was: The Diaries of Malcolm Muggeridge,* ed, John Bright-Holmes (London: Collins, 1981), 353.

233–34 "The political reminiscences" . . . "memoirs of this type": George Orwell, "Review," in *CEJL,* vol. 4, 491–95.

234 "No one was under any illusion": Gordon Bowker, *George Orwell* (London: Abacus, 2004), 405.

234 "Sonia was smart": Wadhams, *Remembering Orwell,* 133.

234 "basically unbelievably unhappy": Ibid., 165.

234 Orwell sat up in bed: Michael Shelden, *Orwell: The Authorized Biography* (New York: HarperCollins, 1991), 440.

234 macabre deathbed wedding: Malcolm Muggeridge, "Knight of the Woeful Countenance," in *World of George Orwell,* ed., Miriam Gross, (London: Weidenfeld & Nicolson), 174.

234 "reading Dante's *Divine Comedy*": Bernard Crick, *George Orwell: A Life* (New York: Penguin, 1980), 577.

234 "has started losing weight": Muggeridge, *Like It Was,* 361.

234 His fishing rods: Orwell, *Diaries,* 567.

235 five books in mind: Muggeridge, "A Knight of Woeful Countenance," in Gross, *The World of George Orwell,* 173.

235 "To be anti-American": George Orwell, "In Defense of Comrade Zilliacus," *CEJL,* vol. 4, 397–98. See also 309, 323.

235 "All the culture": George Orwell, "The Lion and the Unicorn," in *CEJL,* vol. 2, 59.

236 "He looks quite shrunken": Muggeridge, *Like It Was,* 366.

236 "his face looks almost dead": Ibid., 368.

236 to name, "the Cold War": Bowker, *George Orwell,* 307.

236 "melancholy, chilly affair": Muggeridge, *Like It Was,* 376. Muggeridge himself would chart an interesting course after Orwell's death. Just as Churchill had used radio to great effect in the 1940s, in the 1950s Muggeridge embraced the new medium of television and rose to prominence in Britain, becoming perhaps the first "talking head," and certainly one of the best-known journalists of his generation. Orwell had hated his time in the BBC, but Muggeridge rode the network to fame. Visiting Hamburg, Germany, in June 1961, for example, he wandered into a noisy nightclub named The Top Ten. Performing on the small stage, clad in leather and pumped up on amphetamines, was a stomping pop music combo. "The band were English, from Liverpool, and recognized me," he noted in his diary. Had Orwell seen them and heard their accents, he might well have considered the members of the combo to be "proles." One of the band—most likely John Lennon—asked Muggeridge if he was a Communist. No, Muggeridge replied, but he was an oppositionist. "You make money out of it?" the musician wanted to know. Yes, Muggeridge confessed, he did. Muggeridge, *Like It Was,* 524–25. Later that month, when the Beatles went into a recording studio for the first time, the phonograph company gave them publicity forms to complete. In the space that asked for his goals in life, "John W. Lennon" wrote simply, "To be rich." Mark Lewisohn, *All These Years,*

Volume 1: Tune In (New York: Crown, 2013), 434, 446, 451. Within a few years, of course, that band became the supreme media stars of their time. Muggeridge meanwhile became vocally religious, and with his television work and a documentary helped make famous Mother Teresa, the charismatic nun of Calcutta. Orwell had found his beginning as a writer in South Asia; Muggeridge found his last phase there. It seems likely that Muggeridge, in his long and varied life, was the only person to converse with all three of the great "Winstons" of twentieth-century England—Churchill, Orwell, and Lennon.

236 **friend, Anthony Powell:** Shelden, *Orwell*, 443.

237 **Astor bought two cemetery plots:** Ibid., 444.

237 **"a very remarkable book":** Sir Charles Wilson, later Lord Moran, *Churchill: Taken from the Diaries of Lord Moran* (Boston: Houghton Mifflin, 1966), 426.

CHAPTER 15. CHURCHILL'S PREMATURE AFTERLIFE: 1950–1965

239 **Churchill was, like his father:** See Peregrine Churchill and Julian Mitchell, *Jennie: Lady Randolph Churchill, a Portrait with Letters* (New York: Ballantine, 1976), 104.

239 **"It is impossible to re-read":** Roy Jenkins, *Churchill* (Farrar, Straus and Giroux, 2001), 845.

239 **"gorging vast quantities":** Mark Amoy, ed., *The Letters of Evelyn Waugh* (Boston: Ticknor & Fields, 1980), 489.

239 **buttonholed by Frank Sinatra:** Anthony Montague Browne, *Long Sunset* (Ashford, U.K.: Podkin Press, 2009), 220–21.

239 **seven bottles of wine:** John Ramsden, *Man of the Century: Winston Churchill and His Legend Since 1945* (New York: Columbia University Press, 2002), 327.

239 **"No professional historian":** Ronald Lewin, *Churchill as Warlord* (London: Scarborough, 1973), 17.

239–40 **the work "incorrigibly amateurish":** Peter Clarke, *Mr. Churchill's Profession* (New York: Bloomsbury, 2012), 207.

240 **"a paltry little middle-class":** Anita Leslie, *Cousin Randolph: The Life of Randolph Churchill* (London: Hutchinson, 1985), 133.

241 **"His English father":** R. W. Thompson, *Generalissimo Churchill* (New York: Scribner, 1973), 23, 153.

241 **quotes commonly attributed:** "Quotes Falsely Attributed to Winston Churchill," accessed online at the Web site of the Churchill Society.

241 **One quotation has been:** This paragraph is based on "People Sleep Peacefully in Their Beds at Night Only Because Rough Men Stand Ready to Do Violence on Their Behalf," an exposition by Quote Investigator, accessed online.

242 **"He sees clearly":** George Orwell, "Rudyard Kipling," in *The Collected Essays, Journalism and Letters of George Orwell, Volume 2: My Country Right or Left, 1940–1943*, ed. Sonia Orwell and Ian Angus (New York: Harcourt Brace Jovanovich, 1968), 187.

242 **the *National Review* completed:** Peter Kirsanow, "The Real Jack Bauers," *National Review Online*, 11 September 2006, accessed online.

242 **"If Churchill hadn't done":** Juan de Onis, "Castro Expounds in Bookshop Visit," *New York Times*, 14 February 1964, 1.

242 **"I've taken a lot more":** Stephen Rodrick, "Keith Richards: A Pirate Looks at 70," *Men's Journal*, July 2013, accessed online. For references to Churchill's original comment, see Nigel Knight, *Churchill: The Greatest Briton Unmasked* (London: David & Charles, 2008), 144, 374; and Collin Brooks, "Churchill the Conversationalist," in *Churchill by His Contemporaries*, ed., Charles Eade, (Simon & Schuster, 1954), 248.

242 **"There are a terrible lot":** "Miscellaneous Wit & Wisdom," National Churchill Museum, accessed online.

242 **"British governments care":** Max Hastings, "Defending the 'Essential Relationship': Britain and the United States" (2011 Ruttenberg Lecture, Center for Policy Studies, London, July 15, 2011), 3, accessed online.

243 **"I stood by America":** Tony Blair, *A Journey: My Political Life* (New York: Knopf, 2010), 475, 352, 353.

243 **"defender of liberal democracy":** Robin Prior, *When Britain Saved the West: The Story of 1940* (New Haven, Conn.: Yale University Press, 2015), 208.

243 **"I will be with you":** Henry Mance, "Chilcot Report: Tony Blair Rebuked over Iraq Invasion," *Financial Times*, 6 July 2016, accessed online.

244 **"There never has been":** "Text of Blair's Speech," 17 July 2003, accessed online on BBC News Web site.

244 **"The Battle Hymn":** Ramsden, *Man of the Century*, 21.

CHAPTER 16. ORWELL'S EXTRAORDINARY ASCENSION: 1950–2016

245 **"It was a bright":** Zahra Salahuddin, "Will This Blog Be the Last Time I Get to Express Myself," *Dawn*, 21 April 2015, accessed online.

246 **"beat the lot of you":** Michael Shelden, *Friends of Promise: Cyril Connolly and the World of Horizon* (New York: Harper & Row, 1989), 151.

246 **"His influence and example":** Jason Crowley, "George Orwell's Luminous Truths," *Financial Times*, 5 December 2014, accessed online.

246 **50 million copies:** John Rodden and John Rossi, *The Cambridge Introduction to George Orwell* (Cambridge, U.K.: Cambridge University Press, 2012), 98.

246 **"Typically the primary watchword":** John Rodden, *George Orwell: The Politics of Literary Reputation* (New Brunswick, N.J.: Transaction Publishers, 2006), 117.

246 **Neil McLaughlin argues:** Neil McLaughlin, "Orwell, the Academy and Intellectuals," in *The Cambridge Companion to George Orwell*, ed. John Rodden (Cambridge, U.K.: Cambridge University Press, 2007), 170.

247 **"enemy number one":** Arthur Koestler, *The Invisible Writing* (Briarcliff Manor, N.Y.: Stein and Day, 1969), 466.

247 **Orwell's name did not appear:** Rodden, *George Orwell*, 45.

247 **1955 edition of *Bartlett's*:** John Bartlett, *Familiar Quotations,* 13th ed., (Boston: Little, Brown, 1955), 991.

247 **In 1956, Victor Gollancz:** Bernard Crick, *George Orwell: A Life* (New York: Penguin, 1980), 279.

247 **Stephen Spender could dismiss:** "Stephen Spender Recalls," in Audrey Coppard and Bernard Crick, *Orwell Remembered* (New York: Facts on File Publications, 1984), 264.

247 **"If you read his works":** Stephen Wadhams, ed., *Remembering Orwell* (Harmondsworth, U.K.: Penguin, 1984), 104.

248 **"sense of living so dramatically":** Stephen Spender, *World Within World: The Autobiography of Stephen Spender* (New York: St. Martin's Press, 1994, 232.

248 **"My poems from Spain":** Wadhams, *Remembering Orwell,* 105.

248 **"Don't say any more":** Michael Scammell, *Koestler: The Literary and Political Odyssey of a Twentieth-Century Skeptic* (New York: Random House, 2009), 213.

248 **Orwell's reputation began:** Gordon Beadle, "George Orwell and the Neoconservatives," *Dissent,* Winter 1984, 71.

248 **Orwell is elevated:** Peter Watson, *The Modern Mind: An Intellectual History of the 20th Century* (New York: HarperCollins, 2002), v–vi.

248 **most significant nonfiction books:** "The 100 Best Non-Fiction Books of the Century," *National Review,* May 3, 1999, accessed online.

249 **"greatest writer of the twentieth century":** "Pump Up the Volumes," *Guardian,* 26 November 2000, accessed online.

249 **"the most famous English novel":** Robert McCrum, "The 100 Best Novels—Number 70," *Guardian,* 19 January 2015, accessed online.

249 **U.S. Supreme Court:** Scott Dodson and Ami Dodson, "Literary Justice," *The Green Bag,* 26 August 2015, accessed online.

249 **"The Party fights":** Czesław Miłosz, *The Captive Mind* (New York: Vintage, 1990), 42, 215, 218.

249 **"any state forced to devote":** Andrei Amalrik, *Will the Soviet Union Survive Until 1984?* (London: Allen Lane, 1970), accessed online.

250 **"would have been a neoconservative":** Norman Podhoretz, "If Orwell Were Alive Today," *Harper's,* January 1983, 32.

250 **stamps with his image:** Editor's note in George Orwell, *Orwell and Politics,* ed. Peter Davison (Harmondsworth, U.K.: Penguin, 2001), 441.

250 **"the Zionists were white":** Wadhams, *Remembering Orwell,* 122.

251 **"I belong to the Left":** George Orwell, *The Collected Essays, Journalism and Letters of George Orwell, Volume 4: In Front of Your Nose, 1945–1950,* ed. Sonia Orwell and Ian Angus (New York: Harcourt Brace Jovanovich, 1968), 30. Hereafter, Orwell, *CEJL,* vol. 4.

251 **"sort of perverse Toryism":** Ibid., 207.

251 **"Hedonistic societies do not":** George Orwell, *The Collected Essays, Journalism and Letters of George Orwell, Volume 2: My Country Right or Left, 1940–1943,* ed. Sonia

Orwell and Ian Angus (New York: Harcourt Brace Jovanovich, 1968), 30. Hereafter, Orwell, *CEJL,* vol. 2.

251 **became a bestseller:** Rodden, *George Orwell,* 6.

251–52 **introduced the Macintosh computer:** The relationship between Orwell and Apple provides an interesting sidelight into twentieth- and twenty-first-century history. Orwell fans might hope that the company's name somehow related to the crucial moment in *Animal Farm* in which the pigs decided to keep the apples to themselves, but the corporate name actually was a nod to both the apple of knowledge that Eve ate and to the record company founded by the Beatles. (Steve Rivkin, "How Did Apple Computer Get Its Brand Name?," *Branding Strategy Insider,* 17 November 2001, accessed online.) Ironically, thirty-one years later, Noel Gallagher of the British rock band Oasis, irate over Apple Computer's handling of music streaming, accused the company of having "some sort of George Orwell shit going on." (Colin Joyce, "Noel Gallagher Thinks Apple Music Is 'Some George Orwell S—t,'" *Spin,* 4 August 2015, accessed online.) In a final twist, the location of the old Hotel Colón, which had been the Communist Party headquarters in Barcelona when Orwell was fighting there in 1937, and where he espied a machine-gun nest situated behind the middle o in the hotel's sign, became the site of a major retail outlet for Apple products. It is less a store than a sleek Greek temple dedicated to the modern god of Information. On the horizontal, it is all smooth stone, while its verticals— windows, internal walls, and stairs—are thick plate glass, Orwell-like in their clarity. ("Grand Tour of the Apple Retail Palaces of Europe," *Fortune,* 28 April 2014, accessed online.) There is now a new Hotel Colón located elsewhere in the city.

252 **"What he valued":** Wadhams, *Remembering Orwell,* 106.

252 **only serious blows:** Christopher Hitchens asserts on page 156 of *Why Orwell Matters* that the list was revealed in Bernard Crick's 1980 biography of Orwell. But that is a stretch, as there is just one sentence in Crick's book, on page 556, that vaguely refers to a list of suspects Orwell jotted in a notebook.

252 **This act of informing:** Timothy Garton Ash, "Orwell's List," *New York Review of Books,* 25 September 2003, accessed online.

253 **"most important writer":** "Orwell's Century," transcript of *Think Tank with Ben Wattenberg,* first aired on PBS, April 25, 2002.

253 **"Sage of the Century":** William Giraldi, "Orwell: Sage of the Century," *New Republic,* 11 August 2013, accessed online. This article also contains the Hitchens quotation about Orwell owning the century.

253 **"a period piece":** Harold Bloom, ed., *George Orwell: Modern Critical Views* (New York: Chelsea House, 1987), vii.

253 **"*1984* may have little more":** Irving Howe, *Politics and the Novel* (Chicago: Ivan R. Dee, 2002), 251.

254 **"new age of surveillance":** Gabrielle Pickard, "Police Surveillance of Your Life Is Booming Thanks to Technology," *Top Secret Writers* (blog), 8 July 2015, accessed online.

254 **Iraqi writer, Hassan Abdulrazzak:** Charles Paul Freund, "Orwell's *1984* Still Matters, Though Not in the Way You Might Think," Reason.com, 15 January 2015, accessed online.

254 **ten bestselling books:** "What Books Caught Russia's Imagination in 2015?," *Russia Beyond the Headlines,* 25 December 2015, accessed online.

254 **Philippine Airlines took to warning:** Oliver Smith, "Don't Pack George Orwell, Visitors to Thailand Told," *Daily Telegraph,* 6 August 2014, accessed online.

254 **"In Burma there is a joke":** Emma Larkin, *Finding George Orwell in Burma* (New York: Penguin, 2006), 3.

254 **"political terror still survives":** Michael Rank, "Orwell and China, *1984* in Chinese," 2 January 1014, *Ibisbill's blog,* accessed online.

254 **An Islamic radical, reading** *Animal Farm:* "How Orwell's 'Animal Farm' Led a Radical Muslim to Moderation," interview on *Fresh Air,* NPR.org, 15 January 2015, accessed online.

255 **In Zimbabwe, an opposition newspaper:** David Blair, "Mugabe Regime Squeals at Animal Farm Success," *Daily Telegraph,* 15 July 2001, accessed online.

255 **A Cuban artist was jailed:** Pamela Kalkman, "The Art of Resistance in Cuba," *Open Democracy,* 17 September 2015, accessed online.

255 **"Winston could not definitely remember":** George Orwell, *1984 (*New York: Signet, 1981), 30.

255 **"It is a warfare":** George Orwell, *1984,* in George Orwell omnibus (London: Secker & Warburg, 1976), 856.

256 **known as "signature strikes":** Dan DeLuce and Paul McLeary, "Obama's Most Dangerous Drone Tactic Is Here to Stay," *Foreign Policy,* 5 April 2016, accessed online.

256 **"If liberty means anything":** Rodden and Rossi, *Cambridge Introduction to George Orwell,* 107.

257 **"The choice for mankind":** Orwell, *1984* (Secker & Warburg), 895.

257 **"Dear subscriber," it warned:** "Maybe the Most Orwellian Text Message Ever Sent," *Motherboard,* 21 January 2014.

258 **"an economy ruled":** Orwell, *Orwell and Politics,* 207.

258 **"rate of mechanical":** George Orwell, *The Road to Wigan Pier* (New York: Harvest, 1958), 206.

258 **"The processes involved":** Orwell, *CEJL,* vol. 4, 49.

259 **"To adapt George Orwell's motto":** Bret Stephens, "The Orwellian Obama Presidency," *Wall Street Journal,* 23 March 2015, accessed online.

259 **"America is not yet":** Alec Woodward, *"*Republicans Follow Orwellian Agenda," *Emory Wheel,* 13 April 2015.

260 **singer David Bowie:** "David Bowie's 100 Chart-Topper Books," London *Evening Standard,* 2 October 2013, accessed online.

260 **coach of the Birmingham City:** Laurie Whitwell, "Gary Rowett Reads Orwell, Has Banned Mobiles . . . And Rescued Birmingham City After 8–0 Drubbing," *Daily Mail,* 15 January 2015.

260 **Canadian indie duo:** Meaghan Baxter, "Town Heroes Look to George Orwell on Latest Album," *Vue Weekly,* 12 November 2015. The director Paul Greengrass, best known for action movies, announced in 2014 a plan to make a new film version of *1984.* "Paul Greengrass to Direct George Orwell's 1984," BBC News, 20 November 2014. The theater world rediscovered *1984,* with various productions being mounted in London, Los Angeles, and elsewhere. "1984 Announces Return to the West End for a 12 Week Run," *TNT UK,* 29 April 2015, accessed online. Also, Stephen Rohde, "Big Brother is Watching You," *Los Angeles Review of Books,* 4 January 2016. In Leeds, England, a rising ballet company made a dance of *1984.* Annette McIntyre, "Exclusive Behind the Scenes Access Offered to Northern Ballet's *1984,*" *Daily Echo,* 9 August 2015, accessed online. In 2015, Joe Sutton, an American playwright, unveiled *Orwell in America,* a play in which he imagined Orwell on a book tour in the United States to promote *Animal Farm.* Meg Brazill, "Theater Review: Orwell in America," *Seven Days* (Burlington, Vt., newspaper), 18 March 2015. A novel appeared under the title *Burning Down George Orwell's House,* about a man who imitates the author's life and moves to the Scottish island of Jura. Facebook tycoon Mark Zuckerberg, running a book club he created for Facebook members, selected *Orwell's Revenge,* written by Peter Huberas, as a sequel to *1984.* Richard Feloni, "Why Mark Zuckerberg Is Reading 'Orwell's Revenge,' an Unofficial Sequel to '1984,'" *BusinessInsider,* 30 April 2015. Orwell likely would be bitterly amused that the largest pub in early-twenty-first-century Britain, capable of accommodating some 1,700 drinkers, was Manchester's Moon Under Water, named for his minor 1943 essay on the characteristics of the ideal pub. For Orwell's pub, see "The Moon Under Water," at the TheOrwellPrize.co.uk.

260 **new headquarters building:** Katia Savchuk, "Apple's Core: Dissecting the Company's New Corporate Headquarters," *Forbes,* 4 November 2015.

260 **the circular Panopticon:** For the observation that Apple's building resembles Bentham's Panopticon, I am indebted to Richard Wiebe, a San Francisco expert on communications law. Personal communication.

261 **industry publication** *Digital Trends*: Andrew Couts, "'Privacy Is Theft' in the Heavy-Handed Social Media Dystopia of 'The Circle,'" *Digital Trends,* 19 November 2013.

261 **jailed for a night:** Luke Seaber, "Method Research: George Orwell Really Did Have a Stint in Jail as a Drunk Fish Porter," *Science 2.0,* 6 December 2014, accessed online.

261 **to be "pretty useless":** No author, "George Orwell's Time in Hertfordshire as a 'Pretty Useless' Shopkeeper," *Hertfordshire Mercury,* 31 January 2015, accessed online.

261 **income of Orwell's estate:** Robert Butler, "Orwell's World," *The Economist: More Intelligent Life,* January/February 2015, accessed online.

262 **"But all our phrasing":** Ta-Nehisi Coates, "Letter to My Son," *Atlantic,* September 2015, 84.

263 **"did not lose it":** John Lukacs, *Five Days in London: May 1940* (New Haven, Conn.: Yale University Press, 1999), 2.

263 **"Everyone who values freedom":** Paul Johnson, *Churchill* (New York: Penguin, 2009), 166.

AFTERWORD: THE PATH OF CHURCHILL AND ORWELL

265 **They also often were wrong:** Much of this paragraph is drawn from an e-mail exchange with Karin Chenoweth.

266 **The term "psychological avoidance":** Taylor Branch, *Parting the Waters: America in the King Years, 1954–1963* (New York: Simon & Schuster, 1989), 54, 173, 332, 402, 486.

266 **calling it "unwise and untimely":** Jeffrey Aaron Snyder, "Fifty Years Later: Letter from Birmingham Jail," *New Republic,* 19 April 2013; additional details from Branch, *Parting the Waters,* 737.

267 **"right defeated is stronger":** Martin Luther King Jr., "Letter from Birmingham City Jail," from Martin Luther King Jr. Research and Education Institute, Stanford University, accessed online.

268–69 **"the more dynamic" . . . "You begin to liquidate":** Milan Kundera, *The Book of Laughter and Forgetting* (New York: HarperPerennial, 1999), 10–11, 218.

269 **We can all endeavor:** This paragraph owes much to my exchanges with the writer Timothy Noah.

INDEX

All writings of Churchill under Churchill, Winston, writings of;
all writings of Orwell under Orwell, George, writings of.

PHOTO CREDITS

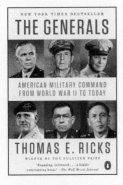

THE GENERALS

American Military Command from World War II to Today

While history has been kind to the American generals of World War II, it has been less kind to the generals of the wars that followed. In *The Generals*, Thomas E. Ricks sets out to explain why and tells the stories of great leaders and suspect ones, generals who rose to the occasion and generals who failed themselves and their soldiers.

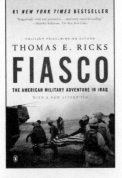

FIASCO

The American Military Adventure in Iraq, 2003 to 2005

Fiasco is a masterful reckoning with the planning and execution of the American military invasion and occupation of Iraq through mid-2006. It is an undeniable account—explosive, shocking, and authoritative—of unsurpassed tactical success combined with unsurpassed strategic failure that indicts some of America's most powerful and honored civilian and military leaders.

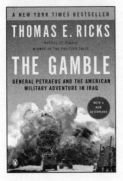

THE GAMBLE

General Petraeus and the American Military Adventure in Iraq

This book is the definitive account of the insurgency within the U.S. military that led to a radical shift in America's strategy. Based on unprecedented real-time access to the military's entire chain of command, Ricks examines the events that took place as the military was forced to reckon with itself, the surge was launched, and a very different war began.